LIBRARY MOVEMENT AND DEVELOPMENT IN INDIA : A STATE WISE SCAN

LIBRARY MOVEMENT AND DEVELOPMENT IN INDIA: A STATE WISE SCAN

By

NASIRUDHEEN. T

Ess Ess Publications
New Delhi

LIBRARY MOVEMENT AND DEVELOPMENT IN INDIA : A State Wise Scan

ISBN: 978-81-936074-6-6

First Published 2018

Published by:
Ess Ess Publications
4831/24, Ansari Road,
Darya Ganj,
New Delhi-110 002.
INDIA
Phones: 23260807, 41563444
Fax: 41563334
E-mail: info@essessreference.com
www.essessreference.com

Cover Design by *Patch Creative Unit*

Printed and bound in India

Dedicated to
My
FAMILY
&
FRIENDS

Contents

Preface

I am extremely happy to submit this work before the LIS community. This can be treated as not only a text book, but also a reference book on Library and Information Science in India. It gives a comprehensive picture of Library movement and development of Indian states. Library movement and development not only means library legislation, but also development of Public libraries in a state, Academic libraries in a state, Special libraries in a state, LIS education in a state and Library organizations and Associations in a state. Thus this book has been organized such a way.

The unique feature of the work is that, almost all sates have been authored by eminent personalities from that states and they have tried their level best to scan the current and historic information on their states. Definitely it will increase the authenticity and depth of the work. The deatails of libraries in the concerned states have been taken from the websites of the respective libraries. The authors are responsible for the information included in their respective chapters.

Acknowledgement

First of all let me thank God, by his grace only I could complete this endeavor. I would like to thank all contributors (Dr. Vahida Beegum, Mrs.Y.sudha rani, Dr. Akhtar Hussain, Mr. Omprakash Patel, Dr. K P Singh and Dipti Gulati, Mr. Raheeb Thottathil, Dr. Geeda Gadhavi, Mrs. Hans, Dr. Dimple, Dr. Shabir Ahmad Ganaie, Mr. Raheeb T, Dr. Mehabubullah, Mr. Nasirudheen.T, Dr. Mahjabeen Aydeed, Dr. Shashank Sonaji Sonwane, Dr. Manoj Kumar Sinha, Dr. Pushpanjali Jena & Nilaranjan Barik , Mr.Baldev Singh, Smt. Dheeraj Pratap Kanwar, Mr. Ashif KM, Mrs. Kalyani KS & Mr.Ashok Kumar A, Mr. Saumen Datta, Dr. Nishat Fatima, Dr. Anil Kumar Dhiman and Mr. Niti Mollah) for their valuable contribution in the form of chapters. Special gratitude is extended to Mr. Abdul Gafoor.M, Mrs.Sheeba Francis and Mrs. Khairunnisa (CHMK Library, University of Calicut) and Mrs. Sangeeda (Dept. of LIS, Calicut University) and Mr. Shukoor (Computer Assistant, dept. of Arabic University of Calicut) for their valuable help in this project.

1

Library Movement in India: An Over View

Dr. Nasirudheen. T
Junior Librarian
University of Calicut, Kerala

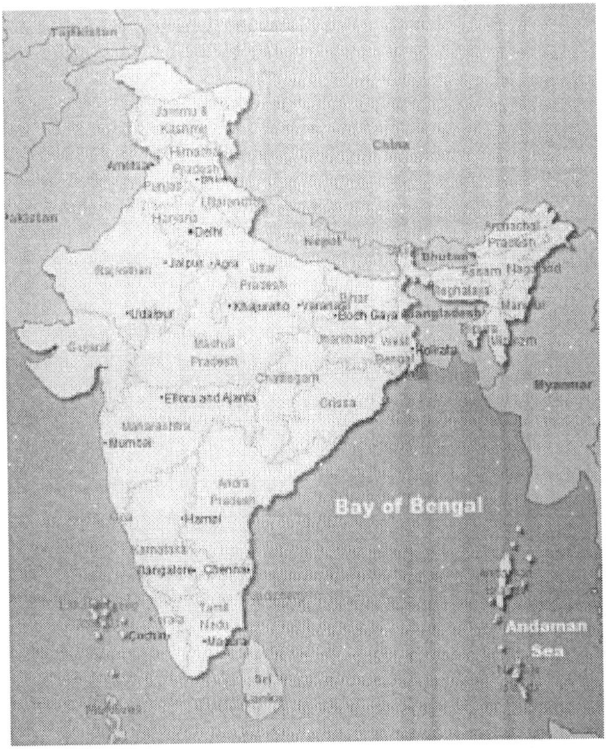

1. INTRODUCTION

The progress of Library Movement is of great importance for the political, social, economic and cultural advancement of a country. Any endeavor which indents the progress and development of library system will come under the title of library movement. Thus the following heading will be coming under the title of library movement in India.

- development of libraries,
- library legislation,
- role of library organizations and associations,
- library policies,
- library commissions and five year plans

2. GROWTH AND DEVELOPMENT OF LIBRARIES IN INDIA

The story of development of the libraries in India can be studied under three distinct headings:

- Ancient Period
- Medieval Period, and
- Modern Period

2.1. Ancient Period

India is a country with unity in diversity. The existence of libraries in India is found from very ancient days when India was reputed for her different seats of learning in the various monasteries *mathas,* temples and Buddhist viharas (monasteries) spread throughout the length and breadth of the country. These seats of learning and centres of culture naturally possessed rich collection of books and manuscripts. These ancient libraries had manuscripts both in Kharosthi and Brahmi scripts inscribed on palm leaves, and other artificial writing materials. Our living testimony of Vedas, the Upanishads and the epics and the Buddhist religious literature indicates, that even at an early date progress in the art of writing was appreciated. Jainism and Buddhism both gave their emphasis upon the systems of organized brotherhoods (Sangam) accommodated *Viharas* or monasteries in the rock cut halls. The Brahamanical systems also followed suit with similar institutions like *Mathas* and other regular colleges.

The availability of written material from the 4th century B.C. points out to the definite existence of places for "stoning" and making manuscripts accessible to the class. The Buddhist system of education and learning indicates the essential requirement of libraries. A few notable examples are those attached to the centers of leaning (Universities) at Nalanda, Rajagriha, Odantapuri, Vallabhi (Kathiawar), Takshsila, Vikramsila, Tamralipta, etc. The University of Takshila (now in west Pakistan) in the 6th century B.C. maintained an excellent library. From the list of specialized subjects taught at the University it can be observed that it must have possessed a vast collection of books and manuscripts on those subjects.

The Nalanda University had a well-equipped library. There was a parallel Buddhist monastery on the other side of Nalanda, the Valabhi, situated near modern Wala in Kathiawar (in Gujarat), which was the capital of the Maitraka kings. It was a famous centre of learning, which attracted students even from far of place like Bengal down to the 12th century A.D. This monastery was equipped with a library. Another famous Buddhist monastery was at Vikramsila which was founded by king Dharmpala in the 8th century A.D. The university possessed a rich and extensive library. There were a large number of books on the religion of the Hindus. On being acquainted with the contents of the books then they discovered that the whole fort was a university.

The University of Sompuri also had its own library. *Navodwipa* in West Bengal, it was the last famous seats of learning Eastern India reached its height of glory from A.D. 1063 to 1106 as a centre of intellectual excellence as well as its rich library facilities. However, this library too was destroyed along with the centre by Bakhtiyar Khilji. The

Nagarjuna Vidyapeeth was situated in South India at Amarawati, on the banks of the river Krishan flourished about the 7th century A.D. Its library housed in the top floor of the five storied building of the university had an enormous collection on the Buddhist Philosophy.

2.2. Medieval Period

The growth and development of libraries in medieval India presents an interesting historical scenario, in which we come across epoch of both high and low profiles of development from the periods of destruction and disregard to the time of committed efforts for the development of libraries. Two factors, during this period, had a far reaching influence on the growth and development of libraries in India. One during the period form 800 A.D. to 1200 A.D, the northern and southern halves of the subcontinent came into closer contact and, the other, the growing literary, scientific, religious and philosophical activities which were promoted more after the establishment of the Mughal Empire in India.

Medieval Indian libraries can be divided into four types i.e. religious libraries, private libraries, academic libraries and public libraries. Each of these libraries had thousand volumes. In Tanjore, Sarabtoji, the last ruling king of Maratha, made a major contribution, organized a massive collection of printed books and manuscripts, and founded the SaraswatiMahal Library, which is till now one of the finest libraries of its kind. We have instances of private collections also in the south and in the north of India. Mahmud of Ghazni maintained a library of more than 30,000 volumes. Mohmud Gavan, a Minister of the Bahamani Sultan owned a library of 3,000 volumes. The king Jalal-ud-din Khilji (1290-96) appointed Amir Khusro as the Director of the Royal Library on a very high salary and also conferred on him the title of Muhafiz-i-Quran (Protector of the Quran).

Many magnificent manuscript libraries were established during the Mughal period (1562-1748). One trait common to all of the Mughal Emperors from Babur to

Aurangzeb, was that they all patronized man of learning and scholarship, and also maintained their palace libraries.

The first Mughal Emperor Babur (1526-30) was very fond of books and took keen interest in the organization and development of library. He regularly used his library which was located in the Old Fort Delhi. After his death Humayun took over the charge of the Empire in 1530 A.D., who was also a scholar and a great lover of books. It is said that Humayun fell down from the stairs of the library and died after sometimes with the injury he had received. Lal Beg was the librarian of Humayun's Imperial Library at Agra.

Akbar the Great (1556-1605 A.D.), succeeded Humayun. The growth and development of libraries reached at its zenith during his reign. The Imperial Library was located in Agra Fort. Faizi (the brother of Abul Fazal) was the librarian of the Imperial library. The books for the imperial library of Akbar were brought from different places like, Gujrat, Deccan, Jaunpur, Kashmir, Bihar, Bengal and so on to enriched its collection.

During the reign of Akbar a separate department of translation was established which translated the important books for the library. The library contained 24,000 illustrated and well bound volumes. The approximate price of the collection was Rs. 64,63,131. Emperor Jahangir (1605-1627 A.D.), further enriched the collection of Imperial library and added a picture gallery to it. The imperial library, he also organized a personal library for his own use containing a number of books on various subjects.

After Jahangir, the Mughal emperors from Shahjahan to Aurangzeb also maintained the imperial library with keen interest. In 1738 A.D., Nadir Shah in his invasion carried away with him the collection of celebrated imperial library. Thus, the Imperial Library of the Mughal emperors met an inglorious end. Among the other contemporary libraries, the valuable collections of Maharaja Chikka Deva Raya of Mysore (1672-1740 A.D.) and Tipoo Sultan deserve special mention.

The decline of the Mughal empire in India form the mid of the 18th century onwards, paved the way for the spread of the British influence.

2.3. Modern Period

The era of transformation of libraries in India began during the middle of the 19th century. It was the time when there were revolutionary changes in social, political, industrial and other phases of life. During the first half of this century, public libraries were established in the three Presidencies Bombay, Calcutta and Madras. In this period, particularly in the context of academic libraries, the important events are (a) The Charter Act of 1813, (b) The birth and progress of the Fort William College and the Serampore Colleges, (c) Sir Charles Wood's Despatch 1854; and (iv) The Hunter Commission 1882-83.

The first library in modern India was established in 1784 attached to the Asiatic Society of Bengal. Next to it was the library of the Asiatic Society of Bombay which was established in 1804. The Madras library society was established in 1818 with a library open to the public. In 1830 another public library, the Bombay General Library was established in Bombay.

Besides these various other public libraries were established around this time. The Indore General Public Library was founded in 1854 by Maharaja Tukoji RaoHolkar II. He founded the present Indore General Library in HuzuryaMahal of the Old Palace and provided a donation of Rs. 500 and a recurring grant of Rs. 12 per month for it. The oldest and premier public library known as 'KitabGhar' till 1866 has had to pass through many vicissitudes during its long and chequered existence. After being shifted from the Palace, the library was shifted to many palaces in the city till 1909 when it occupied the present building situated in the heart of the city "Rajwada Chowk".

The Connemara Public Library at Madras was set up in 1860 which was started as a small museum library owing to the efforts of a captain Jesse Mitchell and was shifted to its present building during the time Dr. Edger Thurston was superintendent of the museum. The KhudaBakhsh Oriental Public Library at Patna, owes its origin to Maulvi Muhammad Bakhsh Khan.

2.3.1. Pre- Independence period

The colonial countries came to India primarily to establish trade and commerce. But some of them were very interested for the enrichment of rich cultural heritage of India. A number of Academic institutions were established during the British period by the East India Company and by the Christian missionaries. The University of Calcutta was established in 1857 and its library was opened in 1873. Other Universities, University of Bombay and University of Madras were established in 1879 and 1907 respectively. There were only nineteen Universities in India before 1947. Universities were equipped with libraries in accordance with the Indian University Act of 1904. The Bengal Royal Asiatic Society set up library in 1784, Bombay Royal Asiatic Society in 1804 and Calcutta Public Library in 1835.

The first three decades of the 20th century can be considered as the golden age of the Indian library movement. In 1902, the Imperial Library Act was passed by Lord Curzon and the Calcutta Public Library was transformed into the Imperial Library. Developments in Baroda were also remarkable in the history of library movement in country. Baroda developed a network of public libraries to serve the entire Public in the State. Maharaja Sayaji Rao Gaekwad III of Baroda, who traveled all over the world, was deeply impressed by the role played by public libraries in the promotion of education in the United States and thought of extending such benefits to his country. In 1911, he brought an American expert, W.A. Borden to organize the public library system for his state. Considering the contribution of Sayaji Rao Gaekwad III to the library movement, he is remembered today as the Father of Library Movement in India.

The contribution of Dr. S.R .Ranganathan to the library development during the pre independence is remarkable. University of Madras created the post of University Librarian in 1923 and Dr. S R Ranganathan was appointed for the post on 4 January 1924. Ranganathan published his Five Laws of Library Science in 1931, Colon Classification in 1933 and Classified Catalog Code in 1934. He also prepared Model Public Library Bill and tried to library legislation in Indian states. He made a tremendous contribution for the development of libraries in India. That is why he is considered as the father of Indian library science.

2.3.2. Post Independent Period

Public libraries in India made a tremendous growth after the independence in 1947. The Connemara Public Library in Madras became the State Central Library in 1950 under the provision of Madras Public Libraries Act 1948, and became one of the three depository libraries in 1955. Delhi Public Library was established in 1951 as the first UNESCO Public Library Pilot Project under the joint auspices of UNESCO and Government of India. In 1954, the Delivery of Book Act was passed. The act obligated every publisher in India to deposit one copy each of its publications to the National Library in Calcutta, the Asiatic Society Library in Bombay, Connemara Public Library in Madras, and Delhi Public Library in New Delhi. In 1979, a library section was established in the Department of Culture under the Ministry of Education, which section was under the charge of an Under Secretary. The objective was to promote the development of public libraries in India.

3. LIBRARY LEGISLATION

The library movement in several countries of the world has been achieved and facilitated through library legislation only. India is not exception in this case. Growth and development of libraries are the responsibility of the states, since public libraries are in the "state list" under the constitution of India. Although the central government has also made enormous efforts by establishing many public libraries in the country, it is essential for each and every state to enact comprehensive library legislation. It is the library legislation which defines sources of funds, structure, functions and objectives of libraries.

Dr. S.R Ranganathan prepared a model public library act in 1930. Based on this act, Madras was the first state to adopt public libraries act in 1948, followed by Hyderabad in 1955. So far 18 states in India have been enacted library legislation. They are – Tamilnadu, Andrapradesh, Karnataka, Maharastra, West Bengal, Manipur, Kerala, Hariyana, Mizoram, Goa, Gujarat, Orissa, Uttarachal, Uttarpradesh, Rajasthan, Chattisgarh, Bihar, and Arunachal Pradesh.

4. LIBRARY ASSOCIATIONS

Library associations have their own role in the library movement of our country. The objective of a library association is to strengthen and expand the library movement in a country. These objectives are fulfilled by conducting local, zonal, national, international workshops, seminars, meetings and discussions. The Andra desa library association was the first library association in India which was formed in 1914. Followed by this a lot of library associations were developed in various parts of the country. Presently separate library associations are functioning in each and every state of our country. ILA and IASLIC are the two leading national level library associations in India.

4.1. ILA (Indian library Association)

ILA is the prominent national level library association in India. Which was formed in the first all India library conference at Calcutta in 1933. The objectives of ILA are-

(a) The furtherance of the library movement in India;

(b) The promotion of the training of librarians;

(c) The improvement of the status of librarians.

(d) Promotion of research in library science;

(e) Co-operation with international organizations with similar objectives. The 1970 amendment to the constitution added following four more objectives:

(f) Publication of bulletins, periodicals, books etc., which tend to the realization of the objects of the association;

(g) Establishment of libraries, documentation & information centres and assistance to their establishment and working;

(h) Promotion of appropriate library legislation in India; and

(i) To do all such other things as are incidental of above mentioned objects.

4.2. IASLIC (Indian Association of Special Libraries and Information Centres)

IASLIC is another prominent national level library association, which was formed in 1955. The objectives of the organization are –

(a) Undertake, support and co-ordinate research and studies.

(b) Organize general and special meetings, seminars, workshops and conferences at national and regional level.

(c) Publish journals, monographs, manuals, newsletters, papers, proceedings and reports.

(d) Conduct short-term training courses.

(e) Collaborate with other fraternal bodies in promoting the interests of the library and information profession.

(f) Undertake such other activities which are incidental and conducive to the attainment of its objects.

5. LIBRARY ORGANIZATIONS

UNESCO, the reputed international organization and UGC and RRLF, the two prominent national organizations have great role in the development of library movement in India. Among these, UNESCO and RRLF have been concentrating on public libraries and UGC on academic libraries.

5.1. NISCAIR

National Institute of Science Communication and Information Resources (NISCAIR) was established in 2002 at New Delhi with the merger of National Institute of Science Communication (NISCOM) and Indian National Scientific Documentation Centre (INSDOC). Both NISCOM and INSDOC, the two premier institutes of the Council of Scientific and Industrial Research (CSIR), were devoted to dissemination and documentation of S&T information.

NISCOM had been in existence for the last six decades (first as two Publication Units of CSIR, which were merged to form the Publications Division, which was later renamed as Publications & Information Directorate and in 1996, as NISCOM). Over the years, NISCOM diversified its activities, and through a host of its information products, comprising research and popular science journals, encyclopaedic publications, monographs, books, and information services, it had been reaching out to researchers, students, entrepreneurs, industrialists, agriculturists, policy planners and also the common man. INSDOC came into being in 1952 and was engaged in providing S&T information and documentation services through myriad activities such as abstracting and indexing, design and development of databases, translation, library automation, providing access to international information sources, human resource development, consultancy, services in setting up modern library-cum-information centres. INSDOC was also host to the National Science Library and the SAARC Documentation Centre.

Now, with the formation of NISCAIR, all the above multi-faceted activities have been amalgamated, making NISCAIR, an institute capable of serving the society using modern IT infrastructure in a more effective manner and taking up new ventures in the field of science communication, dissemination and S&T information management systems and services. Broadly the core activity of NISCAIR will be to collect/store, publish and disseminate S&T information through a mix of traditional and modern means, which will benefit different segments of society.

5.2. UGC (University Grants Commission), New Delhi

The University Grants Commission (UGC) is a statutory organization established by an Act of Parliament in 1956. This is a national body for the co-ordination, determination and maintenance of standards of university education. The UGC serves as a vital link between the Union and state governments and the institutions of higher learning. In addition to its role of giving grants to universities and colleges; the UGC also advises union and state governments on the measures necessary for the improvement of university education. Being an apex body in maintaining the quality of higher education in the country, it has played a major role in promoting library and information services in these universities and colleges.

Some of the functions of UGC in this direction are:-

(a) Financial Assistance to University and College Libraries

(b) Curriculum Development Committee (CDC) on Library & Information Science.

(c) Establishment of National Information Centres

(d) Establishment of INFLIBNET

(e) Modernization of university libraries

(f) National Review Committee on University and College Libraries.

5.3. RRLF (Raja ram Mohun Roy library foundation), Calcutta

Rajaram mohun Roy Library Foundation is the nodal agency of government of India for promoting public library services in the country, which was established in May 1972 on the auspicious occasion of the bicentennial birth anniversary of Raja Rammohun Roy. The Foundation is an autonomous organization, established and sponsored by the Department of Culture, Govt. of India. Its headquarters is located at Calcutta. It works in close collaboration with state and union territories.

The main objectives of the foundation are to promote and support the public library in the country by providing adequate library services and by developing reading and learning habits all over the country. Some of the main objectives of the foundation are-

1. Enunciation of a national library policy and working towards its adoption by the union and state governments and persuading them to enact library legislation where such legislation does not exist;
2. Helping build up a national library system by integrating the services of national libraries, state central libraries, district libraries and other types of libraries,
3. Acting as a clearing house for ideas and information on library development;
4. Providing financial assistance to libraries, to regional and national library associations and to other organisations engaged or interested in the promotion of library development; and
5. Promoting research in problems of library development.

So far, 31,274 libraries have been assisted under various schemes like, construction of library building, increasing book stock, centenary celebration, TV VCP, computer for library application, children section, mobile library services and public library research.

6. RECOMMENDATIONS OF COMMITTEE AND COMMISSION REPORTS

After the independence, Government of India has appointed many committees and commissions for the improvement of libraries in the country. These committees have proposed improvement in the form of various recommendations. On the basis of these recommendations, government has taken many actions to improve libraries time to time.

University Education Commission headed by S. Radhakrishnan (1948) was the first commission set up after independence. Secondary education commission headed by A.L Mudaliyar (1953), and education commission headed by D.S Kothari (1964) submitted their reports with some recommendations on academic libraries in the country. Advisory committee for libraries under the chairmanship of K.P Sinha was set up in 1957 and submitted its report in 1958 with some recommendations for the improvement of public libraries in the country. Report of the UGC library committee, chaired by S.R Ranganathan is the land mark in the history of academic libraries in India. The report was published by UGC in 1959 as, "university and college libraries". The report touched up all aspects of university and college library organization and services and formulated a comprehensive recommendation. The report has also given a blue print for the systematic development of university libraries in the country.

In 1985, a committee was set up under the chairmanship of D.P Chattopadhyaya to formulate a national policy on library and information system (NAPLIS) in the country. The committee submitted its report in 1986 with 60 recommendations.

In 2005, National Knowledge Commission was set up by the Prime Minister of India, Dr. Manmohan Singh under the chairmanship of Sam Pitroda. The main objective of the commission was to prepare a blueprint to tap into the enormous reservoir of our knowledge base so that our people can confidently face challenges of the 21st. Century. The commission has given ten recommendations for the improvement of library services in the country. They are –

1. Set up a national commission on libraries
2. Prepare a national census of all libraries
3. Revamp LIS education, training and research facilities.
4. Re-assess staffing of libraries.
5. Set up a central library fund.
6. Modernize library management.
7. Encourage great community participation in library management.
8. Promote Information communication Technology (ICT) applications in all libraries.
9. Facilitate donation and maintenance of private collections in libraries.
10. Encourage public private partnership in Library and Information Science education.

7. FIVE YEAR PLANS AND LIBRARIES

The economy of India is based on the planning of five years, which is developed, executed and monitored by the planning commission. Five year plans have been giving considerable attention to library and information system in the country.

7.1. First five year plan (1951- 1956)

In the first five year plan Rs. 5 million was set aside for establishment of the national central library, but unfortunately this sum was not used. The improvement of library services was mentioned in this plan for educational development. The spirit of the scheme was to establish the district libraries in each state, which were to be supplemented by a state central library.

7.2. Second five year plan (1956-1961)

This plan contained the same provisions, which were same as in the first plan, plus additional provisions for establishing integrated library service. There were three focuses, firstly the state and district libraries were to be set up in each state; secondly, the library services were to be organized on the basis of legislation; and finally, the district libraries were to form the link between the state central library and village libraries. As a result, the nine states in India established the state central libraries and 254 district libraries.

7.3. Third five year plan (1962-1967)

During this plan period, the system of the central government assistance to the states was changed, and funding for libraries was kept to a bare minimum. Thus, it was up to the individual states to take the plan and develop their public libraries. With the beginning of this plan period, the scheme to support the state governments in establishing state central libraries, district central libraries, and block development libraries were neglected. The central government decided to permit the states for their development. This decision was a major setback to hinder the development of public libraries. During this plan period, four national libraries were to be established at Delhi, Calcutta, Bombay, and Madras. District–level libraries were to be established in all the states. A sum of Rs. 32.3 million was made available to the states for this purpose. In 1962, the central government sent a model Public Libraries Bill to those state governments which had not adopted any library legislation, hoping to persuade these states to show an interest in passing the legislation.

7.4. Fourth five year plan (1969-1974)

In 1972, during this plan period, the central government established the Raja Ram mohan Roy Library Foundation. This foundation was created as an autonomous body under the Department of Culture, controlled by the Ministry of Education, for the development of public libraries in India. This foundation matches the funds of the states for purchasing furniture and books, organizing the conferences and seminars, and providing mobile library service to the rural areas. It also advises the central government on all matters relating to library development in the country. 1972, the Working Group on the Development of Public Libraries was constituted by the Government of India Planning Commission to make recommendations for library development. These recommendations were to be included in the Fifth Five Year Plan.

7.5. Fifth five year plan (1974 -1979)

An adult education program was the emphasis of this plan. This program supported a network of libraries at the village and block levels, and various community centers. Thus, the steps were taken to strengthen not only the village and block libraries, but also the central state libraries, and the district libraries. In 1978, the government adopted the National Adult Education Program, but it did not recognize the public library as an agency that could be assigned a role in solving the literacy problem. In 1979, the Ministry of Education in the Department of Culture established a library section under the charge of an under-secretary. Since then, libraries have not been part of the social education budget. Instead, they have been included in the art and culture component of the budget.

7.6. Sixth five year plan (1980 – 1985)

This plan emphasized minimum essential education of all adults. These efforts were to be supported by post–literacy and continuing education through a network of rural libraries as well as instructional programs conducted through mass communication media. A Working Group on the modernization of the library services and Informatics in the Seventh Plan was appointed by the Planning Commission in 1983.

7.7. Seventh five year plan (1985 – 1990)

During this plan period, the objective of the Planning Commission was to address the needs of 90 million people, aged between 15 years and 35 years through the adult Education Program. The network of libraries was to play a role in the development of literature for neo-literates. An important development during this period was the 1986 adoption of the National Literacy Mission, which emphasized the education of women and also the establishment of rural libraries. A Committee on National Policy on Library and Information System (NAPLIS) was appointed in 1985 by the Government of India, Department of Culture.

7.8. Eighth five year plan (1992-1997)

This plan states that the rural libraries should become the focal points for post–literacy and continuing education programs in those states with an advanced library system. Book promotion is also emphasized in this plan, which was to be promoted by the organization of a National Center for Children's Literature. This national centre should produce 3,000 titles annually. Important books were to be translated into the various Indian languages, and books were to be published for neo-literates. The National Cultural Policy 1993 was the new policy designed by the Government of India. It was created by merging the National Policy of Library and Information Science, the National Book Policy, and other related policies dealt with by the Department of Culture of the Ministry of Human Resource Development.

7.9. Ninth five year plan (1997 – 2002)

During the 9th five year plan, the National Library, Kolkata, undertook several major initiatives to upgrade and modernize its collection building programme, reader services, and conservation of library material. Funds for modernizing and computerization were also provided from central grants to the Connemara Library-Chennai, Maharaja Serovji Sarasvati Mahal Library, Thanjavur and the State Central Library, Mumbai.

7.10. Tenth five year plan (2002 – 2007)

The Tenth Plan focused on upgrading the existing libraries, including the private collections, and widening the programme for bibliographic control and documentation. To make the readers services more comprehensive and effective, the National Library is expected to act as the ultimate referral centre for various subjects. To keep the velocity with the latest developments in the information technology in the public libraries, the upgrading and networking of central and state libraries was also planned.

7.11. Eleventh five year plan (2007 – 2012)

This plan focused on the following areas-

(a) To establish one more National Library in South India, particularly in Bangalore.

(b) To establish the Public Library in every village across the country.

(c) To establishes the Centre for Excellence for Digital Library Development and Research.

(d) To establishes the school Library in every school.

But unfortunately the year plan completed without fulfilling these proposals.

8. Summary

India, the largest democratic and highly populated country in the world could achieve its goals to a great extent related with the library movement through out the years through various programs such as library legislation, establishing library organizations and associations, making library policies, setting up library commissions and five year plans. But unfortunately, even after 65 years of independence, public libraries could not be administered and managed with the clear mandate of law in many states of India. As such, the development of the nation through library services is neglected in some states, and its services are beyond the reach of the rural poor.

REFERENCES

1. Agarwal, Umesh Kumar(1999). Library legislation in India. Jaipur, RBSA publications.
2. Deshpande, K and B.B. Hungund "What Ails our Public Library System", ILA Bulletin, Vol. 24, No.1&2, 1998.
3. Nagar Muralilal (1983) Foundations of library movement in India. Ludhiyana, Indian library institute.
4. Rakesh Kumar Bhatt (1995). History and development of libraries in India. New Delhi, Mittal publications.
5. Sahib singh (2003).Library and literary movement for national development. New Delhi, Concept publishers.
6. Sharma, Jagadish saran (1986). Library movement in India and abroad. New Delhi, Ess Ess Publishers.
7. Sharma, S.K. Pandey (1996). Public libraries in India: Trends and Status. In *Public libraries in developing countries: Status and Trends.* Ed. P. K. Mahapatra, 125-127. New Delhi: Vikas Publishing House
8. Venkatappaiah, V. (1990). State Library Bills And Acts. In: *Indian Library legislation* Ed. P. S.G Kumar. V.2. Delhi : Daya Publishing House.
9. Venkatapaiah (2000) Indian Library Legislation : State Library bills and acts. Delhi, Daya Publishing House.
10. http://www.webpages.uidaho.edu/~mbolin/wani.pdf
11. *shodhganga.inflibnet.ac.in/bitstream/10603/1204/.../09_chapter*
12. http://www.nmlindia.nic.in

2

Library and Information Science (LIS) Education in India : An overview

Dr. Vahida Beegum
Gr-3 Librarian,
Govt. Arts college Meenchanda, Calicut, Kerala

1. INTRODUCTION

Library and Information Science (LIS) education in India has completed its 100 years in 2011. During this period, it was seen a slow and steady growth in LIS education. In India, LIS education was started in 1911 with the establishment of Baroda School by W.A Borden. Presently LIS has grown and developed into a full-fledged discipline; courses are being conducted by university departments, institutions, library associations and specialized institutions in our country.

2. HISTORICAL PERSPECTIVE

In India, the first ever training programme in library science was started in 1911 at Baroda under the directorship of W.A. Borden, under the patronage of Maharaja Sayajirao III, Gaekwad of Baroda. Four years later in 1915, another

American student of Dewey, Asa Don Dickinson, the then librarian of Punjab University, Lahore (now in Pakistan) started a three-months apprentice training programme for working librarians. This training school at Punjab University was considered to be the second library school known in the world, the first being the Columbia school started by Melvil Dewey.

This move was followed by library associations in India through developing training programmes for library professionals. Andhra Desha Library Association started training course in 1920 at Vijayawada, Madras Library Association in 1929 at Madras, and Bengal Library Association training course in 1935 at Banasberia. Among the universities, Madras University under Dr. S. R. Ranganathan took over the certificate course from Madras Library Association in 1931. Andhra University started LIS course in 1935 and Banaras Hindu University in 1941.

Post-independence era of LIS education in India was dominated by university teaching departments. Delhi University started the first postgraduate degree course in 1948 (later changed to Bachelor of Library Science) and in 1957 Aligarh Muslim University initiated the first ever B. Lib. Sc. in India. University of Madras converted their diploma course into B. Lib. Sc. course in 1960. DRTC and INSDOC started two specialized courses in LIS in the year 1962 and 1964 respectively. IGNOU started its BLIS in 1989 and MLIS courses in 1996 through distance mode.

3. PRESENT STATUS AND LEVELS OF LIS EDUCATION IN INDIA.

Presently the LIS education in India is offered at various levels such as certificate, diploma, degree, Associateship in Information Science, M.Phil and Ph.D. These programmes are offered on regular basis as well as through distance education. At present there are about 90 universities in India that are imparting LIS education in different levels.

3.1. Certificate/Diploma in Library Science (CLISc/D.LI.Sc.)

Certificate courses are mainly conducted by library associations. Some departments in universities and affiliated colleges are also conducting this course. The duration of this course is six months to one year. The basic qualification for this course is secondary education. This course prepares students for low level professional positions in libraries such as librarian grade 4, Library Attendant, Library Clerk, etc.

3.2. Bachelor of Library and Information Science (BLISc)

This is a one-year / two semester degree course in library science conducted by universities. The basic qualification of this course is any degree. Bachelor's degree prepares students for professional positions in college and university libraries or as a school librarian. Presently there are around 100 teaching departments of universities/ colleges offer BLISc course in India.

3.3. Master of Library and Information Science (MLISc)

Master of Library and Information Science is imparted as a one-year/ two-semester post graduate degree course in some universities while in some, it is conducted as a two years integrated course. Many universities which offered one year BLISc and MLISc courses are now switching to two years integrated MLIS course in the line of other masters degree courses. The basic qualification of the integrated MILS is any degree, where as the basic qualification of one year MLIS is BLIS.

3.4. Five Year Integrated Course in LIS

In 2010, University of Calcutta introduces five year integrated course in Library & Information Science. It is the first university to launch such course in LIS domain. The basic qualification for this course is 10+2 in Arts / Science or Commerce. Launching of this course will force the learners to choose the LIS by choice and not by chance. It will again help the students to grasp and understand the contents for LIS in a better and exhaustive way.

Associateship in Documentation and Information Science : NISCAIR New Delhi, formerly Indian National Scientific Documentation Centre (INSDOC), has been offering a two-year programme in documentation. In 1977 the programme was renamed as Associateship in Information Science (AIS). The minimum qualification for admission to the course is a

(i) Master's degree; or

(ii) Four-year plus degree like B.E./M.B.B.S.; or

(iii) Bachelor's degree plus B.Lib.Sc. plus one year of relevant experience after B.Lib.Sc.

In 2011 and 2012 notification has not been given for this course.

3.5. Master of Science in library and Information Science

The Documentation Research and Training Centre (DRTC), established in 1962 in Bangalore, offers a Master of Science programme in library and Information science with the primary objective of preparing the next generation information managers. This unique programme offers an ideal blend of courses planning library science, information technology, knowledge management and quantitative studies. The duration of the course is two years and the minimum qualification for the admission of this course is any degree.

3.6. M.Phil (Master of philosophy) in Library & Information Science

M.Phil. in Library and Information Science prepares a student for further advanced research in LIS. The basic qualification for the Mphil course is MLISC or Associateship in Library and Information science from any recognized university. The duration of the course is one year. The Mphil degree holders are exempted from the course work during the PhD programme.

3.7. PhD. Programme in LIS

This is an advanced level research programme being offered after the completion of MLIS or M.Phil degree in library science. The duration of the PhD program is three to five years. Some universities offer integrated Mphil- Phd program. PhD program is given both fulltime and part time mode by Indian Universities. Admission to the PhD programme is given on the basis of entrance test and interview by concerned universities. JRF (Junior Research Fellowship) holders of UGC are exempted from entrance test, and they can join for PhD at any time if a research guide is available. According to new guidelines of UGC, a Ph.D research scholar shall undergo a course work of one-semester duration, which include compulsory class room teaching, seminar and assignment.

3.8. PGDLAN (Post Graduate Diploma in Library Automation and Networking)

This is a one year PG diploma course in library science. The basic qualification of the course is BLIS. PGDLAN aims at equipping candidate in various operations of the library automation and networking. The program also provides practical exposure to enhance technological skills of the learners for independently developing and managing computerized library. PGDLAN course is being provided by a number of universities. Some of them are- University of Hyderabad, Punjab University, Pondichery University, Annamalai University- Thamilnadu, Sambalpur University- Bhubaneswar- Orissa and Indira Gandhi National Open University.

3.9. Post Graduate Diploma in Digital Library and Information Management

This course is being conducted by Tata Institute of Social Sciences (TISS)- Mumbai since 2010. It is a two semester PG diploma course, and the eligibility is BLIS. Main objectives of this course programme are: to prepare students in the application of ICT for selection, organization and preservation of knowledge for use, to bring out the competent human resource to promote access to the traditional and socially useful knowledge by the process of digitization, to involve in capacity building activities to create a development oriented, people friendly learning support system. The course is offered through e-learning platform. It is envisaged that this program will equip librarians with digital information management skills. This is the first course of that kind in India.

4. CORE SYLLABUS OF LIS COURSES

Library and society : This paper includes development of libraries in the world, laws of library science, role of libraries in the society, types of libraries, library legislation, library organizations and library associations.

Library management : This paper includes principles of management, in house operations of library, collection development, book selection principles, various preservation methods, budgeting and library finance.

Knowledge organization : This paper includes theories of cataloguing and classification, various indexing techniques, practical with various classification schemes such as Dewey Decimal Classification, Colon Classification and Universal Decimal Classification.

Information Science : This paper includes various information sources, various information services, reference service and current awareness service.

Information Technology : This paper includes introduction information technology, introduction to computer, computer hardware and software, library networks, library management software, digital library software and internet.

5. CAREER OPTIONS AND JOB SCOPE

The scope of library science is very high. The person

in this field can find employment opportunities in Public libraries, Universities and other academic institutions, News agencies and organizations, research organisations and special libraries, Foreign embassies, news paper libraries, channel libraries, Information centres /documentation centers and Companies and business organisations.

Some of the career options in this field are- Library Attendant, Library Assistant, Semi-Professional Assistant, Professional Assistant, Junior Librarian, Assistant Librarian, Deputy Librarian, University librarian, college librarian, Information scientist, Knowledge manager, Cataloguer and Information Analyst.

6. Problems of LIS education in India

Even though, LIS education has completed its 100 in India, still some problems are there. The following are the major problems,

Absence of a national level accreditation body : To achieve academic excellence, a supreme body to maintain the quality is inevitable. In America, ALA is the accreditation body. Unfortunately there do not exist such a body in India. As a result, new library science schools are opening by following different patterns of education without any criteria. This ultimately results the mass production of LIS professionals with low-standard and having least practical experience.

Abundance of library schools : Library schools and departments are mushrooming without offering basic facilities. The production of this substandard library professionals leads to the un employment in the job market.

Lack of sufficient library facilities : Many LIS schools have either no library, or library with sufficient collection of reference books, text books, and practical tools such as classification schemes and cataloguing codes. As far as LIS students are concerned, library is a workshop to do practical and assignments.

Lack of adequate IT facilities : A Sound IT lab is necessary along with a LIS department/school. Practical training for computerized house keeping operations, computerised information services and digital information management are done with the help of a sound IT lab supported by standard library software packages and digital library management software. But unfortunately, the condition of the most of the LIS schools are pathetic in terms of IT facilities.

Curriculum revision : Time to time revision of curriculum is to be done for the existence of a professional course. Many universities are prevailing the old and outdated syllabus. Then only the LIS professional can face the new challenges of knowledge management.

The LIS courses in Indian states, Universities and colleges have been given in table 1.

Table 1. LIS courses in University Teaching Departments- State-wise List

State	University	CLISc	BLISc	MLISc	Integrated MLIS	PG diploma	MA	MSc	MPhil	PhD
Andhra Pradesh	Andhra University			Y						
	College of Arts & Social Sciences, Department of Library & Information Science		Y							
	Sri Krishnadevaraya University			Y					Y	Y
	Kakatiya University			y						
	Dr B.R.Ambedkar University-Srikakulam			Y						
	Osmania University (OU), Hyderabad		y	y					y	y
	Dravidian University			Y						
Arunachal Pradesh	Arunachal university of studies		Y	Y						
Assam	Guwahati University			Y						y
	Assam University			Y						
	Dibrugarh University		Y	Y						
Bihar	Jai Prakash Vishwavidyalaya (University), Chapra		y							
	Patna University Library		y							
	Veer Kunwar Singh University (VKSU), Ara			y						y

	Babasaheb Bhimrao Ambedkar Bihar University, Muzaffarpur	Y				
	T. M. Bhagalpur University, Bhagalpur	Y	Y			
Chattis-garh	Guru Ghasidas Vishwavidyalaya, Bilaspur	Y	Y	Y		Y
	Pt. Ravishankar Shukla University	Y	Y	Part time Mlisc	Y	Y
Goa	Goa university	Y				
Gujarat	Maharaja Krishnakumarsinhji Bhavnagar University	Y	y			y
	Gujarat Vidyapith deemed university		y		y	
	Gujarat University	y	y			
	University of Baroda,	y	y			y
	Sardar Patel University	y	y	Part time Mlisc	part time	Part and full
	Maharaja Sayajirao University of Baroda	y	y			y
	Saurashtra university	y	y			y
	Hemchandracharya North gujarath university	y	y			
	Veer Narmad South Gujarat University		y			

Haryana	Kurukshetra University,	y	y				y	y
	Kalpana Chawla Govt. Polytechnic for Women (KCGPW), Ambala City				3 year diploma			
	Bhagat Phool Singh Institute of Polytechnic (BPSIP), Khanpur Kalan				3 year diploma			
	Vaish Technical Institute (VTI), Rohtak				3 year diploma			
	SRM University (SRMH), Haryana	y	y					
	Mahatma Gandhi Chitrakoot Gramodaya Vishwavidyalaya	Y	Y				Y	
	Makhanlal Chaturvedi Rashtriya Patrakarita Vishwavidyalaya		Y				Y	
	Rani Durgavati Vishwavidyalaya	Y	Y					
Himachal Predesh	Central University of Himachal Predesh	Y						
	Eternal university	Y						
Jammu & Kashmir	University of Jammu	Y	Y				Y	
	University of Kashmir	y				Y	y	
Jharkand								
Kerala	University of Kerela			Y			Y	Y
	University of Calicut			Y			Y	Y

	Mahatma Gandhi University, Kottayam		Y	Y				Y
	Kannur University				Y			Y
Karnataka	Bangalore University,		y	y				y
	University of Madras			ms				y
	Gulbarga University,			y			y	y
	Mangalore University			Y				Y
	University of Mysore			y			y	y
	DRTC					MS		y
	Manipal university	y		y				
	Karnatak University, Dharwad		y	y				y
	Rani Channamma University, Belagavi			y		MSc	y	y
	Kuvempu University, Jnana Sahyadri, Shankaragatta					Msc	y	y
	Tumkur university			y				
	Karnataka State Women's University, Bijapur	y		y			y	y
Madhya pradesh	AEC Training College And Centre	y	Y					
	Dr Harisingh Gaur university Vishwavidyalaya		y	y				

	Govt. MLB Arts & Commerce Autonomous College		y					
	Awadhesh Pratap Singh University		y	y				
	Devi Ahilya Vishwavidyalaya		y	y		PGDLAN	y	y
	Jiwaji University		y	y				y
	Mahatma Gandhi Chitrakoot Gramodaya Vishwavidyalaya		Y	Y			Y	
	Makhanlal Chaturvedi Rashtriya Patrakarita Vishwavidyalaya		Y				Y	
	Rani Durgavati Vishwavidyalaya		y	y				
	Vikram University Ujjain						y	
	Makhanlal Chaturvedi Rashtriya Patrakarita Vishwavidyalaya, Bhopal		y	Y				
	Mahatma Gandhi Chitrakoot Gramoday University		y	Y				
	IPS Academy		y	y	y	PGDLAN		
Maharastra	University of Mumbay		y	y			y	y
	Sant Gadge Baba	c	y	y				y

	Amravati University				
	Rashtrasant Tukadoji Maharaj Nagpur University		y	y	y
	Chhatrapati Shivaji Shivaji University, Vidyanagar, Kolhapur		y	y	y
	University of Pune	y	y	y	y
	Swami Ramanand Teerth Marathwada University		Y		Y
	SNDT Women's University Mumbai	y	y		y
	Gondwana University Gadchirol				
	North Maharashtra University, Jalgaon		y		
	Tilak Maharashtra Vidyapeeth (TMU), Pune	y	y	y	y
	Dr Babasaheb Ambedkar Marathwada University, Aurangabad		y	y	y
	Vidyapeeth Bhavan, Gultekadi, Pune	Y	Y	Y	Y
Meghalaya	North-Eastern Hill University, Shillong		y		y

Mizoram	Mizoram University		y	y	y
Nagaland	ICFAI University, Nagaland	y	y		
	Kakatiya University		y		
Orissa	Asian Workers Development Instt. Nabakrushna Choudhury Library	Y			
	Utkal University		y		
	Sambalpur University,		y	y	
	SMIT, Berhampur University	Y	Y		
	North Orissa university	Yd	Y		
Punjab	Guru Nanak Dev University	y	y		
	Punjabi University,	Y	y		
	Panjab University Chandigarh	y	y		y
	C V Raman University	Y	Y		
	Baba Farid University of Health Sciences, Faridkot		PG Diploma in Health Sciences Librarianship		
Rajasthan	Mohanlal Sukhadia University (MLSU), Udaipur	y	y		
	Singhania University	y	y		

	University of Rajasthan			Y				
	NIMS UNIVERSITY, Shobha Nagar	Y	Y	Y				
Sikkim	Sikkim University							
Tamilnadu	Annamalai University		Y	Y	5YR INTGTD MLISC		Y	Y
	University of Madrass					Msc		y
	Madurai Kamaraj University			y	PGDLAN			
	Alagappa University		y	y			y	y
	Gandhigram Rural Institute-deemed university							Y
	Bharathiar university							y
	Periyar University Salem	y		y				
	Bharathidasan University, Tiruchirappalli			y	PG Diploma		y	y
	Kakatiya University (KU), Warangal	Y	Y					
Telugana	Osmania University		y	y			y	y
Tripura	Tripura University		y					
	Assam University, Silchar			Y				
Uttar pradesh	Aligarh Muslim University		Y	y			y	y
	Banaras Hindu University			y				Y
	Babasaheb Bhimrao		y					y

	Ambedkar University					
	Dr B.R. Ambedkar University Agra		y	y		
	Bundelkhand University, Uttar Pradesh		y	y	y	
	Lucknow University, Uttar Pradesh		y	y		Y
	Mahatma Gandhi Kashi Vidyapeeth, Varanasi		Y			
	Chhatrapati Shahu Ji Maharaj University Kanpur		y	y		
	Deen Dayal Upadhyaya Gorakhpur University			y		
	Integral University, Lucknow			Y		
	Shri Ramswaroop Memorial University (SRMU), Lucknow	y	y	y		
	University of Lucknow		Y Blisc in arts	Y		
	Galgotias University (GU) Noida		y	y		
	Ram Manohar Lohia Avadh University, Faizabad		y	y		
Uttara-khand	Uttarakhand technical university		Y			
	Vidyasagar University (VU)		Y	Y	Y	

	Himgiri Zee University (HZU)	Y					
	North Bengal University (NBU)	Y	Y				
	Kalyani University (KU)	Y	Y				
West	Jadavpur University,	Y	y				
Bengal	University of Burdwan	y	y			y	
	Calcutta University	Y	Y	5yr intgted		Y	
	Rabindra Bharati University (RBU)		Y	Y			
	Vidyasagar University (VU)	Y	Y			Y	
	North Bengal University (NBU)	Y	Y				
	Kalyani University (KU)	Y	Y				
	Netaji Subhas Open University (NSOU)						
Pondichery	Puducherry University			Y			Y
Delhi	Jamia Millia Islamia	y					
	NISCAIR			5 Years intgted			
	University of Delhi	Y	Y		Y	Y	Y

Table 2. LIS courses in Indian Colleges State- wise list

State	*Name of Institute*	*CLISc*	*BLISc*	*MLISc*
Andra pradesh	Andhra University College of Arts & Commerce, Visakhapatnam			y
	Pragathi MahaVidyalaya, Hyderabad		y	
	Sun Institute of Technical Education & IT (SITE), Hyderabad		y	y
	University College of Arts and Social Sciences, Hyderabad		y	y
	Sri Padmavati Mahila Visvavidyalayam (SPMVV), Tirupati		y	
	Sun Institute of Technical Education & IT (SITE), Hyderabad		y	y
Bihar	Ram Krishna Dwarika College, Patna		y	
	North Bihar Institute of Technology, Muzaffarpur		y	
	Arcade Business College, Patna	y	y	
Chandi-garh	SoftBrain Informatic Technology Pvt. Ltd, Chandigarh		y	y
Himachal pradesh	M.S. Panwar Institute of Communication and Management (MSPICM), Solan		y	y
Hariyana	Kiran Institute of IT & Management (KIITM), Gurgaon		y	y
	VCC Computer Education, Panchkula		y	
Karnataka	SLN Correspondence College (SLNCC), Bangalore			fultime, partime
	St. Philomena's College (Autonomous), Mysore		y	
	SLN Correspondence College (SLNCC), Bangalore		y	y
	Imperial College of Business Studies, Bangalore		y	y
	Guru Mantras Career Development Centre, Bangalore			y
	Rani Channamma University (RCU), Belagavi		y	
	Bright International Education, Bangalore		y	y
Kerala	Ettumanoorappan College, Ettumanoor Kottayam			

	Government College (GC), Nedumangad Trivandrum		y	
	Mahathma Gandhi Education Foundation (MGEF), Alappuzha		y	y
	Mar Thoma College for Women, Perumbavoor		y	
	MES College for Advanced Studies (MESCAS), Edathala			y
	Kuriakose Elias College (K E College), Kottayam		y	
	Regional Institute of Engineering (RIE), Trivandrum			y
	St. Berchmans College (SB College), Changanassery			y
	Divine College of Management Studies (DCMS), Cochin			Y
	Rajagiri College of Social Science		Y	
	Farook College Calicut		Y	Y
Mahar-astra	Abhinav Institute of Technology & Mangement (AITM), Thane (w)		Y	Y
	Dhanwate National College (DNC), Nagpur		Y	Y
	Khandesh College Education Society's Moolji Jaitha College		y	y
	Tilak Maharashtra Vidyapeeth (TMU), Pune		y	y
	Tilak Maharashtra Vidyapeeth (TMU), Pune		y	y
	Vivekanand College, Kolharpur		y	
	Jethro Institute of Distance Education (JIDE), Goregoan (W) Mumbai		y	y
	Mahatma Gandhi Shikshan Mandal's Arts, Science & Commerce College, Chopda	y		
Madya pradesh	Developers Institute of Computer Technology (DICT), Jabalpur		Y	
	Devi Ahilya Vishwavidyalaya, Indore		Y	Y
	Career College, Bhopal		y	y
	Thakur Ranmat Singh (TRS) College, Rewa		y	
	Indore Professional Studies Academy (IPSA)		y	y

	Kamla Nehru Mahavidyalaya, Bhopal		y	
	Mandi Bahuddin (M.B.) Khalsa College		y	
	Katni Arts and Commerce College (KACC), Katni		y	
	Sarojini Naidu Govt. Girls Post Graduate (Autonomous) College (SNGGPGAC), Bhopal		y	y
	Rani Durgawati Vishwavidyalya (RDVV), Jabalpur		y	y
	Sarojini Naidu Govt. Girls Post Graduate (Autonomous) College (SNGGPGAC), Bhopal		y	y
Orissa	Asian Workers Development Institute (AWDI), Rourkela		Y	
	Biju Pattanaik Computer Academy (BPCA), Bomikhal			Y
Rajasthan	B.N.P.G. College, Udaipur		y	
Sikkim	Damber Singh College		Y	
Uttar pradesh	College of Humanities, Social Science, Arts Culture, Allahabad		Y	Y
	Indian Institute of Professional Studies (IIPS), Lucknow		Y	
	Dhanvantari Institute of Professional Education (DIPE)			Y
	Bareilly College, Bareilly		y	
Uttara-khand	Amrapali Group of Institutes, Haldwani		y	y
	Greenway Institute of Management Studies (GIMS), Roorkee		y	y
	Bishamber Sahai Degree College (BSDC), Roorkee		y	
Delhi	Infonet Computer Education (ICE), Delhi		y	y
	Amar Jyoti Research & Rehabilitation Centre, Delhi		Y	
	Ahimsa Women's Polytechnic, New Delhi	y		
	Aarti Institute of Professional Studies (AIPS),		Y	Y

Table 3. LIS courses in India in Distance Mode State –wise list

State	*University*	*CLISc*	*BLISc*	*MLISc*	*Integrated MLIS*	*PG diploma*	*MA*	*MSc*	*MPhil*	*PhD*
Arunachal Pradesh	Sri Venkateshwara Open University	y	y	y		PGDLAN				
Bihar	Jai Prakash Vishwavidyalaya		Y							
	Patna University		y							
	Nalanda openuniversity	y	y	y						
Chandi-garh	University School of Open Learning, Panjab University		y							
Chattis-gargh	Pandit Sundarlal Sharma open University			Y					Y	
Haryana	Maharshi Dayanand University, Rohtak		y	y						
	Kurukshetra University,		y	y	y	y				
Karnataka	Karnataka state open university		y	y						
Madhya pradesh	Madhya Pradesh Bhoj Open University		y	y						
	Dr. Harisingh Gour Vishwavidyalaya Sagar (DHGV-IDE)		y	y						
	Awadhesh Pratap Singh University		y	y						

Maharashtra	Rani Durgavati Vishwavidyalaya Jabalpur		y		
	Yashvantrao Chavan Maharashtra Open University		y	y	
	Bharati Vidyapeeth Deemed University		y	y	
Nagaland	Global Open University		Y		
Orissa	Berhampur University, Berhampur		Y		
	North Orissa University		Y		
	Sambalpur University				PGDLAN
Tamilnadu	Alagappa University	Y			
	Bharathiar university	y	y	y	
Punjab	Punjabi University, Patiala	y	Y	Y	
Uttarakhand	Uttarakhand Open University		Y		
	Kalyani University (KU)				PGDLAN
Uttar paredesh	U. P. Rajarshi Tandon Open University		y	y	
	Aligarh Muslim University		Y		
West bengal	Netaji Subhas Open University		Y		

Delhi	IGNOU	Y	Y	Y		Y	Y
Rajasthan	Jain Vishva Bharati University	Y					
AP	Dr. B. R. Ambedkar Open University (BRAOU), Hyderabad	Y	Y				
Kerala	Mahatma Gandhi University	y					
India	Indira Gandhi National University	Y	Y		PGDLAN	Y	y

7. CONCLUSIONS

In 2011, LIS education has completed its 100 years in our country. Through out these years, both LIS education and profession has achieved tremendous developments. Today, the LIS profession has attained the status of a full-fledged discipline in India. However, it has low recognition and has not been regarded as other well-known professions. In order to make the LIS profession a number one profession, the above mentioned problems of LIS education are to be solved. This can be achieved by taking initiatives by academicians, library organizations and library associations.

REFERENCE

1. Sjitha,MP(2010).Library and Information Science at the critical crossroads, *SRELS Journal of Information Management*, Vol.44, No.3,pp 3-8.
2. Krishan Kumar and Jaideep Sharma(2010), Library and Information Science Education in India:A Historical Perspective, *DESIDOC Journal of Library & Information Technology*, Vol. 30, No. 5, September 2010, pp. 3-8.
3. Vara Lakshmi, R.S.R (2010), Library and Information Science Education in South India: Perspectives and challenges , *DESIDOC Journal of Library & Information Technology*, Vol. 30, No. 5, September 2010, pp. 19-31.
4. Bidyarthi Dutta and Anup Kumar Das, (2001).Higher education in library and information science in India, *ILA Bulletin* , 37(1), 25-30.
5. Singh. SP (2003).Library and information science in India: issues and trends, *Malaysian Journal of Library & Information* Science, Vol.8, no.2, Dec.2003: 1-17

3

Library Movement and Development in Andhra Pradesh and Telengana

Y. Sudha Rani
Librarian(I/C)
Vikrama Simhapuri University,
Nellore, SPSR Nellore
Andhra Pradesh.

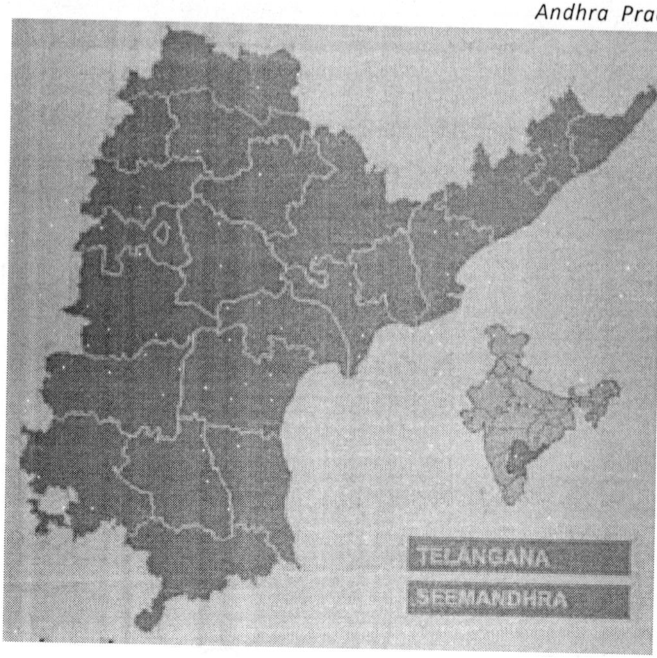

1. STATE PROFILES

Andra Pradesh is one of the oldest Indian states having well set up library system. It has sound history of library movement. Andra Pradesh state gave birth to Telengana state in 2014.

Andhra Pradesh (erstwhile). Andhra Pradesh is regarded as one of the most progressive states of the country today. It has seen a great development on the industrial front, with the IT sector acting as a growth engine. The state has merited visits of world leaders for its impressive achievements. Known as the rice bowl of the South, Andhra Pradesh has an excellent conducive climate for growing food and non food crops. Paddy, pulses, oilseeds, millets are major food crops while tobacco, cotton, chillies, vegetables, fruits, are other commercial and horticulture crops. The state is a leading producer of many of these crops. The State capital of Hyderabad is expanding at a very fast rate, with the development of world class infrastructure. The state will has a world class international airport, express highways, and other infrastructure. The major towns of the state, like Visakhapatnam, Tirupathi, Guntur, Rajamundry, Nellore and Anantapur are now attracting IT and ES investments. Major world players are eager to invest in AP. Services sector contributes 49% to the State's GDP.

Telangana : Telangana is a state in the Southern region of India. It is the newest state of India. It has an area of 114,840 km^2 and is the twelfth largest state in India. Most of it was part of the princely state of Hyderabad (Medak and Warangal Divisions), ruled by the Nizam of Hyderabad during the British Raj, joining the Union of India in 1948. In 1956, the Hyderabad state was dissolved as part of the linguistic reorganisation of states, and the Telugu speaking part of Hyderabad state, known as Telangana, was merged with Andhra State to form Andhra Pradesh. On 2 June 2014, Telangana was separated from Andhra Pradesh as a new 29th state of India, with the city of Hyderabad as its capital.Hyderabad will continue to serve as the joint capital city for Andhra Pradesh and Telangana for a period of not more than ten years. Telangana is bordered by the states of *Maharashtra* and *Chhattisgarh* to the north, Karnataka to the west, and Andhra Pradesh to the south and east. Telangana has an area of 114,840 square kilometres (44,340 sq mi), and a population of 35,286,757 (2011 census). Its major cities include Hyderabad, Warangal, Nizamabad, Karimnagar and Khammam.

2. PUBLIC LIBRARY MOVEMENT

The pioneers of Andhra Library Movement looked at library service as a multifaceted activity to reform and regenerate society. By 1914 about 120 libraries were established by enlighten individuals in the Telugu speaking districts of the Madras Presidency. To coordinate and direct the efforts of individual leaders and librarians the first conference of the representatives of libraries of Andhra desa was held under the auspices of the Rammohan Library, Vijaya wada on 10th April 1914.The prime movers who convened and conducted the conference were Shri Suri Venkata Narasimham and Iyyanki Venkata Ramanaiah. The participants believed that libraries were agents of education and enlightment of the public and instrument of national awakening and development. The Grandalaya Veda was proclaimed by Shri Chilakamarhi Lakshmi Narasimham pantulu in his presidential address .The proclamation of Grandalaya Veda gave direction to the Library movement. Andhra Desa Grantha bhandagara Sangam(Library association), after formation of the state of Andhra Pradesh it was re designated as Andhra Pradesh Grandalaya Sangham.

2.1. Role of Andhra Desa Library Association in promoting the Library Movement (ADLA).

Since the formation of this Association, it becomes the centre for promoting Andhra library movement. The most important section of ADLA was "Granthalaya Sevakas". The sevakas were fulltime honorary workers in the library movement. Shri Iyyanki Venkata Ramanaiah and Shri Paturi Nagabhushanam were devoted nationalists as well as promoters of ADLA. They carried the message of library movement to the villages. Village library was perceived as the centre piece of rural development. It helped in the establishment of several hundred libraries. The village library was an information and community centre. These are arranging lecturers, reading news papers aloud at convenient hours for the benefit of groups of illiterate people. Libraries used indigenous and popular techniques of publicity such as Bhajans, Harikatas, Burrakatha, Tholubommalu (puppet play) and gramphone records to reach the illiterate masses and promote library movement. The association conducted a number of library conferences. These conferences had great publicity value for the library movement.

Library Pilgrimages : The most indigenous method developed by the movement is to popularize library movement through library pilgrimage. This program was devised and ably implemented by Iyyanki Venkata Ramanaiah .A batch Granthalaya Sevakas planned to tour a group of villages. This batch is called Rama Dandu, they propagate library movement in the village. The Association encouraged mobile libraries. Bullock Carts, bicycle etc were used to supply books to people. Shri Paturi naga Bhushanm Conducted mobile libraries on traveling boats for the benefit of passengers.

2.2. Library Movement in Telangana region

The library movement in Telangana area developed on similar lines, and paved the way for social political and cultural renaissance of the people. Sankarananda Granthalayam was started at secuderabad during 1872 with the co operation of Moulana Abdul Quayyam a nationalist and Moulvi syed Hussain Bilgrani which was taken over by the Nizam's Government and opened to the public. The library was converted into Asafia State Library, after the formation of Andhra Pradesh it was renamed State Central

Library, Hyderabad. Shri Krishna Devaraya Andhra Bhasha Nilayam was started in 1901 at Hyderabad by three illustrious personalities, shriyut Ravichettu Rangarao, Kommarraju Laxamanrao and Nayani Venkata ranga Rao. The Library was of great help to the people in the city. Andhra Jana Sangham which was started on November 12th also taken up the causes of libraries in Telangana area. The sangham encouraged the starting of libraries in villages and towns. The Golkonda Patrika was started under the editor ship of Suravaram Pratap reddy in 1926.Through this paper articles and news items enlighten the public to fight against the Nizam's rule. Hyderabad Library Association was started on 26th January, 1951, with main objective of library legislation in Hyderabad state. This Association also started the monthly journal "Granthalaya" in English and Hindi.

2.3. Structure of Public Library system in Andhra Pradesh

The structure of AP public library system is in the form of a pyramid with the State central Library at the apex and the Book deposit centers and Aided Libraries at the bottom. In between two level, there are from top to bottom, the regional libraries, the city central library/the district Central Library, the branch Libraries and the village libraries. The PLs in the state may broadly be divided into three categories: Govt. Libraries, ZGS libraries and Aided Libraries. Government libraries receive full support from the state government. Libraries under Zilla Granthalaya Samsthas are particularly financed by state government fund and partially by library funds. State meets the salary of staff. Aided libraries receive grants from the state and also utilize their own resources.

3. LIBRARY LEGISLATION IN ANDHRA PRADESH

Andhra Pradesh public libraries Act,1960 came in to force with effect from April 1, 1960. It was amended in 1964,and in 1988. Prior to the provision of this Act, public libraries of Andhra region were functioning under the provision of Madras Public Libraries Act of 1948 and public libraries of Telangana region were governed by Hyderabad public library Act of 1955.The objective of this Act is concerned the "establishment and maintenance of Public Libraries in the State of Andhra Pradesh and matters connected therewith".(preamble).

Section 3 provides for the State Library Committee of Andhra Pradesh. It is purely an advisory body. It is not binding on the Government to implement its recommendations. As this committee shall be a Central Authority for carrying out the provisions of the Act, it is necessary to entrust the committee with certain statutory powers and functions. This question has been dealt with from all aspects in the Report of Sri Gopal Rao Ekbote. The committee shall advice the Government on all matters arising under this Act and shall exercise and perform such other powers and duties as may be prescribed.

Andhra Pradesh is the first State in our country to have a separate Department of libraries headed by a separate Director. This is one of the good features of the Andhra Pradesh Public Libraries Act. Section 8 provides for a department of Public libraries and Director of public libraries Section 9 concerned with provision of local library authorities. The Constitution an incorporation of Zilla Grandhalaya Samsthas : 9. (1) For the purposes of organizing and administering public libraries in the state. There shall be constitute Zilla razndhalaya samstha, one for the City of Hyderabad by the name of the Hyderabad City Grandhalaya Samstha; one for the district of Hyderabad excluding the said City by the name of the Hyerabad Zilla Grandhalaya Samstha and one for each of the other districts by the name of the district concerned. The Zilla Grandhalaya Samstha for each district shall consist of the following members, namely -

(a) five members nominated by the Government as follows - (i) One person from among person in the medical profession in the district;(ii) One person from among person in the legal profession in the district; (iii) one head-master or head-mistress of a secondary school in the district; (iv) two persons who have rendered eminent service in the field of education or public libraries.

(b) two members elected from among themselves by the Presidents of the Governing bodies of the Public Libraries, other than those referee to sub-clause (a), (b), and (c) of clause (9) of section 2 in each revenue division in the district.

Powers and functions of Zilla Grandhalaya Samstha are (a) Provide suitable lands and buildings for Public Libraries and also the furniture, fittings, materials and conveniences requisite therefore;(b) Stock libraries with books, periodicals, newspapers, manuscripts, maps, works and specimens of art and science lantern slides, films, cinema projectors, recorders and the like. Section 20 contains provision of Library Cess .Every ZGS shall levy in its area a library cess in the form of a surcharge on the property tax or house tax levied in such area under the relevant laws providing for the levy of such property tax or house tax, at the rate of four naye paise for every rupee in the property tax or house tax so levied ;(b)A ZGS may, with the previous sanction of the Government and shall if directed by them, increase the rate specified in clause (a) so as not to exceed EIGHT naya paise for every rupee.

4. MAJOR PUBLIC LIBRARIES IN ANDHRA PRADESH

4.1. State Central Library

The State Central Library is one of the institution of learning which had its genesis in the year 1891 due to the sustained efforts of Late Moulavi Syed Hussain Bilgrami (Nawab Imadul Mulk Bahadur of H.E.H), the Nizam's Government. The personal library of this great scholar formed the initial corpus of this great institution. It was then known as Asafia State Library after the name of Asaf Jah dynasty and was located in Abids. Mr. Syed Tassaduq Hussian an eminent scholar of Eastern Languages, was appointed as Superintendent of this Library and later he became the first Librarian of State Central Library. In course of time, the Asafia State Library emerged as one of the biggest, finest and richest libraries in the world both in terms of print and manuscripts collection. The year 1941 was another landmark in the history of Asafia State Library, which marked it s Golden Jubilee celebrations. In 1955, after the enactment of Hyderabad Public Libraries Act, Asafia State Library was declared as the State Central Library for the Hyderabad State. After the linguistic re organization of States in 1956, it was declared as the State Central Library for the Andhra Pradesh .

4.2. Gowthami Grandhalayam

The Sri Gowthami Regional Library was started by poet and social reformer Nalam Krishna Rao as Gowthami Grandhalayam in 1898. Initially named Sri Veeresalingam library, since it was backed by the nationalist Kandukuri Veeresalingam Pantulu, it was housed in Nalam Choultry in Innispeta with a very small collection. Around the same time Addanki Satyanarayana established the Vasuraya Library. Gradually, the two merged and were jointly registered in 1920 under the Societies Registration Act. With the increase in collections the library moved to the Town Hall in Rajahmundry. Later land was bought at Lakshmivarapupeta and a rich landlord Kanchumarti Seetaramachandra Rao constructed a building in memory of his daughter Babayamma (one of the first women to complete matriculation in Rajahmundry) who died young. The Babayamma Hall, served as the library building until the 1970s and still exists, behind the new building.. Today Gowthami library has a stock of 82,000 books, and around 400 old manuscripts. Copper plate charters of the 13-14th centuries are also preserved in this library. So is an ancient silver coated ghantam (stylus) on palm-leaf manuscripts.

4.3. Saraswata Niketanam

Saraswata Niketanam library is located in Vetapalem, Prakasam District of Andhra Pradesh. It is one of the foremost research oriented libraries of Andhra Pradesh. This library founded by Late V. V. Shreshti in 1918 with the help of "Pantulu Garu" (Adusumalli Srinivasa Rao) and had the rare privilege and good fortune of its foundation stone being laid by The Father of the Nation Mahatma Gandhi in 1929. This library is the knowledge source for many national and international scholars for archives of information. In spite of its wealth of Telugu literary collection, and over 80 years of colossal service to the Telugu cause, it remains largely undiscovered even among literati. Interesting thing about this library is that since its founding in the pre-independence era in 1918, it has remained a private, family-maintained library. It is a rare institution of its kind in Andhra Pradesh and perhaps in India.

4.4. Sri Krishna Devaraya Andhra Bhasha Nilayam

The library was started on September 1, 1901. The Bhasha Nilayam named after Sri Krishnadevaraya, functioned initially from the Ramkote residence of Jagirdar Ravichettu Ranga Rao, the founding secretary. Later, with a donation of Rs. 3,000 from the wife of Ranga Rao, a small tiled house was bought in Sultan Bazar to house the Bhasha Nilayam. Madapati Hanumantha Rao, who became secretary in 1915, raised more funds for its growth. Among the leading personalities involved in the founding and strengthening of this institution in its formative years were the Munagala Raja, Nayani Venkata Ranga Rao, eminent researcher-historian Komarraju Lakshmana Rao, Pardhasarathi Apparao Bahadur of Palwancha, Suravaram Pratapa Reddy, Madapati Hanumantha Rao, Burgula Ramakrishna Rao, Adiraju Veerabhadra Rao and Raja Bahadur Venkatram Reddy.

The Nilayam was a fountain of knowledge for people starved of intellectual and cultural fare under an oppressive regime. One had no access to reading Telugu newspapers except at the Nilayam. The young and the old turned up in large numbers to hear poets, scholars, politicians speak and to attend cultural and literary events. The Bhasha Nilayam was cradle of the nationalist struggle against the Nizam's rule and a center for Telugu language. Great people in politics, literature and culture considered it a privilege to address the gathering here. There are about 40,000-odd books and old newspapers and magazines.

5. MAJOR ACADEMIC LIBRARIES IN ANDHRA PRADESH

Andrapradesh is a state having a lot universities and other educational institutions. Some of them are mentioned here.

5.1. Indira Gandhi Memorial Library(IGM), University of Hyderabad

IGM Library is one of the important central facilities of the University catering to the information needs of faculty, research scholars and students in Arts, Humanities, Social Sciences, Management, Sciences and Engineering. The main objective is to make the Library the most effective Learning Resource centre to contribute to the quality of higher education. The library also created learning environment by establishing Online Public Access Catalog Searching Area, Internet browsing area for accessing e-resources, Laptop zone with Wi-Fi facility, specialized workstations & software for visually-challenged students.

The library with its excellent IT infrastructure facilities has achieved several distinctions in the country.

- The National Board of Higher Mathematics (NBHM) has recognized IGM Library as their Regional Library for South Zone from the year 1993 to provide facility to faculty and research scholars of other institutions for referring mathematics/statistics books and journals in this library.
- First University Library in India to have fully automated all its house keeping operations by 1997.

- IGM Library has conducted national conferences - CALIBER in 1995, SIS in 1998, NACLIN in 2001 and OCLC Seminar in 2002.
- Library began subscribing online search databases since the year 1998 and full text databases 2001.
- Library is first in the country to offer one year Post Graduate Diploma in Library Automation and Networking (PGDLAN) under Distance Education mode from 1998 with greater emphasis on contact classes, practices and projects.
- UGC INFLIBNET has identified the library one of the 22 resource centres for nation-wide Document Delivery Services to all universities.

5.2. Osmania University Library

The University library system consists of a Main Library and College / Department/Seminar Libraries. The University Library coordinates the library system, which links the libraries in all the campus and constituent college libraries.

The main library was established in 1918 along with the University. The Library was shifted to the present building, which was inaugurated by Dr.S.Radhakrishnan, the then President of India on 3rd August 1963. The main library building departs from the traditional use of the Indo-Saracenic arch, but it seeks unity with the older buildings of the campus through the dominant pillars of the entrance portal. The Library is divided into a number of Sections basing on the collection and services offered. They are Text Book Section, Periodical Section, Reference Section, Acquisition & Cataloguing Sections. Additionally, it has Vision of Osmania, Manuscript Section, Theses Section, CERL Section & U.N. Section, which are highlighted.

5.3. Andhra University Library

The Andhra University Library was started in the year 1927, renamed as V.S.Krishna Memorial Library in 1968 as a mark of respect to the former Vice-Chancellor Dr. V. S.

Krishna. The Library has two branch Libraries, one in Engineering College and other in Law College. The Library is housed in an imposing structure overlooking the sea. The Library has huge collection of books apart from important journals, microfilms, paper and palm leaf manuscript. The Library has been serving the academic and research community over years and presently it is serving more than 17,000 users. The Library User community consists of teachers, research scholars, students and non teaching staffs. In addition to this, it also serves a group of deposit borrowers from outside. Most of them are form local industries and organizations and retired teachers of the University. The resources of Dr.V.S.Krishna Library are also frequently referred as the academic and research purposes by faculty and research students of other Universities.

5.4. Sri Krishna Devaraya University Library

Sri Krishnadevaraya University had its beginning as the Post Graduate centre of Sri Venkateswara University in the year 1968. It gained autonomy in the year 1976. Fulfilling the desires of the people of the region, the Autonomous Post Graduate centre was given the status of the University in the Year 1981. Initially, Sri Krishndevaraya University functioned as a unitary residential University. It was conferred the status of an affiliating University in the year 1987. Presently, it is catering to the higher educational needs of the revenue districts of Anantapur and Kurnool.

The Central library of the University is provided with a rich and varied collection of 114000 books, 190 periodicals and 118 magazines and other holdings enriched primarily on account of the generous support extended by the UGC. There are further one SC/ST Book Bank and a Competitive Examinations Cell in the library for helping the students to prepare for competitive examinations at various levels. INFLIBNET facility, offering a wide range of services, is also available in the university library. Along with software for University Libraries (SOUL).

6. MAJOR SPECIAL LIBRARIES IN ANDHRA PRADESH

The major special libraries in the state are given below.

6.1 National Institute of Rural Development Library, Hyderabad

Centre for Media and Rural Documentation (CMRD) is one of the centres of NIRD consisting of two components viz., Development Communication Wing and Library. The Centre focuses on various issues pertaining to information, communication, and media such as right to information, role of media in development communication, mechanism of information transfer and dissemination to the wider development community comprising of policy framers, researchers, trainers and all those involved in the socio-economic development.

The library acts as a resource centre and a clearinghouse of information on rural development in India. Government publications, research reports, and data apart from journals and other unpublished material form a massive resource base of the library. It has developed a computerized database of the resources in its collection. The computerized database consists of nearly two lakh references. The library has also fully automated its day-to-day operations.

The library has a strong database of books, monographs, governmental reports, seminar and conference proceedings, research reports and other gray literature relating to rural development and allied aspects. A growing collection of video cassettes covering subjects ranging from environmental issues to safe drinking water, sanitation, science and technology, gender and other development related issues, is maintained in the video library.

6.2. Indian Institute of Chemical Technology Library

IICT-CCMB Library is a combined facility for two National Laboratories viz IICT and CCMB and it is known as Information Management Area. It has precious internationally acclaimed reference collections in frontier areas of Chemical, Engineering and Life Sciences. It plays a vital role in acquisition, organization and dissemination of knowledge. It is consulted not only by the institutional users but also by researchers in and around Hyderabad. It has an impressive collection of both print and electronic resources including books, journals, technical reports, standards, patents, theses and other material. It has adequate infrastructure to meet its requirements. Main thrust of the library continues to be the improvement of quality services and facilities, achieving higher degree of user satisfaction and modernization of its activities and operations. Print holdings include Books, Dictionaries, Handbooks, Encyclopedias, Reference book series and back volumes of journals. These total print collections are more than a lakh in number, library subscribes to around two hundred national and international journals in every year. Apart from this access to around three thousand electronic journals has been provided through e-journal consortia of CSIR.

6.3. National Institute of Mentally Handicapped Library

The library was started in the Institute in 1984 to provide bibliographical and documentation support to the teaching and research programmes of the Institute. The NIMH library is a specialized library established to cater to the needs of different types of clients. The NIMH Library has a variety of documents such as books, periodicals, dissertations reports, off-prints, video films and CDs etc. It has a specialized and representative collection of books in the area of Mental Retardation and allied areas. The holdings are not limited to these areas alone. It has a substantial number of books on subjects like psychology, special education, child development, medical books (Pediatrics & Psychiatry), Social work, counseling the families of the Mentally retarded and so on in order to support research activities of inter-disciplinary nature. It has a well –balanced document collection. The library is being extensively used by the students of different courses numbering to about faculty members and research staff of the institute. In addition the use of the library is extended to the professionals of NGO's research scholars from colleges, parents and general public with prior permission.

6.4. Small Enterprises National Documentation Centre (SENDOC)

The Small Enterprises National Documentation Centre (SENDOC) was set up in 1970 when, was SIET, to energies MSMEs in India and the developing countries around the world with information and knowledge. Since then, it has been functioning as a clearing house of information both for entrepreneurs and extension agents. The Centre has emerged as a one - stop global and IT powered information centre for a wide spectrum of MSMEs, academia, students, research institutions, industry associations. The library of the SENDOC possesses 70,000 books, 18,000 back volumes of journals, 30,000 reports, 65,000 journal abstracts, 7,500 product profiles, and subscribes to 140 national and international periodicals. It has also a collection that provides information on statistics, economics, production, finance, marketing, technology, machinery and equipment, raw materials, consultants, Government policies and programmes, exports and imports, investment, trade and area literature, licensing, etc. Experts working in the Centre scan and arrange information systematically for quick retrieval using LIMS (Library Information Management System) package. The information is accessible through the website www.nimsme.org. It also provides reprography and consultancy service, product profiles, and organises training programmes for clientele on cost.

7. LIBRARY ASSOCIATIONS IN ANDHRA PRADESH

Andhra Pradesh Library Association

Andhra Desa Grantha Bhandagara Sangham, established on 10th April, 1914, is the first library association in India and it was later named as Andhra Pradesh Library Association. The Andhra Pradesh Library Association was born with a noble mission of spreading literacy, knowledge and awareness among the public. This Association has been harbinger of the public library movement in the state of Andhra Pradesh and most of the libraries in existence were established by learned individuals by providing restricted access to the readers. In the first step of its function, the association fostered the physical growth of libraries in number as well as size and there by the number of libraries increased to 586 by 1919. The association gave wide publicity to the importance of role of libraries in social and economic development in the country and it strongly advocated the need for learning by the public and the importance of establishing more and more number of Libraries that are accessible to the Public.

The Association is a role model for the library associations in the country. They had started periodicals long back. The first periodical published in 1915 was Granthalaya Sarvaswamu and Some more periodicals were published now and then but they did not last long and all of them ceased to function after a brief spell. Granthalaya sarvasamu and Andhra granthalayam were prominent among them. Formerly they were giving traing for library professionals in the state. 1989 onwards the association has been giving a five months certificate course in library science. The association has started a public library and its name is Sarvottama Granthalayam. Library conferences and seminars are being conducted by the association time to time.

8. LIS EDUCATION IN ANDHRA PRADESH

LIS education in Andhra Pradesh is currently passing through a turning point and has become a fast developing subject with multi disciliplinary approach. Today LIS education not only includes the library –specific subject but has extended to subjects like computer application, statistics, and information science and management studies. With the changing scenario modern librarianship has become a profession with diversity of opportunities and challenges for LIS students and professionals.

Andhra University is the first University started LIS course in 1935. The first open University is Andhra Pradesh open University now Dr.B.R.Ambedkar Open University was established in Hyderabad in 1982,which offers the LIS course in Distance mode. Following are the other Universities offering LIS education in Andhra Pradesh. Kakatiya University, Nagarjuna University, Osmania University, Sri Krishna Devaraya University and Sri Venkateswara University. LIS education in Andhra Pradesh is offered at various levels such as certificate, diploma, degree, M.Phil and PhD. Andhra Pradesh Library Association offered Certificate course in Library science at vijayawada. These programs are offered on regular basis and distance mode with part time and full time. University of Hyderabad offers Post Graduate Diploma in Library Automation and Networking (PGDLAN).

CONCLUSION

Andhra Pradesh and Telengana states have a good history of library movement. the public library legislation, public libraries and library associations, Library and Information Science education and library association in the sate are ideal and role models to any other states of India.

REFERENCE

1. Gangadhar Rao, P & Ramesh Babu, B (1990). Recent trends in Library and information Science Education in South India. International Library Review.22(3),181-190.
2. Krishan Kumar (1995). Library Organization. New Delhi: Vikas.
3. Raju, AAN (1988). Library Movement in Andhra Pradesh. New Delhi: Ajanta.
4. Raju, AAN (1992). Constraints on the Public library services in Andhra Pradesh. CLIS Observer, 7 (3), 69-72.
5. Ramesha & Ramesh Babu, B (2007).Trends, Challenges and Future of Library and Information Science Education in India. DESIDOC Bulletin of Information technology. 27(5), 17-26.

6. Rout, RK (1986). Library Legislation in India: Problems and prospects. New Delhi: Reliance publishing.
7. Venkatappiah, V (1997). Nurella Grandalaya Udyamum (1886-1986). Hyderabad: Telugu academy
8. http://www.osmania.ac.in/oulwebpage/About%20Library.htm
9. http://igmlnet.uohyd.ernet.in:8000/
10. http://www.andhrauniversity.edu.in/library/index.html
11. http://www.skuniversity.org/Facilities%20&%20Services/Central%20Library.asp
12. http://www.nimhindia.org/Library.html
13. http://www.nimsme.org/page.php?id=102
14. http://www.iictindia.org/Support.aspx?idc=39
15. http://www.nird.org.in/library.aspx
16. http://en.wikipedia.org/wiki/Sri_Krishna_Devaraya_ Andhra_Bhasha_Nilayam
17. http://www.telupu.com/vetapalem.html
18. http://en.wikipedia.org/wiki/Rajahmundr
19. http://en.wikipedia.org/wiki/State_Central_Library,_Hyderabad

4

Library Movement and Development in Bihar

Akhtar Hussain
Librarian & Information Officer,
King Saud University, Riyadh,
Kingdom of Saudi Arabia
Ziaul Hassan Bakhshi
Assistant Professor (Bio-Statistics),
Saudi Electronic University,
Riyadh, Kingdom of Saudi Arabia

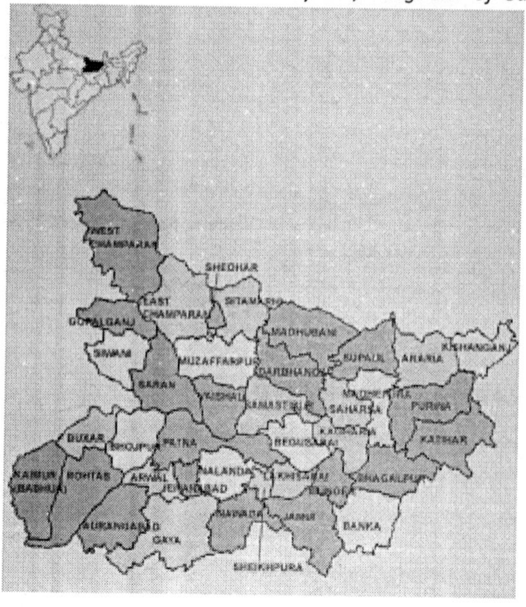

1. BIHAR: A PROFILE

Bihar is located in the eastern part of the country. It is an entirely land–locked state, although the outlet to the sea through the port of Kolkata is not far away. Bihar lies mid-way between the humid West Bengal in the east and the sub humid Uttar Pradesh in the west which provides it with a transitional position in respect of climate, economy and culture. It is bounded by Nepal in the north and by Jharkhand in the south. The Bihar plain is divided into two unequal halves by the river Ganga which flows through the middle from west to east.

Bihar was a centre of power, learning and culture in ancient and classical India. From Magadha arose India's first and greatest empire, the Maurya empire, as well as one of the world's most widely adhered-to religions, Buddhism. Magadha empires, notably under the Maurya and Gupta dynasties, unified large parts of South Asia under a central rule. Its capital Patna, earlier known as Pataliputra, was an important centre of Indian civilization. Close to Patna, Nalanda and Vikramshila were centres of learning which were established in the 5th and 8th century respectively in Bihar, and are counted as amongst the oldest international universities of the time.

2. LIBRARY MOVEMENT IN BIHAR

In 400 A.D., there came into being one of the biggest known universities, the Nalanda university , why by 450 A.D. became a renowned seat of leaning, its fame spreading beyond the boundaries of India. Nalanda, near Patna grew to be the foremost Buddhist monastery and an educational centre. Most of what we know of the Nalanda University during the 6th and the 7th centuries A.D. is due to the account left by Hieun-tsang who lived in the institute for 3 years in th first half of the 7th century.

Information on the Nalanda University Library is also found in the Tibetan Accounts; from we understand that the library was situated in a special area known by the poetic name the Dharmaganja (Piety Mart) which comprised three huge buildings called Ratnasagara, the Ratnodadhi and the Ratnaranjaka. Ratnasagara was a nine- storied building and housed the collection of manuscripts and rare sacred works like prajnaparamitasutra etc. The library at Nalanda had a rich stock of manuscripts on philosophy and religion and contained texts relating to grammar, logic, literature, the vedas, the Vedanta etc.

Bihar has its importance in being the land of Buddha (for Buddhist) and Mahavira (for Jains). Bihar like U.P. has significantly contributed to Hindi and Urdu literature in the past. It has a lead in the country with its oldest Nalanda Odantipura & Vikramshila University Libraries. The Library patronage of the Mughal Governors of Bihar was very well continued to some extent, by their descendants and Abu Zafar Nadvi stands testimony to this (Nadvi,1945,1946).While there were libraries in each period in this land, these were not an instrument of mass education, hence these libraries wound not form a part of the present sense of public library structure. A true pattern of such a structure emerged only since a hundred years.

The literacy rate in this state are 10% in 1951, 185 in 1961; 20% in 1971; 26.21 in 1981 and 18% in 1961; 20% in 1971: 26.21% in 1981 and 38.54 in 1991;63.8% in 2011. It is one of the least literature states, and is the crux of the problem for the public libraries in particular and librarianship in general. The khuda Baksha Oriented Public Library Patna, owes its origin to Maulvi Muhammad Bakhsh Khan, who at the time of his death in July, 1876, left a collection of 14,000 volumes.

It was opened to the public in 1981 through a "Trust Deed". 34 In December,1969, the Government of India, through an Act of Parliament, declared it as an 'Institution of National Importance' and since July 1970 it is being governed as an autonomous institution by a Board of Management constituted by the Government of India with Governor of Bihar as its ex-officio Chairman, it is one of the richest public libraries in oriental manuscripts.

The Bhagalpur Institute Library is the oldest known library. The special features of the library is it was open to public every evening – to say it was beginning of public libraries and humble attempt was made by making it part-time service. The Gaya Public library founded in 1855 was founded on the basis of subscriptions and donations. The Khuda Bakhsh Oriental Library was founded in 1888 has a lead in royal Patronage in the city of Patna.

Patna University was established in 1999. The Sinha (19240 was converted into the state library in the year 1956. This state library is managed by a private trust. It has a collection of 1,50,000 Volumes by a private trust. The Public library Movement received impetus from the ministry setup in 1935, under the ministry of education, Dr. Syed Muhammad. In status of Bihar growth of library is going on smoothly and government of Bihar also aware for set new library and information centre from secondary education institution to higher education institution.

3. PUBLIC LIBRARY ACT OF BIHAR 2008

Bihar State Public Library and Information Centre Authority came in shape in September 2012, under Bihar State Public Library and Information Centre (Amendment) ACT 9, 2012 (25 May 2012). First of all to organise and develop all the libraries spreaded in various forms in different parts of state, Bihar State Public Library and Information Centre Act 17, 2008 was enacted by the Legislature of Bihar in the Sixty third year of Republic of India. After the appointment of Rtd. Prof (Dr.) Ram Vachan Rai as honorary Chairman, who has been facilitated with the rank of Cabinet Minister, in September 2012, office has been opened near Dak Bungalow Chauraha, Patna in April 2013. Libraries have been divided into five categories – Block to State level. While there is also a provision for the development of Library at Panchayat, Village & Private level. For this purpose Rs. 96144240/- has been proposed in Current Budget. STATE

LIBRARY FUND has also been established in this. Bihar has become 13th to implement Library Act.

4. ACADEMIC LIBRARIES IN BIHAR

There are so many universities in Bihar state. Most of them possess well established libraries. Along with universities AIMS-Patna and NIT- Patna have their own sound libraries. Some of the important academic libraries in the state have been mentioned here.

4.1. Nalanda University Library

The memory of the iconic library that distinguished ancient Naland is undiminished even eight hundred years after destruction. Infact, nothing denotes the violent end to the knowledge enshrined at Nalanda more than the image of the burning library : a library whose vast resources are captured in the vivid image of available and all convey the deep significance of this building with its untold treasures.

As with the ancient Nalanda, the present day Nalanda University too envisions its library as the central and striking feature of the master plan for the university: both in terms of its design and its relevance. Aspiring to be Indian's leading space for research the library will provide a vast resource for scholars and learners alike.

4.2. Bihar Agricultural University Library

The library was established in 1908 with the start of Agricultural Experiment Station and Agricultural School at Sabour. It continued with its basic activities of information resources development by collecting, processing, organizing, storage and retrieval of information; maintaining liaison with other related University libraries for resource sharing and exchange of information; providing need based current awareness, reference and bibliographic services and facilitating online access to wide range of information resources in print and electronic versions. Open access system is followed in the Library and the books are arranged as per Dewey Decimal Classification scheme and catalogued as per A.A.C.R.-II.

4.3. Central University of Bihar

The University believes that library is the most important element in the facilities of an educational institution and hence the University has developed a well-equipped Central Library for both the Campuses (Patna and Gaya) to cater the information requirements of students and faculty members for their academic accomplishments. The library has built a balanced collection of more than 18,500 books to support academic curricula, teaching and research in various science and social science subjects. All the books are bar-coded and organized using Dewey Decimal Classification (DDC) Scheme. An Online Public Access Catalogue (OPAC) of Library books is made available to students, faculty and officials on every computer in the University premises. At present, the Central Library is having 11 staff working hard to fulfill the needs of Library Users of both the Campuses.

4.4. NIT (National Institute of Technology) Patna

The Central library of the institute owns a vast stock of over 75,000 books catering to the needs of all the relevant fields of engineering. It has a resourceful stock of over 10,000 computer related books and clearly demarcated section for every engineering branch and architecture. In addition to the engineering pertinent books, the central library is self-sufficient in a vivid category of other business and current affairs related magazines, pamphlets and journals.

The Central Library is fully automated and all operations are performed with the help of Libsys-Library Automation Software. The students can issue a sufficient no. of books for use throughout the semester and an additional no. of books for special reference.

5. SPECIAL LIBRARIES IN BIHAR

The Khuda Baksh Oriental Public library is the

prominent public library in the state. It is special library in the sense of its collection.

5.1. Khuda Baksh Oriental Public library

Khuda Bakhsh Oriental is one of the national libraries of India. It was opened to public in October, 1891 by Khan Bahadur Khuda Bakhsh with 4,000 manuscripts, of which he inherited 1,400 from his father Maulvi Mohammed Bakhsh. It is an autonomous organization under Ministry of Culture, Government of India, and is governed by a Board with the Governor of Bihar as its ex officio Chairman, and is known for its rare collection of Persian and Arabic manuscripts. It also hosts paintings made during the Rajput and Mughal eras of India. It is also a designated 'Manuscript Conservation Centre' (MCC) under the National Mission for Manuscripts.

The library finds its origin in private collection of a bibliophile Mohammad Bakhsh and expanded by his son Khuda Bakhsh, who inherited 1,400 manuscripts and continued to add to the collection and eventually converted it into a private library by 1880. The library was opened to public upon its inauguration by Sir Charles Elliot, Governor of Bengal on 5 October 1891. In 1969 through a Federal Legislation, an Act of Parliament, namely 'Khuda Bakhsh Oriental Public Library Act' (1969), the Government of India declared Khuda Bakhsh Oriental Public Library a centre of national importance and government took over the funding, maintenance and development of the library. Today it continues to attract scholars from all over the world.

The Library specializes in Islamic Studies, Tibb (Unani Medicine), Tazkira (Biography), Tasawwuf (Islamic Mysticism), Comparative religions, Medieval History, South East Asian History, West Asian History, Central Asian History, Medieval Science, Literature on Freedom Movement and National Integration as also Urdu, Persian and Arabic Literatures. It contains about 21,000 manuscripts in Arabic, Persian, Urdu, Turkish, Hindi and Sanskrit and Palm-Leaves. It includes splendors of arts of Iranian, Mughal, Central Asian,

Kashmiri and Rajasthani schools besides Calligraphic Masterpieces. Listed in the Survey of Manuscripts in India.

6. BIHAR LIBRARY ASSOCIATION

The Bihar Library Association was founded in October 1936, with Pandit Ganga Prasad Tiwari as the main driving force. In 1937, the association prepared a draft scheme for the development of libraries in Bihar state and submitted to the state Government in 1938. It was accepted by the Ministry of Education in 1939- 40, and an amount of Rs. 30,000 was provided in the budget for libraries. Also the association gave full support to the Mass Literary Campaign, begun in April 1938. Under the inspiration of Dr. Sved Mahmud, the Education Minister of the Bihar.

Since 1952, the Association has been known as the Bihar Rajya Pustakalaya Sangh. In august 1954, the sangh started training camps for librarians. It also holds periodical conferences.

7. LIBRARY SCIENCE EDUCATION IN BIHAR

Library and Information Science education being imparted in the universities as well technical colleges in Bihar is at four levels, i.e., Diploma, Bachelor, Master and research (MPhil/PhD).Government Women's Polytechnic, Muzaffarpur and Government Women's Polytechnic, Patna offer diploma courses.While Nalanda Open University conducts diploma course in libarry and information science.

B.R Ambedkar Bihar University, Muzaffarpur, Jai Prakash University, Chhapra,Patna University, Patna and Veer Kunwar Singh University, Ara offers B.L.& I.SC. Similarly.Magadh University, Bodh Gaya,Nalanda Open University, Patna offer B.L.& I.SC and M.L. & I.SC. Tilak Manjhi Bhagalpur University offers B.L. & I.SC., M.L.& I.SC and PhD in library and Information science.

Promotions of research work Khuda Bakhsh oriental Public Library; patna encourages scholars and provides them all research facilities including free accommodation. It awards 10 research fellowships - 3 Senior and 7 Junior - for a period of 2 years and helps they do Ph.D./D.Litt. It also assigns different projects to them, for example, editing of manuscripts, compilation of descriptive catalogue of manuscripts, indexes of Urdu periodicals, subject bibliographies, etc.

8. CONCLUSION

Library is repository where information is acquire, process and disseminate to the right user, right place and at the right time. Growth and development of library in India as a continuous process, that is, from agricultural society to information societies. In status of Bihar growth of library is going on smoothly and government of Bihar also aware for set new library and information centre from secondary education institution to higher education institution.

REFERENCES

1. Amjad ali. Oriental libraries of India and their collections. 2004. Ess ess publication, New Delhi. P 58.
2. Dasgupta (R K). India. *In* wedgenworth (robert), *ed.* Ala encyclopedia of library and information services. Ed2; 1986. Ala, Chicago. P 353.
3. Dhiman (anil kumar) and yashoda rani. Learn library and society. 2005. Ess Ess publications, New Delhi. P 6.
4. Dhiman (anil kumar) and yashoda rani. *Op.cit.* P 7.
5. Dictionary for library and information science. 2005. Rain tree, chennai. P 404.
6. Dutta (d n). Libraries and their users. 1975. World press, Calcutta. P 1.
7. Encyclopedia Americana. International ed. V 17; 2002. Grolier, Danbury. P 311.
8. Grover (b l). New look on modern history from 1707 to the present day. Ed7; 1984. S. Chand, New Delhi. Chap 27.
9. Khanna (j k). Library and society. 1987. Research publications, kurukshetra. P 1- 2.
10. Khuda bakhsh oriental public library annual report 2004-2005. Khuda bakhsh oriental public library, Patna. P 1.

11. Mchenry (robert), *ed.* New encyclopedia Britannica. V7; 1993. Encyclopedia Britannica, Chicago. P 333.
12. Mishra (jogesh). History of libraries and librarianship in modern India since 1850.1979. Atma ram & sons, Delhi. P 23.
13. Moghe (v s). Public libraries of Indore souvenir. 27th – 30th dec.; 1968. ILA 17th all India library conference, university of Indore, indore. P 67.
14. Notes and news. *Herald of library science.* 7 (1); 1968; 358-359.
15. Ramaiah (l s). Public library legislation. *In* jain (m k) and others, *eds.* 50 years library and information services in India 1988. Shipra publications, Delhi. P 40.
16. Ranganathan (s r). Reference service and bibliography. V 1; 1940. Madras library association, madras. P 25.
17. Sengupta (benoyendra) and chakraborty (bhubaneswar). Library, library science and librarianship. 1981. World press, Calcutta. P 41.
18. Sharma (pandey s k). Libraries and society. Ed 2; 1922. Ess Ess publication, New Delhi. P 205.
19. Sinha (arun kumar). Library and librarianship: history and philosophy. *In* Vashishth (cp) and Satija (m p), *eds.* P.S.G. Kumar festschrift library and information profession in India. V1.reflections and redemptions, 2004. B.R. Publishing, Delhi. P 27-28.
20. Swami Nathan (s). Libraries in India: yesterday and today. *In* library science today: ranganthan festschrift. V 1; 1965. Asia publishing house, Calcutta p 358.
21. Trehan (g l). Libraries in ancient and medieval India. *In* sen (n b) *ed.* Development of libraries in new India. 1965. New book society of india, New Delhi. P 99.
22. Trehan (g l). *Op.cit.* P 102.
23. Unesco. Public libraries for asia: Delhi seminar, UNESCO public library manual no. 7. 1965, UNESCO, Paris. P 9
24. Young (heartsill). Ala glossary of library and information science. 1983. American library association, Chicago. P 130
25. Esperanza,m.(1995),library and information science: emerging Trends, Agrawal, s.p. ed. concept publishing .company., New Delhi, 1995.

5

Library Movement and Development in Chhattisgarh State

Omprakash Patel
Librarian
Shri Shankaracharya Mahavidyalaya
Bhilai, Chattisgarh.

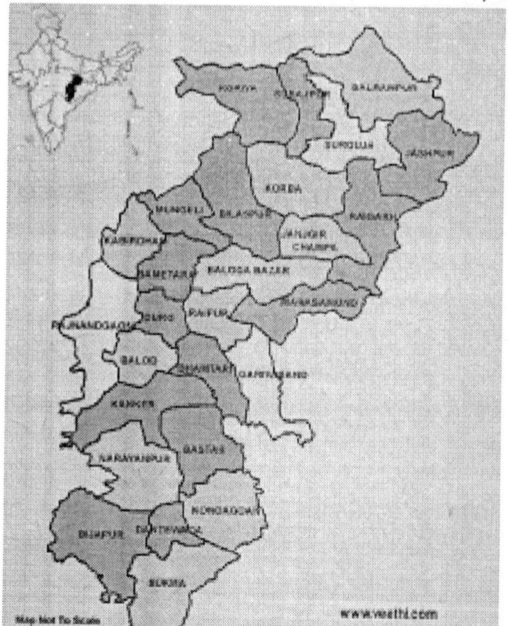

1. CHHATTISGARH : A PROFILE

The Chhattisgarh carved out of Madhya Pradesh come into being on 1st Nov. 2000 as the 26th state of the Union. It fulfills the long-cherished demand of tribal people. In ancient time the region was known as kaushal his finds mention in Ramayana and Mahabharata also. Between the sixth and twelfth century Sarabhpuri, Pandhuvanshi, Somvanshi, Kalchuri and Nagvanshi rulers dominated this region. Kalchuri ruled this state from 980-1791 AD. With the advent of Britishers in 1854 Raipur gained dominance instead of capital Ratanpur. In 1904 Sambalpur was transferred to Orissa and states of Surguja were transferred from Bengal to Chhattisgarh.

Chhattisgarh is situated in the central part of India. It is bounded by northest Jharkhand in north and Andhra Pradesh in south. Chhattisgarh cons are of about one third of farmer Madhya Pradesh geographical area and population. This area comes 44 Approx Percent of MP's total forest land.

2. LIBRARY MOVEMENT IN CHHATTISGARH STATE

The History of Chhattisgarh Library Act is not a very old. After the separation of Madhya pradesh Library Act also demanded from here. The demanded of the Library Act have been taken by the former Prof. and Students by the Guru Ghasidhas University Bilaspur but that demanded did not reach to Government.

In 2003 when Chief Minister Presented as a chief guest in Indira Gandhi Agriculture University they have been declared Library Act. After that some little activities would be done. The enlightened persons of Guru Ghasidhas - University Bilaspur and Pt. Ravishankar Shukla - University Raipur they are related to Library Science played an important role for making Library Act. The Former commissioner of Chhattisgarh Higher Education Department also played important role for that. The Library Act was constituted in 2008.

3. CHHATTISGARH PUBLIC LIBRARIES ACT, 2008

The Chhattisgarh public libraries act, 2008 has eight chapters.

Chapter -1 : Preliminary (Short Title, extent and commencement)

- This is Act may be called the Chhattisgarh Public Library Act 2008.
- It extends to whole of the state of Chattisgarh.
- It shell come into 10 September 2008.

Definition

- Book includes- every volume, a part r division of a volume and pamphlet, in any language, newspaper, periodicals, serial publication and manuscripts, sheet of music, map, chart or plan separately printer or lithographed, audio-visual, audio and visual materials such as tapes, cassettes, films, filmstrips, micro card, microfilm computer, floppy, compact disk, photograph etc.

Chapter -2 : Advisory Committees

2.1 As soon as may be after the commencement of this Act. The state government shall by notification constitute for the purpose of this act a council to be called the state library council.

2.2 The State library Council shall consist of:-

- The minister, school education department, Govt., of Chhattisgarh, chairperson.
- The Principal Secretary to the Govt. of Chhattisgarh, school education department charge of the public library, Vice-chairperson.

2.3 Constitution and function of the state standing committee:-

- The Principal Secretary to the Government of Chhattisgarh, School Education Department,

Chairman.

- The Secretary to the Government of Chhattisgarh, Higher Education Department, Member.
- The Secretary to the Government of Chhattisgarh, Finance Department or his nominee net below the rank of special secretary, Member.
- The Secretary to the Government of Chhattisgarh, Planning Department or his nominee net below the rank of special secretary, Member.
- The Director, School Education Department, Chhattisgarh, Member.
- The Additional Director, Department of Higher Education Chhattisgarh, Member.
- The official on Special duty (Library cell) school education department Government of Chhattisgarh, Member/Secretary.
- The tenure of the members specified at series 11 to 13 shall be two years.
- The Headquarter of the council shall be at Raipur.

2.4 Constitution and function of a District Library committee:-

There shall be a District Library Committee in each district of the state consisting of -

- The District Collector, Chairperson.
- The chief Executive officer, Zila Panchayat, Vice-Chairperson.
- The Principal, District Institute for Education and Training, Member.
- The Librarian District Government Library if any Member/Secretary.

Chapter-3 : Director of Public Libraries

The Director of Secondary Education Chhattisgarh shall be the director of Public Library and be responsible for the proper administration and operation of the Act.

Chapter-4 : Structure of Public Library system and Function of Various state centres Libraries.

State level Library : There shall be State Level Libraries in the state, of which one shall be the state Central Library at Raipur and the other shall be the state Reference Library at Bilaspur.

Chapter-5 : Finance

The Library development plan shall from an integral part of the centralized and decentralized annual and five year plan and non plan budget of the state. The State Government, if it considers necessary may also find means and ways to raise additional resources support and develop the Public Library System.

Recognition and De-recognition

- The state Government may recognize any library run by the voluntary organizations registered under the Chhattisgarh society Registrikaran Adhiniyam, 1973, or any library run by local authority open for use to the public as public library for the purpose of payment of grant in aid or other assistance to it.
- To state Government may, in accordance with the rules recognize any public library association in the state registered under the Chhattisgarh Society Registrikaran Adhiniyam, 1973 for the purpose of grant in aid or other financial assistance to it.

Chapter-7 : Reports and Inspection

- Every person who is in charge of the management of public library and every person is in charge of public library association shall submit such reports and returns and furnish such information as the state Government may from time to time require.
- The Director or an officer authorized by him in this

behalf shall be have power to inspect public Libraries and public library association or any institute attached thereto or any institute conducting the training courses in library service and library information science receiving financial assistance, for the purpose of satisfying himself that the provisions of this Act and the rules made there under are being carried out.

- Within six months from the close of every year, the director shall prepare an annual report on the working and administration of and the progress made by, public libraries and public library associations in that year together with such information and particulars as may be prescribed and submit the same to the state government.

Chapter-8 : Miscellaneous

- All the members of the council while acting or purporting to act in pursuance of the provisions of this Act or any rules and regulations made there under be deemed to be public servants within the meeting of section 21 of the Indian Pencil Code.
- No suit, prosecution or other legal proceedings shall lie against the council or any member or servant thereof for anything done or intended to be done in good faith in pursuance of the provisions of this Act or the rules and regulations made there under.
- The State Government may be notification make rules for carrying out the purposes of this Act.
- The council may make regulations not inconsistent with the provisions of this Act and the

4. THE STATUS OF PUBLIC LIBRARIES IN CHHATTISGARH

In chhattisgarh the last few years are very important of establishment of Public Libraries. In Chhattisgarh state public Libraries are situated in Raipur, Bilaspur, Dhamtari, Bhilai and Rajnandgaon district. Public Library situated in Bhilai was established by Bhilai steel plant. The name of this library is Central Library, Bhilai Steel Plant.

The public library situated in Durg district is called Central Library which is operated by Nagar Nigam, Durg. It was established in 1975.

In Durg district a District Library (Jila Granthlaya) is situated it's new name is "Maithalishran Gupta Vachnalaya" It was established in 1955.

In Rajandgaon District a District Library is situated it's name is "Government Jila Granthlaya Rajnandgaon" It was established in 1981. At present there are 37464 Book in this library and the number of journals and Magazines are 53. It has a very big building with reading rooms.

5. ACADEMIC LIBRARIES IN THE STATE

Almost all universities have well established libraries. The universities in the state are - Indira Kala Sangeet University- Khairagarh, Pt. Ravishankar Shukla University- Raipur, Guru Ghasidhas University Central University- Bilaspur, Indira Gandhi Agriculture University- Raipur, Hiduttlah National Law University- Raipur, Kushabhau Thakre Patrakarita University- Raipur, Pandit Sunder lal Sharma (Open) University- Bilaspur, Swami Vivedanand Technical University- Bhilai, Dr. C. V. Raman University- Bilaspur, MATS, University- Raipur, Bastar University- Jadalpur, Surgurja University- Ambikapur, Ayush and Health Science University- Raipur, Bilaspur University Bilaspur- Bilaspur, Maharishi University of Management of Tech- Bilaspur, Kamdhenu University- Durg, Guru Ghasidhas University- Bilaspur, Indira Kala Sangeet University- Khairagarh Pt. Ravishankar Shukla University- Raipur, Indira Gandhi Agriculture University- Raipur, Hiduttlah National Law University- Raipur, Kushabhau Thakre Patrakarita University- Raipur, Pandit Sunder lal Sharma (Open) University- Bilaspur, Swami Vivedanand Technical University- Bhilai, Bastar University- Jadalpur, Surgurja University- Ambikapur, Ayush and Health Science University- Raipur, Bilaspur University Bilaspur- Bilaspur, and Kamdhenu

University- Durg.

6. SPECIAL LIBRARIES IN THE CHHATTISGARH

6.1. Desbandhu Library Raipur

Desbandhu Library is the richest reference library in Central India. It is also, perhaps, the biggest library in the non-governmental sector in Chhattisgarh. The Raipur based library has some 30,000 books on a variety of subjects and more than 60,000 reference dockets covering a whole range of topics. The library has three separate sections. -Text Book Section, Research and Documentation Centre public Reading Room and Children's library.

The Library caters to the needs of various groups- books lovers, media persons and other visitors from the state and out of state visitors, civil society organisations, social activities, political parties and persons, cultural activists, students, researcher's government department, national and international agencies and diplomatic missions etc.

Efforts are afoot to make Deshbandhu Library more user- friendly and upgrade it to meet the changing needs of the visitors. This task is being accomplished with the support of National foundation of India, New Delhi. A grant from NFI has enabled us only in air-conditioning and computerisation of the Library, but also in making it more systematic and focused.

6.2. Indiara Gandhi Krishi Vishwa Vidyalaya Library (Nehru Library)

The Nehru Library is an important educational center of the university and working as Central Library of Indira Gandhi Krishi Vishwavidyalya. Nehru Library functioning as Central University Library for constituent and affiliated colleges of Indira Gandhi Krishi Vishwavidyalya viz. nine constituent Colleges and fifteen private colleges, Research Stations and Krishi Vighyan Kendras (KVKs).

The Nehru Library established in 1987 after IGKV came

in to existence by bifurcation from JNKVV Jabalpur. Before that it was the library of College of Agriculture, Raipur. It has been recognized as Regional Library of Central India by the Indian Council of Agricultural Research in 2005. The Nehru Library of IGKV has been well equipped with the latest communication media and information technologies like web based information, CD Rom database search, OPAC, internet browsing as it is well connected through LAN/ BSNL leased line. This library has become a HUB connected on LAN with all automated centralized facilities and acting as a nodal center for disseminating all kind of agricultural information to its users. The library is linked with various consortiums for online journals. Nehru Library maintains around less than 60000 collections of books, reference book, reports, theses, monograph, back volumes, journals, CD ROM Database and e-resources. This was possible by the help of ICAR through NATP/NAIP. Chhattisgarh Government supported for its infra structure development and provided other facilities.

6.3. Hidayathullah National Law University Library

The Law Library is an integral division of the HNLU. The library of the HNLU is considered as a laboratory of a scientific institute, where the apparatus for the law students are the classic law books, case law reports and journals that are available in full sets. The students would perform legal research like experiments to augment their studies by using these equipments. The HNLU Library has adopted an open access system so as to make it easier for the readers to access to the library resources thereby saving precious time. To assist the students and research scholars in locating their desired legal literature and other information, efficient library automation package has been installed

The HNLU Library also conducts library orientation programme for the fresh students to acquaint them with the library system, services and resources so that they may exploit the available resources for their maximum benefit..

The library automation software also helps the staff in maintaining inventory and house-keeping jobs. There are quite a few P IV workstations placed in the library hall for the students to browse legal resources from West Law, Manupatra and other on-line sources, apart from Grand Jurix which is available for search off line.

6.4. Indian Institute of Management (IIM) Library

The Library is one of the critical resources during MBA and is being expanded constantly to become a reservoir of knowledge for the coming batches. The present library already has over 10,000 books. Apart from books, the library has subscribed to the leading periodicals, research magazines and business magazines of note. The Library also provides access to several key Online Databases like EBSCO, Emerald, Econlit, ProQuest, Capitaline, Business Beacon, CMIE, CRISIL, Euromonitor, Huddle, Industry Analysis Services, Prowess, and Science Direct amongst others.

7. LIS EDUCATION IN THE STATE

7.1. Degree and PG courses in LIS

The subject of LIS (Library and Information Science) is relatively a younger one compared to those like Chemistry, Physics, Literature, and Philosophy in Chhattisgarh it is taught as short term certificate level to postgraduate research degree level. Universities conduct BLIS and MLIS courses separately of one year duration each. Admission to these courses is strictly on merit basis depending upon the performance at the graduation level followed by personal interview. The following universities offer BLISc or MLISc courses. They are - Indira Kala Sangeet University – Khairagarh, Pt. Ravishankar Shukla University – Raipur, Guru Ghasidhas University Central University - Bilaspur, Indira Gandhi Agriculture University – Raipur, Hiduttlah National Law UniversityRaipur , Kushabhau Thakre Patrakarita University – Raipur, Pandit Sunder lal Sharma (Open) University Bilaspur, Swami Vivedanand Technical University-

Bhilai, Dr. C. V. Raman University Bilaspur, MATS, University – Raipur, Bastar University – Jadalpur, Surgurja University – Ambikapur, Ayush and Health Science University Raipur, University Bilaspur – Bilaspur, Maharishi University of Management of Tech.- Bilaspur and Kamdhenu University-Durg.

7.2. Conduct of the M. Phil Courses

Some Universities conduct LIS M. Phil courses separately of one year duration each. Admission to these courses is strictly on merit basis depending upon the performance at the post graduation level followed by personal interview. The universities which offer MPhil course in library science are - Pt. Ravishankar Shukla University – Raipur and Dr. CV Raman University – Bilaspur.

7.3. Ph. D. Programme

Admission to these courses is strictly on merit basis depending upon the performance at the Ph. D. programme level followed by personal interview. The following universities offer PhD. in library science. They are - Pt. Ravi Shankar Shukla University-Raipur, Dr. CV Raman University-Bilaspur, Guru Ghasidhas University-Bilasur, Pt Sunderlal Sharma (open) University - Bilaspur and Mats University-Raipur.

8. CONCLUSION

Chhattisgarh has a well set up of library and information scenario. There are a number of well established public, academic and special libraries in the state. What the state lack presently is the lack of a strong library association.

REFERENCE

1. Latha, J.K., Nagarajan, M & Nithyanandam, N. (2010). ICT Infrastructure development in special libraries in Tamilnadu. 'Pearl- A journals of Library and Information Science'. 4, (2),76-81.

2. Rama rao., & K. Krishna (1965). Philosophy of Librarianship in Development of Libraries. New India
3. Sharma, S.K. Pandey (1996). Public libraries in India: Trends and Status. In *Public libraries in developing countries: Status and Trends*. Ed. P. K. Mahapatra ,.125-127. New Delhi: Vikas Publishing House.
4. Venkatappaiah , V.(1990). State Library Bills And Acts. In: *Indian Library legislation* Ed. P.S.G Kumar. V.2. Delhi : Daya Publishing House
5. http://www.bvvjdp.ac.in.html.
6. http://www.en.wikipedia.org/wiki/digitallibrary
7. http://msfraipur.org/DESHBANDHU%20LIBRARY/libindex.htm
8. http://www.pssou.ac.in.
9. http://www.hnlu.ac.in.
10. http://www.iksvv/lib.html.com.
11. http://www.chhattisgarheducation.net/university/Krishi_Vishwaidyalaya/index.aspx
12. http://www.prsu.ac.in/about.html.
13. http://www.ktujm.ac.in/inaugu.html.
14. http://www.en.wikipedia.org/wiki/csvtu.ac.in/html.
15. http://www.Sua.nic.in/abus.html.

6

Library Movement and Development in Delhi

K P Singh
Senior Assistant Professor & Principal Investigator
Department of Library and Information Science,
University of Delhi, Delhi
Dipti Gulati
Assistant Librarian,
Institute of Information Technology and Management.
D-29, Institutional Area,
Janakpuri, New Delhi-110058

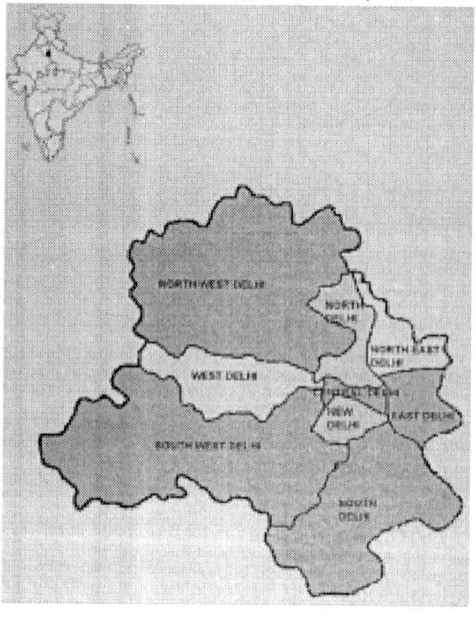

1. DELHI : A PROFILE

The national capital territory of Delhi with an area of 1,484 sq. km. is situated between the Great Himalayas and the Aravalis range in the heart of Indian Sub-continent. It is surrounded by three sides by Haryana and to the east, across the river Yamuna by Uttar Pradesh. The major part of territory lies on the western side of river Yamuna, only some villages and the urban area of Shahdara lie on the eastern side of the river. The population of Delhi is around 6.75 million, which includes Male-8,987,326 and Female-7,800,615 having a Literacy Rate of around 86.21%.[2]

Delhi has seen the rise and fall of several empires which have left behind a plethora of monuments exhibiting the grandeur and glory of bygone ages. A city which traces its history to Mahabharata, the great epic tale of wars fought between estranged cousins, the Kauravas and the Pandavas for the city of Indraprastha. The Mughals ruled Delhi in succession starting from Qutab-ub-din to Khiljis, Tughlaqs. The city of Delhi passed on to the hands of the British in 1803 AD. It was only in 1911, when the capital of British Empire was shifted from Calcutta to Delhi, when Delhi received its present prestige. After independence, autonomy was conferred on the capital, although it largely remained a chief commissioner's regime. In 1956 Delhi was converted into a Union territory and gradually the chief commissioner was replaced by a Lt. Governor. In 1991, the national capital territory Act was passed by the parliament and a system of diarchy was introduced under which, the elected Government was given wide powers; except law and order which remained with the central Government. The actual enforcement of the legislation came in 1993. Not much is known about the existence of libraries in Delhi in the early period of history, as Delhi with its own romantic antiquity and continuity comprised an unparalleled urban tradition of trade and commerce which was necessary for a stable population and growth.

2. DEVELOPMENT OF LIBRARIES IN DELHI

Delhi being the national capital of the country and a house of the several central institutes and universities; has a great history on the growth and development of libraries. Based on the literature, the libraries of Delhi are grouped into four basic categories:

- Public Libraries
- Academic Libraries
- Special Libraries; and
- Government Libraries

3. PUBLIC LIBRARIES IN DELHI

A Public library is largely regarded as the People's University. Until independence, there was no significant development in Delhi which could be responsible for the growth and development of libraries. In striking contrast to the library movements in other states of Baroda, Madras and many more, Delhi lacked an enthusiasm for establishing libraries. There are several reasons for the lack of public libraries in Delhi, such as, destruction of social and political structures during the renaissance period of Delhi, lack of educational facilities, particularly higher education; attitude of the authorities was also responsible for lack of public libraries, lack of library legislation and movement in Delhi. Presently there are 12 public libraries which are in the service of people living in Delhi.

3.1. Hardayal Municipal Public Library

It is located near old Delhi Railway Station, which was established as the Lawrence Institute and is the oldest public library in Delhi in 1862. In 1970, the library was rechristened as the Hardayal Municipal Public Library after the famous freedom fighter and intellectual Lala Hardayal. The library has a collection of more than 1,70,000 books in Hindi, English, Urdu, Arabic, Persian and Sanskrit.

3.2. Delhi Public Library

The second major public library which was established in 1961 as the 1st UNESCO pilot project sponsored by UNESCO and the Government of India. The DPL which is governed by DPL governing board and Director General known as CEO are responsible for the administration of the DPL and its branch libraries. The DPL has a network of Zonal Libraries, Branches & Sub-branches, R C Libraries, Community Libraries, Deposit Stations, Mobile Library and Braille Library spread all over Delhi and has a collection of more than 18 lakh books in Hindi, English, Urdu, Punjabi & other Indian Languages-almost all subjects are represented in its collection. The DPL is the public library in the Delhi, which is fully automated using KOHA software. In addition to, in the country, the DPL is also a repository of the Indian published books under the Book Delivery Act 1950.

3.3. Marwari Public Library

It was set up by Seth Kedar Nath Goenka, a cloth merchant of Delhi, on the Vijaya Dashmi day in 1915 with a collection comprising 30,000 volumes. It still continues to function from the same old place as in 1915. The collection of the library includes more than 50,000 books mostly in Hindi and the library caters to more than 300 members and researchers.

4. ACADEMIC LIBRARIES IN DELHI

An academic library is a library that is attached to an academic institution above the secondary level, serving the teaching and research needs of students and staff. There is a phenomenal growth and development of academic institutions in Delhi, especially after the independence and after it received the status of Delhi as a state, many state based universities have been established. The movement of the Academic Libraries in Delhi has been put into following sections:

4.1. University of Delhi Library

It is the premier university of the country and is known for its high standards in teaching and research and was established in 1922 which is a network of more than 86 colleges some of the famous colleges which has a great impact on education in India was established before Delhi University St. Stephen's College founded in 1881, Hindu College founded in 1899 and Ramjas College founded in 1917. In addition to this, it is also consists of 16 faculties, 77 academic departments and 132435 enrolled students. To cater to the information needs of the students, faculties and staff of the university, the Delhi University Library System (DULS) came into existence in 1922. DULS is split into 8 other libraries namely, Arts Library, Central Library, Central Science Library, Ratan Tata Library, South Campus Library, Law Faculty Library, FMS Library, East Asian Studies Library. The present holdings of the DULS include: Over 14,04,000 volumes, subscription for about 2000 journals, 4000 journals are available online through Campus-Wide Networking, 13,000 Ph.D Theses and M. Phil Dissertations, 700 manuscripts of which Sanskrit and Persian account for 480 and 153 respectively.

4.2. Jawaharlal Nehru University Library

The Central Library, a knowledge hub of Jawaharlal Nehru University provides comprehensive access to books, journals, theses and dissertations, reports, surveys covering diverse disciplines. The Library collection is made up of over 50,0000 books, audiovisual items, over 10,000 journals in print format offering online access to more than 20,000. It has been developed with 2 aims that are to support the academic programmes of the University and to support the research pursuits of the teaching community and the research scholars. The holdings of the Library are particularly rich in Social Sciences and Humanities.

4.3. Jamia Milia Islamia Library

Jamia Millia Islamia, an institution originally established at Aligarh in United Provinces, India in 1920 became a Central University by an act of the Indian Parliament in 1988. In Urdu language, Jamia means 'University', and Millia means 'National'. The story of its growth from a small institution in the pre-independence India to a central university located in New Delhi—offering integrated education from nursery to research in specialized areas—is a saga of dedication, conviction and vision of a people who worked against all odds and saw it growing step by step. Dr Zakir Husain Library named after the ex-President of India, (Late) Dr. Zakir Husain in 1973, is the Central Library of the Jamia Library System, which includes the Faculty and Center Libraries. Stocking a rich collection of over 3.57 Lacs learning resources in all major discipline taught in the university.

4.4. Indira Gandhi National Open University Library

IGNOU was established in 1985, to build an inclusive knowledge society through inclusive education. Today, it serves the educational aspirations of over 4 million students in India and 36 other countries through 21 Schools of Studies and a network of 67 regional centers, around 3,000 learner support centers and 67 overseas centers. The IGNOU library is the most resourceful information centre in the country in the field of Distance Education. The library has the largest collection of books, journals and other related materials in the field of Distance Education, throughout the country. It was established in 1986 in tune with the objectives of IGNOU. The Central Library caters to the needs of Academic, Administrative and Supportive staff and students at the headquarters.

There are 11 Deemed Universities some of the major one are discussed below:

4.5. Jamia Hamdard Library

Jamia Hamdard, Deemed University, established in 1989, is located in the surroundings of Tughlaqabad adjoining the Jahanpanah forest and overlooking the historic Tughlaqabad fort in the east. Jamia Hamdard was conceived as a seat of higher learning in Unani Medicine, Islamic Studies, Biosciences, Pharmacy, Nursing and other areas of knowledge by its founder as a means of fulfilling the objects of the Wakf. The Hamdard University library system consists of central library and six faculty libraries. The central library of the university was named as 'Hakim Mohammed Said Central Library' after the name of younger brother of the founder Hakeem Abdul Hamid. The total library holdings exceed 1.46 lakh including 1,05,000 English, Urdu, Arabic, Persian, Hindi, etc. books. 17,000 bound volumes, 20,000 rare collections and 4500 manuscripts, mostly in Urdu, Arabic and Persian languages.

4.6. Shri Lal Bhadhur Shastri Rastriya Sanskrit Vidyapeeth Library

The Vidyapeeth was established by All India Sanskrit Sahitya Sammelan on Vijaya Dashmi day in 1962 and was named Akil Bharatiya Sanskrit Vidyapeeth. It was renamed as Shri Lal Bahadur Shastri Rashtriya Sanskrit Vidyapeeth on 2nd October, 1966. The Vidyapeeth library is housed in a commodious building having a total floor area of 586 Sq. M. on the ground and first floors with 290 Sq. M. of stocking accommodation. It has about 63926 books of various subjects of learning. In view of the current requirements, 35 journals are subscribed by the library.

4.7. Indian Agricultural Research Institute Library

Got established in 1905 by the Government of India was located at Pusa, Bihar. In 1934, the institute shifted to New Delhi. Currently, the Institute has 20 divisions 5 multi-disciplinary Centers situated in Delhi. IARI Library is one of the largest and the finest agro-biological libraries in South

East Asia housing a total of 6 lakh publications including 1 lakh books/monographs, 3,50,000 journal volumes, 45,000 bulletins, 15,000 post graduate theses, 10,000 pamphlets, 30,000 news clippings, 30,000 reports, and other reference materials. The Library has, on its role, 2000 members, viz., students, scientists and technical staff. It also serves about 8,000 visitors every year. The library functions as the depository of FAO, IDRC and AVRDC publications and also as the National Depository for CGIAR institutes publications.

4.8. National University of Educational Planning and Administration Library (NUEPA)

NUEPA was established in 1962 by the Ministry of Human Resource Development, Government of India, as a premier organization dealing with capacity building and research in planning and management of education. It has an outstanding multi-disciplinary faculty and a library, which is well stocked with a large number of books, national and international journals and official documents in the area of educational planning and administration. In addition to its multifarious activities, it offers M. Phil., Ph.D and Part-time Ph. D. programmes in educational policy, planning and administration from a broader inter-disciplinary social science perspective. The Library has a wide collection of more than 53500 volumes on educational planning and management including books, documents, government publications, annual reports, project reports.

4.9. Indian Institute of Foreign Trade Library

IIFT was set up in 1963 by the Government of India as an autonomous organization to help professionalize the country's foreign trade management and increase exports by developing human resources; analyzing and disseminating data; and conducting research. The Library at IIFT is one of the largest of its kind in the developing world, with a holding of around 84,000 volumes and subscriptions to 800 journals with complete online cataloguing, is a veritable storehouse of information.

4.10. National Museum Library

NML collects books and journals related to the fields of history, art and culture of the World for specialized research and reference. It covers a large variety of themes such as anthropology, archaeology, conservation, decorative arts, history, literature, museum studies, painting, philosophy and religion. It contains more than sixty thousand volumes of books, bound journals as well as several Indian and international journals and magazines.

4.11. Guru Gobind Singh Indraprastha University Library

Guru Gobind Singh Indraprastha University established by Government of NCT of Delhi under the provisions of Guru Gobind Singh Indraprastha University Act, 1998 read with its Amendment in 1999. The University will stimulate both the hearts and minds of scholars, empower them to contribute to the welfare of society at large; train them to adopt themselves to the changing needs of the economy; advocate them for cultural leadership to ensure peace, harmony and prosperity for all. The IP University has affiliated more than 70 Institutes in Delhi. The Library is referred to as an Information Resource Centre. The collection includes books, CDs, journals and magazines etc. The Library has about 15,690 books and subscribing 250 journals.

4.12. National Law University Library

National Law University, Delhi is an institute of excellence striving for all round development and holistic growth to create enterprising, sensitized, socially aware legal personalities. In the five years since its inception, the university has managed to strike a balance between academics, extra-curricular and co-curricular activities with phenomenal success at national as well as international moot court competitions, debates and sporting events.

4.13. Bharat Ratna Dr. B.R. Ambedkar University Library

The Bharat Ratna Dr B.R. Ambedkar Vishwavidyalaya

(Ambedkar University, Delhi or AUD) was established by the Government of the National Capital Territory of Delhi through an Act of Legislature in 2007 and was notified in July 2008. AUD library has specialized collection of more than 16000 books, 130 national and international print journals, magazines and 18 leading online publisher's journal database (more than 13500 e-journals) in the area of humanities and social science.

In addition to the above university libraries, there is one international university i.e. South Asian University established in the year 2010 by the eight member nations of South Asian Association for Regional Co-operation (SAARC) viz. Afghanistan, Bangladesh, Bhutan, India, Maldives, Nepal, Pakistan and Sri Lanka. South Asian University Library was established to fulfill academic and research need of the students, faculty members and other users of the library. The library has text and reference books covering different subjects i.e. computer science, mathematics, biotechnology, sociology, economics, law, international relation etc. There are about 5,600 volumes of book available at the Library.

5. SPECIAL LIBRARIES IN DELHI

Special libraries often have a more specific clientele than libraries in traditional educational or public settings, and deal with more specialized kinds of information. Delhi is a big network of the libraries and information centers of following organizations:

5.1. Council of Scientific and Industrial Research Library (CSIR)

CSIR was established in the year 1942 with an aim to provide industrial competitiveness, social welfare, strong S&T base for strategic sectors and advancement of fundamental knowledge. CSIR has a headquarter in Delhi and 5 National Laboratories namely, Central Road Research Institute, Institute of Genomics and Integrative Biology, National Physical Laboratory, National Institute of Science

Communication and Information Resources and National Institute of Science, Technology and Development Studies.

5.2. Indian Council of Agricultural Research Library (ICAR)

ICAR is an autonomous organization under the Department of Agricultural Research and Education (DARE), Ministry of Agriculture, Government of India. Formerly known as Imperial Council of Agricultural Research, it was established on 16 July 1929 as a registered society under the Societies Registration Act, 1860 in pursuance of the report of the Royal Commission on Agriculture. The ICAR has its headquarters at New Delhi, One Deemed University–Indian Agricultural Research Institute, 3 Research Institute namely National Research Centre on Plant Biotechnology, National Centre for Integrated Pest Management, National Centre for Agriculture Economics & Policy Research, 3 Directorates namely, Directorate of Knowledge Management in Agriculture, Directorate of Floriculture Research, Directorate of Maize Research, 1 National Bureaux-National Bureau of Plant Genetics Resources.

5.3. Indian Council of Medical Research Library (ICMR)

ICMR was established in 1949 as the apex body in for the formulation, coordination and promotion of biomedical research, is one of the oldest medical research bodies in the world with its headquarters in Delhi and three other Organizations namely, National Institute of Malaria Research (NIMR), National Institute of Pathology (NIP), National Institute of Medical Statistics (NIMS).

5.4. Indian Council of Social Science Research Library (ICSSR)

Indian Council of Social Science Research (ICSSR) was established in the year of 1969 by the Government of India to promote research in social sciences in the country. In Delhi, ICSSR affiliated organization are five namely, Institute of Economic Growth (IEG), Centre for the Study of Developing Societies (CSDS), Centre for Policy Research

(CPR), Centre for Women's Development Studies (CWDS), Institute for Studies in Industrial Development (ISID).

5.5. Defense Research Development Organization Library (DRDO)

DRDO was formed in 1958 from the amalgamation of the Technical Development Establishment (TDEs) of the Indian Army and the Directorate of Technical Development & Production (DTDP) with the Defence Science Organisation (DSO). In Delhi, DRDO is functioning with 10 Laboratories namely, Center for Fire, Explosive and Environment Safety (CFEES), Defence Institute of Physiology & Allied Sciences (DIPAS), Defence Institute of Psychological Research (DIPR), Defence Scientific Information & Documentation Centre (DESIDOC), Defence Terrain Research Laboratory (DTRL), Institute of Nuclear Medicine & Allied Sciences (INMAS), Institute of Systems Studies & Analyses (ISSA), Laser Science & Technology Centre (LASTEC), Scientific Analysis Group (SAG) and Solid State Physics Laboratory (SSPL).

In addition to many other prominent special libraries such as

5.6. National Council of Educational Research and Training Library (NCERT)

NCERT was set up by the Government of India in 1961 as an autonomous organization to assist in formulation and implementation of the policies and major programmes in the field of education, particularly for qualitative improvement of school education. The Division of Library, Documentation and Information (DLDI), located in Pt. Govind Ballabh Pant Block, is the Learning Resource Centre and Service Division of NCERT. The role of an institutional library is to help the institution to realize its objective. The main objective of DLDI Library is, therefore, to supplement the efforts of the Council in fulfillment of its objectives.

5.7. National Council for Applied Economic Research Library (NCAER)

The NCAER Library is one of India's premier research libraries in applied economics. Ever since its inception in 1956, the library has been an integral part of the institution, providing research support to the Council's economists as well as to policy makers, administrators, consultants, students and others from all over the country. The library plays a vital role in collecting, organizing and disseminating information for the benefit of researchers.

5.8. Indian National Science Academy Library

The National Institute of Sciences of India, now the Indian National Science Academy, was inaugurated on 7 January 1935 at Calcutta and functioned with its HQ at Asiatic Society of Bengal till 1946 and their after shifted to Delhi in 1951. INSA Library is well equipped with modern information technology tools for retrieval and dissemination of information. It has a collection of 19,000 books, 800 scientific journals.

5.9. Indian Islamic Cultural Centre Library (IICC)

IICC also provides a forum where scholars from all fields of learning can interact with each other to promote brotherhood, friendship, peace and amity amongst the various cultural and religious groups in India and also to strive for a peaceful co-existence. *Bureau of Indian Standards* - BIS came into existence in the year 1986 with a broadened scope and more powers taking over the staff, assets, liabilities and functions of erstwhile Indian Standards Institution (ISI). The Technical Library of the Bureau is a National Clearing House for information on standards and related matters and meets the needs of industry, trade, Government, researchers and consumers alike with its headquarters Library (New Delhi).

Government Libraries in Delhi

Many Government Libraries have been established before and after the independence in order to meet the information needs of the government officials. The major Government Libraries housed in Delhi are:

5.10. Central Secretariat Library (CSL)

CSL is one of the oldest libraries of the Government of India. It dates back to 1891 when the Imperial Secretariat Library was established in Kolkata (Calcutta). With the shifting of the Capital, the Library was also moved to Delhi and since 1969 it is housed in G-Wing of the Shastri Bhawan. In terms of size of collection (5, 50,000 volumes + non-print material), it is the second largest Central Government library after the National Library, Kolkata. Its Hindi & Regional Languages Wing (Tulsi Sadan Library) is located at Bahawalpur House and branch library at R.K. Puram, New Delhi. CSL is funded and administered by the Ministry of Culture of the Government of India.

5.11. Parliament Library

Parliament Library is the largest library in Delhi and second largest library in India after the National Library. It is one of the richest repositories of books in India and was established in the year 1921 to assist members of the Indian Legislature. A modest functional Library, was established in the year 1921, with a small collection of publications comprising mainly of Departmental reports, proceedings of Legislatures, Statutes, etc., for the first time to cater to the members of the then Central Legislative Assembly. Books and other important publications, when required by members, were obtained on loan from the Libraries of the Legislative Department and the Imperial Secretariat. This Library continued to serve members on a modest scale for a number of years.

5.12. Election Commission of India Library

The library & Resource Centre of Election Commission of India is a unique information resource centre involved to collect, store and disseminate democracy, election and electoral rolls related information to the researchers, scholars, Commission staff and other community who need it for the benefit of different kind of the society.

5.13. Supreme Court of India Library

Supreme Court of India came into existence in 1950 and is located on Tilak Marg, New Delhi. Supreme Court Judges Library is a "Reference and Research" wing of the Apex Court. It has to keep a close watch over the multifarious literature requirements of the Hon'ble Judges and Court functionaries and functions as throbbing heart of the Apex Court. It was established in 1937, and then known as Federal Court Library. It contains significant legal literature to support the need of the Hon'ble Judges and the Courts. It is a grid of libraries. It maintains workable collection in 15 Bench Libraries and 31 Residential Libraries of Hon'ble Judges. Delhi is also considered as the house of some of the country-based libraries, whose primary role is to disseminate the knowledge or information generated in their respective country such as

5.14. American Information Resource Centre Library (AIRC)

AIRC which was set up in 1946 as the USIS Library with 3000 books, 2000 pamphlets, 200 periodicals and seating for 24 readers. The main purpose of the American Central Library is to provide information on United States, its institution, its history, its arts, and literature and its people. At present, the library has a collection that includes 27,000 volumes, over 200 periodicals, 5 leading American Newspapers and 70 videotapes.

5.15. British Council Library

British Council Library is the gateway to a world of

opportunity which offers books on Economics, Engineering, Information Technology, Law Management, Medicine and Science & technology. The Collection of the library includes 24,000 books, newspapers, journals and magazines.

The *Max Muller Bhawan Library* houses a selection of the latest print and audiovisual media in German and translations to keep people informed about the latest trends and current issues.in Germany. Around 40% of their collection consists of books and media in English language.

6. LIS EDUCATION IN DELHI

The root of formal LIS education in the country started from the University of Delhi, when a full-fledged department parallel to the other disciplines was established in 1946 through the efforts of Padmashree late Prof. S R Ranganathan and Dr. S D Gupta, and started a regular course in Library Science known as Diploma in Library Science later known as Bachelor of Library and Information Science.

The Delhi University was the first university in the country which also started Masters, M. Phil. and Research programmes in Library and Information Science in 1946, 1985 and 1957 respectively. In addition to the Delhi University, earlier NISCAIR under the CSIR conducts a two-year specialized courses in LIS i.e. Associateship in Information Science in the year 1962. Since 2012 this course has been ceased by NISCAIR. IGNOU in response to the demand for a large number of trained personnel in libraries, documentation and information centers, the University launched its Bachelor's Degree in Library and Information Science Programme (BLISC) in 1989 and MLIS courses in 1996 through distance mode right from late eighties and this move was followed by different dual-mode state universities.

In Jamia Milia Islamia, Dr. Zakir Husain Library has been offering Bachelor's degree in Library and Information Science course to meet the needs of the Library and Information Science profession since 1985. The degree programme in Library and Information Science is intensive in nature and thereby demands students who are highly motivated and dedicated to learning.

Apart from the universities, some Library Professional Associations and Polytechnics have also started courses in library science. The Delhi Library Association has been conducting training courses at the certificate level since 1955. In view of the heavy rush, the School of Library Science is obliged to select every year about 100 candidates from amongst the applicants. It is a part-time course, conducted in two shifts. The Diploma in Library and Information Technology was started in 2003 which is of six months duration. The DLA is also running a certificate course in library science which is certified by the Govt. of India. Meera Bai Polytechnic also started two years Diploma in Library Science.

7. LIBRARY ASSOCIATIONS IN DELHI

7.1. Indian Library Association

ILA is a premier association committed to the cause of Library Movement and Development. It is the national association which represents those who work in or advocate for Indian libraries. ILA members work in college, university, public, special (corporate, non-profit and government) and school libraries. ILA has provided a wide variety of services and programs to its members and others in the library community since its formation in 1933. ILA publishes one journal i.e. Journal of Indian Library Association, a peered reviewed quarterly journal and one newsletter i.e. Newsletter of Indian Library Association.

7.2. Delhi Library Association

The DLA was founded in 1939 with the objective to promote library movement in Delhi; to provide training facilities in library science; to strengthen co-operation among libraries in Delhi and work for the improvement of library service; to improve the status and the working conditions of persons employed in the libraries; to take up publication work in library science; to co-operate with other organizations having similar objectives. It is one of the oldest and most pronounced Library associations which embarked upon several programmes and undertaken projects during its existence. The Library Herald is a quarterly journal of the Delhi Library Association has completed 44 successful volumes.

7.3. Satija Research Foundation for Library and Information Science

At the time of superannuation of renowned Professor (Dr.) M P SATIJA on 30th June 2008 from the Department of Library & Information Science, Guru Nanak Dev University, Amritsar (Punjab), the admirers, students and research scholars throughout the country and abroad came together and decided to have a Research Foundation in his name and dedicate it to their great teacher to express their love, affection and devotion.

8. CONCLUSION

The role of libraries in providing widespread and inclusive access to knowledge has also been acknowledged by the National Knowledge Commission, Government of India and its core recommendation i.e. Census of Libraries in India is a very ambitious programme in order to know the actual status of libraries in terms of physical infrastructure and services. But unfortunately, there is no authentic survey or study which tells the story of census of libraries in India. Through this article an effort has been made to highlight the major activities of the major libraries housed in Delhi. The public library movement in Delhi should be strengthening in order to fulfill the objective of library recommendations by National Knowledge Commission i.e. to make public library as a community information centre. Therefore, it is the need of hour that library legislation should be implemented by the Government of Delhi.

REFERENCES

1. Bhatt, R K. History and Development of Libraries in India. Mittal Publication, Delhi. 1995. P172-176
2. Kumar, PSG. Library Movement and Library Development in Delhi and Chandigarh. BR Publishing House, Delhi. 2010. P-7.
3. http://en.wikipedia.org/wiki/History_of_libraries
4. http://shodhganga.inflibnet.ac.in/bitstream/10603/1204/9/09_chapter%202.pdf
5. http://www.ggsipu.nic.in/urc/digital.htm
6. http://insaindia.org
7. http://www.iiccentre.org
8. http://www.csl.nic.in
9. http://www.bis.org.in
10. http://www.parliamentofindia.nic.in
11. http://eci.nic.in
12. http://supremecourtofindia.nic.in
13. http://dlaindia.wordpress.com
14. http://www.ilaindia.net
15. http://www.srflisindia.org

7

Library Movement and Development in Goa

Sathi. M C
Assistant Librarian
Kerala Veterinary and Animal Sciences University
College of Veterinary and Animal Sciences
Pookode, Wayanad Kerala

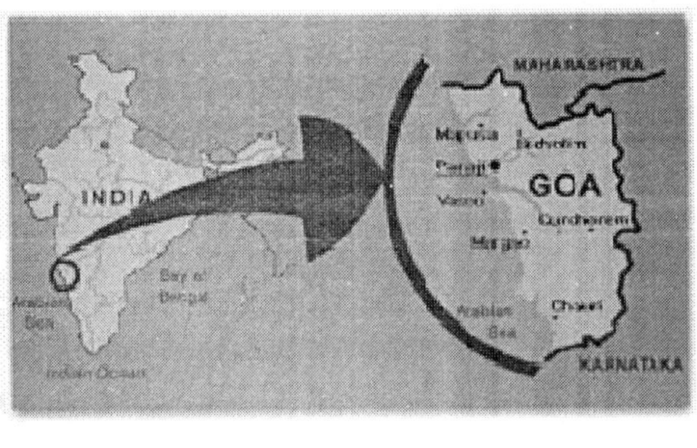

1. GOA : A PROFILE

Goa is India's smallest state by area and the fourth smallest by population. Located in West India in the region known as the Konkan, it is bounded by the state of Maharashtra to the north, and by Karnataka to the east and south, while the Arabian Sea forms its western coast. Goa is India's richest state with a GDP per capita two and a half times that of the country as a whole. It was ranked the best placed state by the Eleventh Finance Commission for its infrastructure and ranked on top for the best quality of life in India by the National Commission on Population based on the 12 Indicators.

Panaji is the state's capital, while Vasco da Gama is the largest city. The historic city of Margao still exhibits the cultural influence of the Portuguese, who first landed in the early 16th century as merchants and conquered it soon thereafter. Goa is a former Portuguese province; the Portuguese overseas territory of Portuguese India existed for about 450 years until it was annexed by India in 1961. Goa is visited by large numbers of international and domestic tourists each year for its beaches, places of worship and world heritage architecture. It also has rich flora and fauna, owing to its location on the Western Ghats range, which is classified as a biodiversity hotspot.

2. LIBRARY MOVEMENT IN GOA

The Portuguese ruled Goa for about 450 years. During their rule, they did two notable things. They started 1st printing press in Goa in 1556 and also established the 1st public library in Panaji in the year 1832. It was started as "Public Livraria" by their Vice Roy Dom Manuel de Portugal e Castro. This library is one of the oldest public library of modern India and Asian continent.

The above name was changed several times i.e. 'Bibliotheca Public', 'Bibliotheca Publica de Mova Goa", "National Library", "Bibliotheca National Vasco de Gama".

In 1889, Saraswat Vidyapeeth Pustakalaya was established at Marcel in Ponda taluka.

In 1898, Goa Hindu Pustakalaya was started. In 1907, two public libraries were established. One was Shri Mahalaxmi Prasadic Hindu Vachan Mandir Panjim and another Shri Durga Vachan Mandir at Mapusa. In 1913, Shri. Saraswati Mandir Library, Panajim came into existence.

After liberation the Bibliteca National de Goa was

renamed as central library in1964. In the year 1975 Govt. took initiative in starting Govt. Taluka and Village libraries. In 1978 the Govt. of Goa had constituted an expert committee under the chairmanship of Dr. K.S. Deshpande ,University Librarian, Karnataka University, Dharwad to suggest ways and means to improve existing library facilities in the state.

"Goa Public Libraries Act" was passed in 1993.

3. PUBLIC LIBRARIES IN GOA

3.1. Goa State Central Library

The State Central Library is the oldest Public Library in India. It was established on 15th September 1832 by Vice Roy Dom Manuel de Portugal e Castro as 'Publica Livraria.' It had a beginning as 'Academia Militar de Goa' (Military Training Institute). In 1836 the name was changed to 'Bibliotheca Publica' and enriched with bibliographical repository transferred from the Convents run by religious orders that were suppressed in the1834. In the same year the Library was shifted to premises where the Municipal Proceedings were held, however, the collection on Mathematics and Military sciences was left in Academia and books on Administrative and Legislative matters were transferred to Secretariat Library.

On 15th February 1897 the status of Library was raised to that of a National Library and renamed as 'Bibliotheca Nacional de Nova Goa'. In March 1925, it was annexed to the academic and cultural institution, (Instituto Vasco da Gama) and redesignated as "Biblioteca Nacional Vasco da Gama'. By Decree Law no. 38684 dated 18th March 1952, the privilege of 'Deposito Legal' (Delivery Act) was made applicable to this library and by virtue of it the library received all publications from Portugal and her overseas Provinces. From September 1959, the Bibliotheca was detached from the Institute and put under the administrative control of 'Servicos de Instruccao e Saude' (Education and Health Services); it was then renamed as Biblioteca Nacional de Goa. The collection of pre-liberation period consists mainly of Books and Journals in Portuguese, French, Latin, English and very few books in local language like Konkani and Marathi. The total pre-liberation collection was about 40,000 volumes.

The Library is named as Krishnadas Shama Goa State Central Library the founder of Konkani prose and father of Konkani literature in the written word of 16th century. The library has more then 1.8 lakhs book in different languages like English, Hindi, Marathi, Konkani, Portuguese since its inception. The Goa State Central Library is under the administrative control of Government of Goa, Directorate of Art & Culture and Curator is the Head of State Central Library-Goa.

3.2. Dr Francisco Luis Gomes District Library

The Dr Francisco Luis Gomes District Library is the major library in the district of South Goa, Goa, India. It is run and funded by the Government of Goa and was set up on 21 November 2010. The District Library located at Navelim, Salcete, Goa — just outside the South Goa headquarters city of Margao — is named after the intellectual and former Parliamentarian from Navelim, Dr. Francisco Luis Gomes, who was born on May 31, 1829. Dr. Francisco Luis Gomes came to be known as a great Goan Parliamentarian, a linguist, thinker, master of several European and Indian languages, medical doctor, writer, orator, economist, campaigner for rights and social worker. The foundation stone for the District Library was laid on February 5, 2007.

The Library covers area of above 8000 square metres, comprising five floors, providing various services to the users. An estimated 40,000 books in diverse languages—English, Marathi, Hindi, Konkani and Sanskrit—besides newspapers and periodicals, are homed in this library. Braille section and Goa section are the special features of this library.

3.3. Taluk Libraries

Along with state and district libraries, there are seven

Taluk libraries. They are - Govt. Taluka Library, Bicholim, Goa, Govt. Taluka Library, Canacona, Goa, Govt. Taluka Library, Curchorem, Goa, Govt. Taluka Library, Mandrem Pernem, Goa, Govt. Taluka Library, Ponda, Goa, Govt. Taluka Library, Sanguem, Goa and Govt. Taluka Library, Valpoi, Goa.

4. LIBRARY LEGISLATION IN GOA

One of the most important contribution of the government of Goa towards the library movement in the state was that it passed the Goa public Libraries Act in 1993. This demand for the library legislation to Goa was initiated by Goranatak Granthalaya Sangh in 1970 and it was fulfilled after a gap of 23 years. Many individuals and organizations made continuous efforts for enacting of Goa public libraries act. Much of the credit goes to Shri KT Satarwala, governor of Goa who was also the chairman of state library advisory board. In June 1982, he had reconstituted the state library advisory board under his chairmanship and had appointed a sub committee to draft a library bill by taking a model of Public Libraries Act of Maharastra 1967.However it did not receive the assent of the government. The Goa public libraries bill 1989 was introduced by the then MLA Shri. Domnic Fernends during the mansoon session of the assembly on 16th July 1993 and was passed on November 1997, and its implementation started from May 30, 1997, after being amended on 24th April 1997.

The act has novel feature which is not found in any public libraries act or is not in practice any Indian state that the act stipulates the compulsory enrolment of every student in public libraries on reaching standard 8. By going one step ahead, the act further stipulates the compulsory production of membership certificate of the public libraries by the unemployed youth during the registration in employment exchange. The act has provision of establishing district libraries and directorate of libraries. The amended act makes provisions for a sate library development cell under the directorate of school education with the state library officer as its head and for libraries at the state / district/ taluka and panchayat level. the finance is provided at the rate of 1% of the education budget for promoting public library service in the state. Goa government has imposed a library cess in the excise duty at the rate .5paise per liter of liquor/beer. New the library cess is being collected as per th4e Goa public libraries act 1993.

5. SPECIAL LIBRARIES IN GOA

5.1. The International Centre Goa Library

The International Centre Goa ICG) is a non-profit autonomous society founded in June 1987, under the Societies Registration Act, 1860. It was inaugurated by His Excellency, the former President of India, late Dr. Shankar Dayal Sharma, on 18th June 1996. The Centre was conceived as a forum to bring together thinkers, scholars, academics, achievers, sociologists, industrialists and creative people from India and around the world. The existing renovated Library cum Business Centre was inaugurated by the Mr. Shrinivas Dempo – Life Trustee of the ICG in February 2010. The renovation was financially supported by the Dempo Charity Trust. The Library, with its pleasant and relaxing atmosphere, offers a remarkable collection of over 1400 books covering a variety of subjects ranging from Economics to Philosophy, with special collections on Goa and bestsellers as well as over fifteen popular periodicals including the ones published in Goa.

6. ACADEMIC LIBRARIES IN GOA

6.1. Goa University Library

Goa University, established in June 1985 by an Act of Goa Government, is located on a picturesque campus spread over 427.49 acres area of Taleigao Plateau overlooking the Zuari Estuary, within close vicinity of the capital city of Panaji, in North Goa. The Goa. University Library and Information Centre was set up in 30th of June 1985 around the nucleus of the Library of the Centre for Post Graduate Research and Instruction, University of Bombay. The initial collection numbered 37,678 books and several bound volumes of periodicals. Today, the holdings have crossed one lakh forty thousand books covering a wide range of disciplines under Humanities, Social Science and Pure and Applied Sciences especially Microbiology, Marine Science, Environmental Science, Computer Science, Geology, Management and other disciplines including a special collection on Latin America and The Caribbean. The Library also has a large collection of titles in Konkani, the state language of Goa and a foreign language section which includes titles in Portuguese, French and Spanish. The Library acquires around 3000 books and over 350 periodicals every year. It also receives more than 150 periodicals gifted by various organisations and institutions. Goa University Library is a designated Repository Library of United Nations publications since 1996.

Along with the Goa University library, there a number of good academic libraries, such as BITS Pilani Library, NIT Goa Library, Goa Institute of Management Library etc.

7. LIS EDUCATION IN GOA

7.1. Goa University department of Library and information

Goa University department of Library and information science offers BLISc course.

8. LIS ASSOCIATIONS IN GOA

8.1. Academic Library Association Goa (ALAG)

Academic Library Association Goa (ALAG) Professional Association of Librarians working in the Academic Institutions in the state of Goa.

Aims and Objectives of the ALAG

- To promote fellow feeling, social interaction between the librarians, self help, self reliance and self respect among librarians working in the academic institutions in the state of Goa.

- To unite all librarians in Goa by holding conferences and meetings for the discussion of questions affecting the library profession and matters affecting libraries or their regulation or management or otherwise. To work for improvement in the conditions of service, social status and prospects of the librarians working in the academic institutions in the state of Goa; Scope of the association is restricted to Goa state.
- To protect and safeguard the rights of the librarians working in the academic institutions in Goa by constitutional methods; To take all lawful action, including legal action, in order to protect professional and those areas of public interest affecting, or related to, the profession. To do all such other lawful things as are necessary and as advisable for the advancement of its interests.
- To initiate, sponsor, undertake, encourage and promote scholarly study, research and consultancy work in the fields of library science and services. The Association shall constantly strive to relate its academic work to social needs of the community, and shall focus its research and consultancy work to socially relevant themes. To provide consultancy service to private / corporate and other educational institutions in the field of library and information Science.
- To provide opportunities for self education and self improvement among librarians working in the academic institutions;
- To celebrate Dr. S.R. Ranganathan Birth anniversary by conducting book exhibitions, lectures, seminars, workshops and other instructional programmes to further the aforementioned objectives of the Association.
- To publish (print and online) books, newsletters, journals, bulletins, etc., on topics of interest to professionals as well as public relating to library and

information services.

- To suggest ways and means to improve the conditions of the libraries on behalf of the library community in Goa and to make an appropriate recommendations to Government and other higher authorities and organizations for protection of the profession.
- To co-operate with other state, national, international and other organizations with similar objectives.
- To do all such other things as incidental or conducive to the attainment of the above mentioned objectives.

9. CONCLUSION

Library movement and development of Goa is very interesting. It has long history of libraries during the French period. Its library legislation has its own special features such as compulsory membership for students and youth and inclusion of tax for library in liquor/ beer. The one of the shortage is the lack of higher education in Library and Information science in the state.

REFERENCE

1. Kumar, PSG (2008). Library movement and library development in Maharastra and Goa. New Delhi , B.R. Publishing Corporation.
2. Satpute, BB (2009).Development of public libraries in Goa. *Library Herald*, Vol 47(2), 115-123.
3. Sharma, S.K. Pandey (1996). Public libraries in India: Trends and Status. In *Public libraries in developing countries: Status and Trends.* Ed. P. K. Mahapatra ,125-127. New Delhi: Vikas Publishing House
4. Venkatappaiah , V.(1990). State Library Bills And Acts. In: *Indian Library legislation* Ed. P.S.G Kumar. V.2. Delhi : Daya Publishing House.
5. Venkatapaiah (2000) Indian Library Legislation : State Library bills and acts. Delhi, Daya Publishing House.
6. www. http://centrallibrary.goa.gov.in
7. http://en.wikipedia.org
8. *shodhganga.inflibnet.ac.in/bitstream/10603/1204/.../09_chapter*
9. http://www.nmlindia.nic.in

8

Library Movement and Development of Gujarat

Shishir H. Mandalia
University Librarian(I/c)
Sardar Patel University, VallabhVidyanagar
Anand-388120, Gujarat

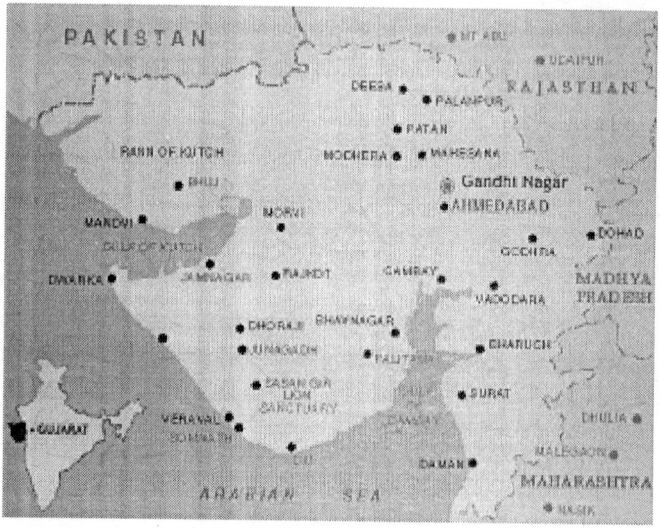

1. GUJARAT : A PROFILE

Gujarat is a state in the western part of India known locally as Jewel of the West. It has an area of 196,204 km^2

(75,755 sq mi) with a coastline of 1,60 km (99mi), most of which lies on the Kathiawar peninsula, and a population in excess of 60 million. The state is bordered by Rajasthan to the north, Maharashtra to the south, Madhya Pradesh to the east, and the Arabian Sea as well as the Pakistani province of Sindh to the west. Its capital city is Gandhinagar, while its largest city is Ahmedabad. Gujarat is home to the Gujarati-speaking people of India.

The state encompasses major sites of the ancient Indus Valley Civilization, such as Lothal and Dholavira. Lothal is believed to be one of the world's first seaports. Gujarat's coastal cities, chiefly Bharuch and Khambhat, served as ports and trading centres in the Maurya and Gupta empires, and during the succession of royal Saka dynasties from advent of the Western Satraps era, whose geographic territories included Saurashtra and Malwa: modern Gujarat, South Sindh, Rajasthan, Maharashtra and Madhya Pradesh states. Gujarat was known to the Ancient Greeks, the various Persian Empires, the Roman Republic, and familiar in other Western centers of civilization through the end of the European Middle Ages. of the First Century'.

2. HISTORY OF LIBRARY MOVEMENT IN GUJARAT

The first considered public library in Gujarat was called, "Himabhai Institute of Library" established in 1849 in Ahmedabad. Other pioneer public libraries were Andrews Library established in 1850, Lang Library in 1857, Lakhajirao Pusthakalaya in 1868, Bhagavatsihji Library in 1884, State Library in 1865, Barton Library in 1882, Takhsinhi Library in 1877, and Victoria Jubilee Library in 1891. There are 2 State Central libraries, 18 District Libraries in all the districts, 45 Taluka Libraries, 129 Mahila Libraries run by voluntary organizations, more than 300 Book Service Centers and Mobile Library service.

3. GUJARAT PUBLIC LIBRARY ACT 2001

Objective of Gujarat Public Libraries Act provided in

its preamble is to provide for the promotion and development of public libraries in the State of Gujarat and for that purpose to constitute State Library development Council and for the matters connected therewith or incidental thereto. Important features of this act are:

1. Constitution of State Library Council with Minister – in-charge of Libraries as its Chairman;
2. Establishment of Public Library Department with Director as its head of office;
3. Establishment of District and Taluk Libraries at the headquarters of Taluk;
4. Constitution of District and Taluk Library Advisory Committee;
5. Formation of State Library Development Fund;
6. Recognition of libraries run by voluntary organizations.

Characteristics of the Gujarat Public Libraries Act

1. It is quite appreciable that clarification of maximum number of library related matters are comprised in definition at the beginning of the act.
2. Not only conventional books but also printed and non-printed matters in them are invaded in the definition of books which are core at library. Also computer which is the vehicle of information age today has been rendered priority. This a commendable effort is made as keep pace with modems technology and simultaneously, the intellectual treasure of India Manuscripts are also not forgotten. Hence the sublime traverse of library is from manuscript as e-book which is really exemplary.
3. Gujarat state Library council is an integral factor as entire act. It is the merit of the act that recognizing the significance of the council the act presents the comprehensive and adequate information about it in chapter 2 immediately introduction.

4. The invasion of Gujarat Library Academy and Gujarati Literary council and their chairmen in the act as really praiseworthy which shall play a vital role in Gujarati Literary world. The synergy of Gujarati Littérateurs and leaved librarians will prove to be efficacious in furnishing and organizing bibliographies of scattered library wealth.
5. An attempt is mate to remove ambiguity by delineating the scope of "Gujarat State Library Development Council"
6. There is a provision that govt. will facilitate the headquarter of 'Gujarat State Library Development Council' in Gandhi nagar or anywhere in the state, so it can be perceived that govt. does not give importance at Gandhi nagar only but also arouse faith and confidence in citizens other than of capital through regionalizing its foundation. In a way the library act will be helpful in bringing about enormous public wariness.
7. Section 15 envelopes the provision of constituting the advisory committee of district and Taluk libraries. Adequate number of sub-sections is allotted for the committee members and as the act is crystal clear regarding the some there remains no question of complication.
8. The titles in themselves district and Taluk library advisory committees stand for their nature as advisory.
9. It is a welcome factor that – besides library experts. The representation of primary secondary and higher education is maintained in member of advisory committee of district library.
10. The formation of Taluk library advisory committee will benefit the development of Taluk libraries.
11. The provision of females librarian representation in district library advisory committee and Taluk library advisory committee exhibits the noble tendency of

government as harmonize all segments of society and its commitment at women empowerment.

12. Chapter – 4 of section – 13, has the provision to establish new libraries.
13. The duties and responsibilities of public library director are well defined.
14. There is a provision of government donation for development, management and maintenance of public libraries and a provision of "State Library Development Fund" which is very important on account of which a regular source of income has emerged for public libraries.
15. It is essential that its employees ought to be well equipped with sophisticated technology in order that libraries may keep pace with shifting sands of time. For this purpose, training classes and financial provisions are chalked out.
16. The act also specifies and depicts the blue print of developmental project to be followed by the director so that public money may not be squandered and remain beyond the clutches of director's nepotism.
17. The director has to use funds after negotiating with govt. as it clearly mentions who and with whose counsel money will be spent.
18. It is the responsibility of library director to give affiliations to unions in Gujarat Library Act..
19. Coordination will be sustained in library activities as the director is obliged to formulate Taluk and district library advisory committees.
20. There is a provision to appoint two persons having the minimum experience of 10 years in higher education in State Library Council.

4. MAJOR PUBLIC LIBRARIES IN GUJARAT

4.1. Gujarat Vidyapith: Central Library

Started since the foundation of the Vidyapith in 1920, the Central Library has grown over the years to become one of the richest repositories of books, journals and manuscripts in Gujarat. The library remains open 364 days a year, remaining closed only on the first day of the Vikram Samvat. The membership of the library is open to the public at a nominal fee. Its membership stood at 36,864 but in 2005-06 the total active members are 3006. The Central Library of the Vidyapith is the statutory referral library of the state for the purpose of copyright. The copyright section has 1,08,635 books as in the year 2005. The library comprises of the main book storage facility, reference section, copyright section, a separate hall for Gandhian studies, the magazine and journal section, a reading hall and a children's section.

4.2. The Lang Library

Based in Rajkot, Gujarat, Lang Library has a rich collection of Gujarati literature because of which it has gained eminence across the state as well as nationally. This library has an enviable and desirable assortment of Gujarati and Kathiawadi literature. Some of these are bound in leather covers and some older books available here are made of handmade paper and written with gold. The library holds more than 3 lakhs books along with a good collection of some recently launched e-Journals and e-Books. This makes Lang Library the best option for those with a keen interest in Gujarat literature. The library adds thousands of recent published books each year and subscribes to hundreds of printed journals and periodicals on a variety of subjects. A storehouse of books, periodicals and journals, this library is situated in the great Jubilee Gardens.

4.3. Andrews Library

The Library was started in 1850 a building near Sardar Patel Museum in Chowk Bazaa and later shifted to the existing building. The library was started as part of the efforts to improve educational infrastructure by British offcials leading Parsi and Surti citizens. "says historian Mohan Meghari. The restoration and renovation will be undertaken by Andrews and Naginchand Zaveri Manav Vikas Sanstha at Rs. 21 lakh. The structure has Andrew's Library on ground floor while Naginchand Zaveri Hall on first floor. Currently the library has collection of more than 30,000 books. As part of the renovation, the ground floor will be turned into centrally air conditioned hall with modern racks for books.

4.4. Sayaji Vaibhav Public Library Navsari

The Sayaji Vaibhav Public Library, located in Navsari. is one of the largest libraries of the Gujarat state. This is the only library in Gujarat to have received the prestigious Late Motibhai Amin Library Award five times by the Government of Gujarat.

4.5. K J Choksi Public Library

The Library was founded by Mr. G K Choksi in 2008 in the memory of his father Mr. K J Choksi. Mr. K J Choksi was a freedom Fighter, Mayor of Bharuch City and headed the local library for several years. The primary objective of setting up the library is the promotion of reading habits among public at large. The trustees wish to make reading a popular hobby among students and young generation, which is influenced by lot of other entertainment avenues. The Library is not for profit and is fully funded by Kantilal J Choksi Charitable Trust.

5. ACADEMIC LIBRARIES IN GUJARAT

5.1. Gujarat University Library

Gujarat university library was started along with its parent body the Gujarat University . The University Library moved to its newly constructed building in May 1967. The Library have more than 3,50,457 books. 11,600 E-Books and 7,500 E-Journals. The Library adds about 5000 books every year and subscribes to about 250 Printed periodicals in various subjects. This library caters to the needs of the students and teachers of the University at large. In addition, there are small libraries attached to each school / department in which house texts and reference books on courses being currently offered by the respective school / department are provided. These books are issued from the Central Library on long-term basis to each school / department. The department and school libraries offer books and reading-room facilities to their students and teachers. Also there is a reading room attached to the Central Library. The reading room can accommodate 600 readers. They can sit and read at the same time. For those students who find the Central Library away from their residence, nearer centres are provided by the university in the Ahmedabad city, such as centers at Hajipur, Saraspur and Khokhra-Mehemdabad.

5.2. Maharaja Sayajirao University of Baroda – Shrimati Hansa Mehta Library

Shrimati Hansa Mehta Library, the University Library of M S University of Baroda was established on May1, 1950. At the time of establishment of the M. S. University of Baroda, a collection of 25,000 books belonging to the two State Libraries (Huzur Political Office and Secretariat Library) was handed over to the University Library. There were several colleges in Baroda - Baroda College (for Arts), Science Institute, Commerce College, and Secondary Teacher's Training College etc. These colleges had libraries of their own. These libraries continued to remain as Faculty Libraries and were administered independently. Thus the University Library System was established on 1-5-1950, which was housed in the central block of Old Residency Office Building

5.3. Saurashtra University Library

The Saurashtra University was established on 23rd May 1967, with the Head Quarters located both at Rajkot and Bhavnagar.Consequently upon the formation of the

Bhavnagar University in 1979. The Head Quarters of the Saurashtra University is now at Rajkot. The Saurashtra University Library started functioning along with the University in 1967 in a rental building 'Dharampur No Utaro'. On the 1st Aug 1967 the Library was shifted to another building called 'Nand Vihar' in the Jagnath Plot Area. The library was finally shifted to its own newly constructed building at the University Campus on 20th June 1973 with the area of 3056.15 Sq. Mt. The Saurashtra University Library which begun its services with a collection of 3200 books in 1967- 68, has presently over 154 000 books. The current growth rate is approximately 3000 books per year along with 350 bound volumes and 100 theses/Dissertations per year.

5.4. Hemchandracharya North Gujarat University Library

The library was started along with the establishment of the University in the year 1986. The library was established on 15th January, 1988. Initially It was housed in the Gandhi Memorial Hall. The University received a donation of Rs. 51 lakhs from Dr. M.S.Patel Trust, Mumbai for the construction of the library building, hence the library is named as Shivabhai Umedbhai Patel Library.

5.5. Maharaja Sayajirao University Library

Shrimati Hansa Mehta Library, the University Library of M S University of Baroda was established on May1, 1950. At the time of establishment of the M. S. University of Baroda, a collection of 25,000 books belonging to the two State Libraries (Huzur Political Office and Secretariat Library) was handed over to the University Library. There were several colleges in Baroda - Baroda College (for Arts), Science Institute, Commerce College, and Secondary Teacher's Training College etc. These colleges had libraries of their own. These libraries continued to remain as Faculty Libraries and were administered independently. Thus the University Library System was established on 1-5-1950, which was housed in the central block of Old Residency Office Building.

6. SPECIAL LIBRARIES IN GUJARAT

6.1. INFLIBNET Centre Library

Information and Library Network (INFLIBNET) Centre is an autonomous Inter-University Centre of the University Grants Commission (UGC) of India. It is a major National Programme initiated by the UGC in March 1991 with its Head Quarters at Gujarat University Campus, Ahmedabad. Initially started as a project under the IUCAA, it became an independent Inter-University Centre in June 1996. INFLIBNET is involved in modernizing university libraries in India and connecting them as well as information centres in the country through a nation-wide high speed data network using the state-of-art technologies for the optimum utilisation of information. INFLIBNET is set out to be a major player in promoting scholarly communication among academicians and researchers in India. .

The INFLIBNET Library plays a vital role in the collection development and dissemination of scientific and technical information to meet the present and future needs of the Centre. The INFLIBNET Centre has a small, specialized library consisting of 2000 documents on computer, communication, information and library science. The library is fully computerized using SOUL integrated library management software. The collection of the library is available online through the web OPAC facility of the SOUL. The INFLIBNET Library plays a vital role in the collection development and dissemination of scientific and technical information to meet the present and future needs of the Centre. The Library maintains databases of - participants who attended various training programmes at INFLIBNET Centre; SOUL installations; and universities and its contact details including e-mail and website addresses. These databases are accessible through the library website at http://www.inflibnet.ac.in/universitydirectory/.

6.2. Indian Institute of Management (IIM) Ahmedabad-Vikram Sarabhai Library

The Vikram Sarabhai Library (VSL) is named after Dr. Vikram Sarabhai, world renowned physicist and founding Director of IIMA. It was set up in 1962 and is one of the best management libraries in Asia. The four storeyed building, spread over 20120 sq. ft. is divided into two wings by a central staircase. One wing is stack area and another wing has a reading hall. Reference books are placed in the reading hall. Open carrels are provided in the stack area for individual study. Circulation counter is situated at the entrance. Main Reading Hall is situated on second floor.

The library is open 24x7. The strength of the library is its digital collection of 67 databases, accessible from any networked computer within the campus which provides scholarly, company and industry information. The library provides specialized tools like EBSCO Discovery, journal title search (A to Z), remote login (restricted to internal users) and institutional repository searching.

6.3. Sardar Vallabhai Natioanal Institute of Technology, Surat Library

The Central Library, SVNIT Surat is one amongst major technological libraries in the area of science, engineering and technology. The Library was established in 1968. It has completed nearly 35 years and has built a large collection of books, journals and non-book materials. It also has a rich collection of resources in electronic media available locally on the Institute Intranet and accessible on the Web. It caters to the needs of large groups of users including more than 2000 students, 200 faculty, 150 research scholars and equally large number of supporting staff. It has computerized all its house-keeping activities using a global software that is being maintained and updated regularly. It also facilitates industries, individual consultants and corporates to access online database and journals. It uses state-of-the-art technology in its functioning and services. Not only having a very good reference section, Library has been subscribed to access INDEST by MHRD.

6.4. Anand Agricultural University Library

The history of Dr M.D. Patel Library dates back even prior to our Independence. In 1942, this Library was an accessory to the then SMC School of Dairy Science. After the inception of the B.A. College of Agriculture in 1947, it grew as the Central Library, merging the collections of BACA and SMC College of Dairy Science. In 1983, it was named after Dr Maganbhai Dahyabhai Patel (Dr. M. D. Patel Library).

Looking to the striking advances made by the Information Technology Center at Anand campus in the erstwhile Gujarat Agricultural University for the development of Agricultural Education as per SAU model under ARIS and ISD, ICAR had taken Dr. M.D. Patel Library to be an integral part of its 18-Regional Library Consortium project and selected Dr. M. D. Patel Library as the Regional Library in the western zone. The launching of National Agriculture Technology Project by ICAR, New Delhi, on Library Improvement and Networking (LIS O&M) drastically altered not only the fiscal statistics, but also the Library's status as well, as the Library became an inextricable part of a nation-wide consortium, towards digitization, automation and establishment of modern Cyberary with 20 mbps Internet and 36 work-stations, thereby obtaining the esteemed position of Regional e-Library.

7. LIBRARY ASSOCIATION IN GUJARAT

7.1. Gujarat Granthalaya-Seva Sangh

Full name of the association is Gujarat Granthalaya-Seva Sangh. It is an outcome of the concentrated efforts of the active and enthusiastic librarians and information Scientist of Gujarat State. The membership of this Association is spread throughout the Gujarat State. Gujarat Granthalaya-Seva Sangh came into existence in 1971. its head office is located at Ahmedabad.

8. LIS EDUCATION IN GUJARAT

There is a well established education set up for library information science. Almost all levels of courses are being provided in the state. The following university departments offer various course in library and information science. Maharaja Krishnakumarsinhji Bhavnagar University, Gujarat Vidyapith deemed university, Gujarat University, University of Baroda, Sardar Patel University Maharaja Sayajirao University of Baroda, Saurashtra university, Hemchandracharya North gujarath university and Veer Narmad South Gujarat University.

REFERENCES

1. Barua, B. P. (1994). Raja Ram Mohan Library Foundation and Library Movement in India. *39th All India Library Conference, Delhi, Indian Library Association*.
2. Kumar, PSG (2009). Library Movement and Library Development in Gujarat, Dadra and Nagar Haveli and Daman and Diu. New Delhi, B.R Publishing Coroporation.
3. Mohammed Taher (2001). Libraries in India's national developmental perspective: a saga of fifty years since independence: New Delhi: Concept publishing.
4. Sharma, S.K (1996). *Public library in India: trends and status.* P.K.Mahapatra (Ed.), Public libraries in developing countries (pp.121-127). New Delhi: Vikash Publishing House.
5. Venkatapaiah (2000) Indian Library Legislation : State Library bills and acts. Delhi, Daya Publishing House.
6. http://www.shreeprakashan.com
7. www.en.wikipedia.org
8. *shodhganga.inflibnet.ac.in/bitstream/10603/1204/.../09_chapter*
9. http://www.nmlindia.nic.in

9

Library Movement and Development of Haryana

Amrita Devi
Senior Research Fellow,
Natioanal Dairy Research Institute
Karnal – Haryana

1. HARYANA: A PROFILE

Haryana is a state in north India with its capital at Chandigarh. It came into existence on 1 November 1966 as a newly created state carved out of the Indian Punjab (East Punjab) state on the basis of language. It has been a part of the Kuru region in North India. The name Haryana is found mentioned in the 12th century AD by the Apabhramsha writer Vibudh Shridhar (VS 1189–1230). It is bordered by Punjab and Himachal Pradesh to the north, and by Rajasthan to the west and south. The river Yamuna defines its eastern border with Uttarakhand. Haryana also surrounds the country's capital Delhi on three sides, forming the northern, western and southern borders of Delhi. Consequently, a large area of south Haryana is included in the National Capital Region for purposes of planning for development.

Location of the state was home to prominent sites of the Indus Valley and Vedic Civilizations. Several decisive battles were fought in the area, which shaped much of the history of India. These include the epic battle of Mahabharata at Kurukshetra mentioned in the Hindu mythology (including the recital of the Bhagavad Gita by Krishna), and the three battles of Panipat. Haryana was administered as part of the Punjab province of British India, and was carved out on linguistic lines as India's 17th state in 1966. Haryana is now a leading contributor to the country's production of food grain and milk. Agriculture is the leading occupation for the residents of the state, the flat arable land irrigated by submersible pumps and an extensive canal system. Haryana contributed heavily to the Green Revolution that made India self-sufficient in food production in the 1960s.

2. HISTORY OF LIBRARY MOVEMENT IN HARYANA

Before the creation of this separate state, some public libraries were already established, Guru Gobind Singh Municipal Library (formerly Fyson Library) in 1926, Shri Parmeshwari Yuvak Librray in 1927, and Sri Bal Amar Samiti Library in 1932. A State Central Library (Jagnayak;1999;67) was started in 1967 by th4 Government of Haryana. Besides it has started 12 District Libraries, 11 Sub- Divisional Libraries and 11 Municipal Libraries. Many philanthropic trusts and local 51 bodies/organizations had also established public libraries, which took active role in the promotion of reading habits and library services in the state. The Haryana Library Association was founded in 1967. The Haryana Public Libraries Bill was passed in 1989 and independent Directorate of Libraries was established in January 1993. Mobile library services to reach the interior of the remote villages with reading facilities were started and the people are very much encouraged for the development of libraries at villages and panchayat levels as a social education center and community information center as well.

3. HARYANA LIBRARY LEGISLATION 1989

Mr. ML Bhagi, former librarian of the state central library, Haryana took initiative to start the Haryana Library Association in 1967. During 1971m, he presented a paper in Haryana Book festival on "public library services and the draft bill for library legislation". This was submitted to the director of Higher education of Haryana. Again in 1989, Haryana Library Association organized a seminar on "library Legislation in Haryana" in July 1989.. As a follow up the organizing committee submitted the library bill go the government. It was passed in that year in the Haryana Assembly. Haryana is the eighth state in India with library legislation.

Salient features of the Act

The salient features of the Haryana Public Libraries Act are given below

1. Constitution of the state Library Authority to advice the government on all matters in promotion of library services in the state.
2. Formation of a state Library Directorate to implement the programmes approved by the state authority.
3. Establishment of the State Central Library with state reference library section and state lending library section.

4. Constitution of a District library committee for each district.
5. Constitution of a city and town library committee for each city with a population of not more than one lakh, constituted in accordance with such rules a s may be framed by the district library committee concerned.
6. Constitution of Block Library Committee and Panchayat Library committee by district library committee.
7. Constitution of the state Library fund, district library fund, city or town or block or village library fund meant for the development , improvement and maintenance of the library services.
8. Levy of library cess in a form of surcharges on property tax and house tax at such a rate decided by government from time to time.
9. Provision to recognize state library associations and cooperative institutions by the state library authority.

4. PUBLIC LIBRARIES IN HARYANA

4.1. State Central Library – Haryana

The State Central Library was built during British rule in India in 1920 for education purposes. It is located at Ambala(formerly it was Ambala district library). It was turned into Library in 1957. Now it is Haryana's state central Library. The library consists of 64000 books which are available in many languages like Hindi, Punjabi, Urdu and English.

4.2. Other Public libraries in the state

The other prominent public libraries in the sate are - Gobind Singh muncipal library, Kirori Mal Library, Kishan Lal Seva Sadan library, Mathura Parsad Trust Library, Sultanpur Park's library, Gandhi Memorial Library, Jatton Mohalla Library, Police Library, Arya Samaj Library, Manav Sewa Sangh Library, Partap Library, Jain Library, Vidya Vihar

Gurukul and Gita Bhawan Library, Kamalia Bradari Library and Sthaneshwar Public Library.

5. ACADEMIC LIBRARIES IN HARYANA

5.1. Central University of Haryana

Central University of Haryana Library System having more than 33000 volumes in multidiscipline to serve the academic community. There are 4869 high quality e-Journals being made available through campus network to teachers, students and research scholars. CUHL also promotes Open Access e-resources. The main services of the library are - Circulation & Reader Services, Issue,Return, Renewal of Books, Reference and Enquiry Service, Library Orientation, Modern and attractive reading tables and chairs, A/C Reading Room and A/C E-Library.

5.2. Kurukshetra University Library

The University Library was started in Kalsia House with Sanskrit books and later on continues to be housed at two places i.e the main library in the College of Education and Indic Studies Section in the top floor of the Administrative Block. library was shifted in its new building in July 18, 1972 having plinth area 33000 Sq ft in three storeys' Later on during 1984-85 due to shortage of space the building was extended and presently has plinth area 49230 sq. ft. In order to provide adequate reading space 57500 sq ft. area was added in the golden jubilee year of the university. This reading area now known as Golden Jubilee Reading Hall. After adding this library has area of 1,06,730 sq ft. Library reading capacity has increased from 470 users to 1270 users. Library has 1270 reading seat capacity.

5.3. Deenabajdhu Chhotu Ram University Library

The University Library is housed in Saraswati Library Complex which is a four story building, a perfect and beautiful blend of aesthetics, latest technology and green architecture. The University Library has a seating capacity of

500 members. The University Library has a 54, 480 books and other reading materials and 343 e-books. The University Library subscribes 101 printed Indian Journals. It also subscribes 67 Magazines and 19 Newspapers to cater the needs of users for current awareness and leisure reading. The University Library has undertaken the subscription to the Online Journals of J-Gate (Social and Management Science – 6936), Emerald – 150 (Management – 150), EBSCO (Art and Architecture – 239) and IEEE/IEL.

5.4. Mahrshi Dayanand University Library (Vivekananda Library

Maharshi Dayanand University came into existence as an autonomous body in 1976. Though the establishment of this Library coincides with the establishment of Regional Centre of Panjab University Chandigarh in 1966, the year 1989 is a land-mark in its history, as the present library building was officially dedicated to the University community in particular, State in general and the country at large in this year. Vivekananda Library, named after Swami Vivekananda The Library has five satellite libraries – Law Library, IMSAR Library, and UIET. Library, Math Library and Hotel & Tourism Library.

6. SPECIAL LIBRARIES IN HARYANA

6.1. Natiaonal Institute of Technology- Kurukshetra Library

The Library initially set up in 1965 has grown in size, collection and services. Presently NIT Kurukshetra has a very spacious Library with good collection of documents which includes text and reference books, video cassettes, CD- ROMs and large number of Print & Online Journals and e-books. With its growing resources, space & services, the Library caters to the need of faculty, research scholars and students.

6.2. Gur Jambheshwar University of Science and Technology Library

The University Library building has a total area of 4875

sq. meter. The Library has two Reading Halls with a total capacity of 250 seats. The Library has processed the subscription of 169 Indian Journals in the year 2013. The Journals already subscribed in the Library were reviewed keeping in view their utilization pattern. The Library subscribes 58 magazines and 19 newspapers to cater to the general information needs of the University. The access to more than 6000 electronic journals of 17 publishers have been provided through the INFONET programme of UGc. The access to the electronic journals and databases is provided through Campus Wide Network for use by the Faculty and the Students.

7. LIS EDUCATION IN HARYANA

7.1. Kurukshetra University (K U), Kurukshetra

The Kurukshetra University was established in 1956 as a unitary residential University and its foundation stone was laid by late Dr. Rajendra Prasad, the first President of India. Located in the holy city of Kurukshetra, land of the historical battle of 'Mahabharata' and the great message of Bhagwad Gita. The Department of Library and Information Science came into existence in 1969 to impart quality education and modern skills in the field of Library and Information Science. The Department has the distinction of being the pioneer in Haryana in LIS education. On the persistent demand of the students, the Department also started offering Master's degree Course in 1986 and at present four Courses i.e. B. Lib. & Inf. Sc., M. Lib. & Inf. Sc., M. Phil. and Ph.D. are being run The Department is also disseminating knowledge through distance mode by actively participating in three courses viz - Diploma in Library Science (one year), B. Lib. & Inf. Sc. and M. Lib. & Inf. Science.

7.2. Maharishi Dayanand University (MDU), Rohtak

Maharshi Dayanand University established as Rohtak University, Rohtak, came into existence by an Act No. 25 of 1975 of the Haryana Legislative Assembly in 1976 It had a unitary and residential character in its nascent stage, but became an affiliating University in November 1978. The Department of Library and Information Science recently came into existence in 2010 to impart quality education and modern skills in the field of Library and Information Science. Initially, it is headed by Professor Prem Singh and manning by three Assistant Professors. Atpresent two year integrated course of M. Lib. & Inf. Sc. is being run by the department. The Department is also disseminating knowledge through distance mode by actively participating in two courses viz - B. Lib. & Inf. Sc. and M. Lib. & Inf. Science.

7.3. Vaish Technical Institute (VTI), Rohtak

Vaish Technical Institute is situated in the Western end of Vaish Education Society Complex at Rohtak. Vaish Technical Institute came into existence in 1957 with a humble beginning by introducing a diploma in Civil Engg. At present it is offering diploma courses in 8 branches of engg. and 2 branches of non engg.field which include diploma in Library Science. The department of LIS was started in 1984.

7.4. Bhagat Phool Singh Institute of Polytechnic (BPSIP) , Khanpur

Kalan Bhagat Phool Singh M ahila Polytechnic Khanpur Kalan was established in1984, situated far from 10 Km from Gohana and firstly it started with two diploma courses Library & Information Science and Commercial Practice & Stenography with 60 students. Department of Library and Information Science is running 3 year diploma course in Library science.

7.5. Kalpana Chawla Govt. Polytechnic for Women (KCGPW), Ambala City.

The KCGPW was established in 1968. It is the oldest and a premier Women Polytechnic among the only three Women Polytechnics in Haryana. It was opened for up liftment of Women section of the society. The Department of Library and Information Science was established in 1969 and initially, it was headed by Meenakshi Bansal and is running 3 year diploma course in Library science. Library is considered as the mother of all science and is a fountain of knowledge.

8. LIBRARY ASSOCIATIONS IN HARYANA

Haryana Library Association (HLA)

Haryana Library Association(HLA) was established in 1967. The association was the mind and hands behind the public library legislations in Haryana state. The association regularly organize seminars on library related issues. HLA organized a national seminar in 1982 on "public library system in Kurukshetra". In 1989 the association again conducted a seminar on "Library legislation in Haryana". This seminar became success and in that year the government of "Haryana passed Haryana Public library Act 1989".

REFERENCE

1. Barua, B. P. (1994). Raja Ram Mohan Library Foundation and Library Movement in India. *39th All India Library Conference, Delhi, Indian Library Association.*
2. Kumar, PSG (2011). Library Movement And Library Development In North-West India Vol 1 Haryana, Himachal Pradesh And Jammu Kashmir. New Delhi, B.R Publishing. Coroporation.
3. Mohammed Taher (2001). Libraries in India's national developmental perspective: a saga of fifty years since independence: New Delhi: Concept publishing.
4. Praveen Kumar (2012).Present scenario of Library and Information Science eductation in Haryana. In Asian Journal of Library and Infoarmation Science, pp 2-9.
5. Sharma, S.K (1996). *Public library in India: trends and status.* P.K.Mahapatra (Ed.), Public libraries in developing countries (pp.121-127). New Delhi: Vikash Publishing House.
6. http://revenueharyana.gov.in/html/gazeteers.
7. *shodhganga.inflibnet.ac.in/bitstream/10603/1204/.../09_chapter*
8. http://www.nmlindia.nic.in

10

Library Movement and Development in Himachal Pradesh

Arun Kumar
Research Scholar
Department of Library and Information Science
Central University of Himachal Pradesh
Dimple Patel
Department of Library and Information Science
Central University of Himachal Pradesh, Dharamshala (HP)

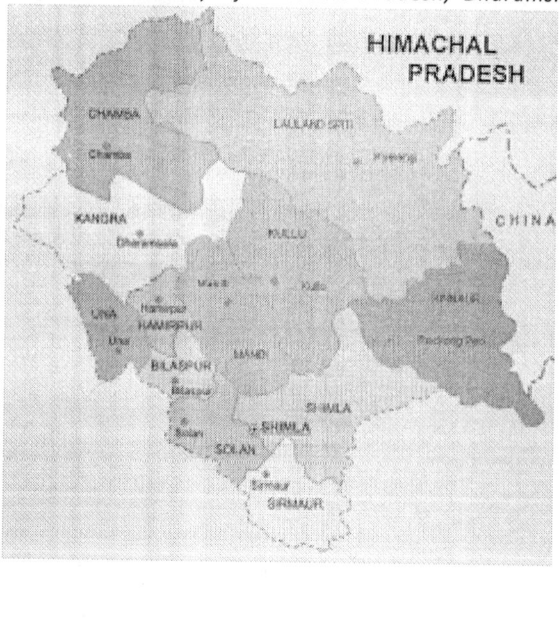

1. HIMACHAL PRADESH : A PROFILE

Himachal Pradesh is the northern state and it lies in the Himalayan region of India. It is spread over 21,495 sq mi (55,670 km^2) with 1500 to 22000 feet above the sea level and average rainfall of 63.45", and is bordered by Jammu and Kashmir on the north, Punjab on the west and south-west, Haryana and Uttarakhand on the south-east and by the Tibet Autonomous Region on the east.

Himachal Pradesh was formed as a union territory in April 15, 1948 by the merger of 30 former Punjabi princely states. The small state of Bilaspur was merged with it in 1954. In 1966 five more districts and parts of two others from Punjab were added to the territory. Himachal Pradesh became a state in 1971. It has 12 Districts, 77 Blocks, and 20118 Villages having population of 68.65 Lakhs as per2011 census, 3,481,873 males and 33,82,729 females, population growth rate of 12.94%, literacy rate 83.78% . It is governed by a chief minister and cabinet responsible to an elected unicameral legislature and by a governor appointed by the president of India.

2. LIBRARY MOVEMENT AND PUBLIC LIBRARIES

Public library system in Himachal Pradesh, had its starting point in the library development in 1950's when Central State Library Solan with the establishment of 6 district libraries. By 1985 the state had apart from the state central library, 12 district public libraries and 3 Tehsil / Community Centre public libraries, 2 Rural public Libraries, 5 Community center Libraries, 50 Paragna village libraries, 12 Paragna (Integrated village libraries, 9 block libraries under the education department of the state. Further there are 5 municipal committee/corporation libraries, 138 small panchayat libraries financed and administered by municipal committee/corporation and Directorate of Panchayat Raj.

Interestingly, during the seventh plan period much development took place. With re-organization of boundaries of the state in 1996, it received from Punjab 3 district libraries.

A state central library at Shimla was also established, among other libraries. This library is being developed as a multilingual library in a phased manner.

Administratively, the state public library system is under the control of director of education. The whole system is run by the state govt. as there is hardly any privately managed library system. Annual budget allocation is by the grants which the state government gives and the matching grant received from RRLF. There is no cess or any other source of income.

Realizing the importance of library legislation, a draft Library Bill was prepared. The unique feature of the Bill is that the academic libraries are also involved in the library system. The action taken by the Government of Himachal Pradesh on this Bill so far is not known.

3. ACADEMIC LIBRARIES IN HIMACHAL PRADESH

3.1. Information Resource Centre, Central University of Himachal Pradesh

The Central University of Himachal Pradesh is established under Central Universities Act 2009 (No.25 of 2009) enacted by the parliament. The University is funded and regulated by University Grant Commission (UGC). The university became functional on 20th January 2010. Pending the development of its own infrastructure and permanent campuses, the university is presently operating from its Temporary Campuses.

Information Resource Centre of Central University of Himachal Pradesh is functional in TAB, Shahpur Campus, which is being further developed with adequate number of books, journals, and reference material related to the disciplines in which programmes of studies are being offered. Library automation using SOUL V2.0 is in progress, DDC 22nd edition is used for classification of library documents.

3.2. Himachal Pradesh University Library

The Himachal Pradesh University Library is a multi-storied building having the features of a modern library like its architecture, space management, ventilation, and optimum use of day light. The Library maintains comprehensive collection of 1,82,738 books including bound volumes, and 308 periodicals. Central Library has different sections like Circulation Section, Text Books Section, General Reference Section and a Periodical publications Section in the subject field of Humanities, Social Sciences & border line disciplines and three Sectional Libraries in the subject fields of physical and Biological Sciences, Law and Education. Besides a separate Maps, Dissertations and Thesis, careers and Courses, Bibliographies, Micro documents and moral and Spiritual Studies are in the process of being set up.

3.3. Central Library, ARNI University

The Library has a collection of around ten thousand books, 45 Print Periodicals, 12 national newspapers, and the Library has a collection of over 300 CDs/ DVDs on different subjects. The duplex library is stylishly furnished and it can seat 200 students at a time in its spacious reading halls & Students can also access 35 Computers for internet access. The serene atmosphere in the library with rows of neatly stacked books plays a major role in attracting the students to the library for serious study and supplementing their class notes. The Library remains open on all the days of the years except some special holidays.

3.4. Central Library, Baddi University

Baddi University Library has a collection more than 35000 volumes and 150 print journals, and 14 national newspapers, and access to a full range of electronic resources including e-journals(Springer, ASCE, ASME, IEEE, BENTHAM, JGate, ProQuest, NPTEL video lectures and collection of CDs/DVDs. Library is automated using KOHA software, an open source Integrated Library Management system. Library is a member of DELNET network for providing inter-library loan service, membership of British Library, Chandigarh.

3.5. Central Library, Eternal University

The central library has a collection of 22000 volumes, 54 periodicals. 300 CDs/ DVDs on different subjects. The Library subscribes to online resources through J-Gate and has access to over 1435 scholarly Engineering & Technology Journals. The library is automated using PHI Alma Library Automation Software, 22nd edition of Dewey Decimal Classification Scheme is used for classifying the books.

3.6. Learning Resource Center, Jaypee University

The Learning Resource Center is a three floor library and is capable of accommodating 325 users at a time. LRC has wide collection of books and journals (international and national) in ICT related areas. It has subscription to journals larger number of e-journals through INDEST Consortia. E-journals subscribed are IEEE/IEE, Springer, ACM, ASCE, Emerald Management Xtra. LRC is an active member of Developing Library Network (DELNET) for resource sharing, and IndiaSTAT Databases for statistical information. LRC has the latest books, journals and CD-ROMs on bioinformatics, biotechnology, computer science, information and communication technology, electronics and communication engineering, management, humanities and social sciences

3.7. Central Library, Maharishi Markandeshwar University

Maharishi Markandeshwar University is having more than 14 Libraries including central library, and departmental libraries. The Library collection comprises of Books, Cd's, Videos, Thesis, Standards and back volumes in all Campus Libraries with the collection about 155388 with 30520 of titles. The Central Library subscribes 5078 journals. It has a seating capacity of more than 1500 users at a time. Central Library is member of National Networks, such as: INFLIBNET and DELNET etc. Libraries are automated using Library Automation Software SOUL. The Central Library have subscribed electronic resources by Lippincott Williams & Wilkins e-collection, EBSCO-Management, IEEE, ASME, ASCE, Bentham Science, EBSO Dentistry, and Gale Info Trac Medical.

4. SPECIAL LIBRARIES IN HIMACHAL PRADESH

4.1. Library and Information Centre, Institute of Himalayan Bio-Resources and Technology (IHBT-LIC)

The Institute is a prestigious national laboratory under the Council of Scientific & Industrial Research (CSIR). The IHBT Library and Information Centre (IHBT-LIC) of the IHBT was established in the year 1982-83. LIC is a special resource Centre by its nature as it is serving the scientific and technical community. Institute of Himalayan Bio-resource Technology (IHBT) is providing R&D services on economic bio-resources in western Himalayan region leading to value added Plants, Products Process for industrial, societal & environmental benefit.

IHBT-LIC is specialized in subject area of plant science. It procures the resources in plant sciences including biotechnology, biochemistry, floriculture, tissue culture, genomics, natural products, biodiversity, medicinal plants, and floriculture. The center has separate building required seating and reading space, and leased line connection for internet. LIC is automated using KOHA library automation software.

4.2. Directorate of Mushroom Research

Central Library, Directorate of Mushroom Research has a specialized collection in mushroom science and related sciences to support research and consultancy in the relevant areas. This is a sole referral library in Mushroom literature in India not only of DMR but also from different Institutes of ICAR, State Agricultural Universities, private organizations and individuals both in print and electronic format.

Library holds a good collection of 1694 books, 2500 back volumes of journals. Collection includes reference books, textbooks, abstracting and indexing periodicals, annual reports, reprints, conference proceedings, CD- ROM databases and on-line journals to the information needs of scientists, students, mushroom growers and trainees. The library subscribes national and international journals in subjects of Enzymology, Biochemistry, Plant Pathology, Mycology, Microbiology, Genetics, Horticulture, Food Sciences, and Agricultural Sciences. An addition collection of books of general interest and Hindi language are also available.

4.3. Library & Documentation Unit, Central Potato Research (CPRI)

The Library & Documentation Unit of Central Potato Research Institute (CPRI) was set up in 1956. It provides scientific and technical information resources and services support towards attainment of research mission of the Institute. CPRI Library is one of the best Indian Bio-science library on POTATO and most sought after for potato and agricultural research information. It is a well-stacked Library having WEBOPAC of its holdings (more than fifty thousand) of research documents in print, digital and online form for serving scientific community. Library is divided into sections as Resource development & technical processing, Periodicals and resource management, Reference section, documentation and users' services, Computer & Internet based services, and Xerography unit.

4.4. Central Library, Indian Institute of Technology, Mandi

Central Library currently holds more than 12400 books, provide access to more than 2000 e-journals, and 17 print journals in the field of Engineering, Science & Technology and related areas Library stands as a unique Knowledge Centre that offers access to essential and specialized information resources and services to meet the growing information needs. Library operations are automated using KOHA Library Management Software.

Library provides access to full text databases of ACS, ACM, AIP, APS, ASME, IEC, IEEE/IET, JASTOR, SIAM, Science Direct, Springer Link, Taylor & Francis, ProQuest.; Bibliographic databases Web of Science, MathSciNet, and SciFinder.; E-books from ASME, Cambridge University Press, Elsevier, IEEE, Pearson Taylor& Francis, World Scientific, Tata McGraw Hill, Wiley, and Ebrary e-book collection.

4.5. Central Library, National Institute of Technology Hamirpur

The Central Library was set up in 1986 in one room of Government Polytechnic Hamirpur. In 1988 it was shifted to its permanent campus in Visvesvarya Block. The library has the collection of 52000 Books, 10449 Book Bank General, 1734-Book Bank SC/ST, 1896-TDP Book Bank, 1963-ISI Codes, 2622-Bound Back volumes of Journals, 1872-Video Cassettes, 393-Reports, and 382-CDROM. Total 71033, as on March 31, 2012. Library has subscribed the 14 e-journals databases through INDEST consortium, Knimbus and JCCC, which provide the searching within library subscribed e-journals at one place. Library is automated and have its OPAC to search the catalogue. Central Library provides the Book Bank service for economically backward students, Reference Service, Inter Library Loan, and Reprographic Service.

4.6. Central Library, IGMC Tanda

The Central Library is located in the middle of the hostels. It is an air-conditioned library providing peaceful atmosphere for its readers, with provision of all the modern facilities. Library presently possesses more than 8400 reference & text books. Latest edition of reference & text books are available in the library. Library has more than 800 bound back volumes of Medical journals. Library has 300 hundred CD's of medical books.

4.7. College Libraries of Himachal Pradesh

At present there are 240 colleges in Himachal Pradesh affiliated to Himachal Pradesh University. In which 66 are Government colleges, 5-Government Sanskrit colleges, 59-Private Degree Colleges, 71-Private B. Ed. Colleges, 09-Private M.Ed. colleges, 03-Private B.P.Ed. Colleges.17-Private Sanskrit Colleges, 06-Private Law Colleges, 04-Govt. & Self Financing B.Ed. Colleges, at most institute have traditional libraries, and also they lack of Library professionals.

4.8. School Libraries of Himachal Pradesh

Presently there are 841-Govt High Schools (GHS), and 1548-Govt Senior Secondary Schools (GSSS) in Himachal Pradesh affiliated to HP Board, Dharmshala. Out of these very few schools have the libraries, which are traditional libraries.

5. LIS EDUCATION IN HIMACHAL PRADESH

LIS education in Himachal Pradesh is in nascent stage. Presently only one university is offering integrated MLIS course i.e. Central University of Himachal Pradesh. The Department of Library and Information Science, of Central University of Himachal Pradesh is functioning from the TAB located at Shahpur, Kangra. The department is offering Post Graduate and Research Degree Programmes in Library and Information Science.

5.1. PG Programme

The Department of Library and Information Science offers an integrated dual degree Programme in Library and Information Sciences in the School of Mathematics, Computer and Information Sciences. Students are admitted through a common entrance test called FEAT (Further Education Admission Test), with a total intake of 30 students. A student admitted to M. Lib. Sci. (Integrated dual degree Programme), if opts out after successfully completing two semesters with 40 PG credits, shall be awarded the degree of

B. Lib. Sci. Those who thus opt out shall be eligible to lateral entry if they return to the University within the next two years to complete remaining two semesters and get the desired degree of M. Lib. Sc.

5.2. RD Programme

Students in RD programmes (M. Phil. /Ph.D.) are admitted through a common entrance test called TREAT (The Research Entrance Aptitude Test). Completion of M. Phil. Programme requires 60 credits whereas Ph.D. is of 120 credits. Presently department has undertaken research in areas of Knowledge Management and Digital Libraries. The RD programme involves compulsory coursework of 6 months under the guidelines of UGC before starting the research.

6. LIBRARY ORGANIZATIONS AND ASSOCIATIONS IN HIMACHAL PRADESH

Presently there is no professional library organization or association in Himachal Pradesh.

7. CONCLUSION

Development of libraries, library schools and the library profession have a long way to go in Himachal Pradesh. Though there are libraries in the state associated with all academic and research institutes, the library movement never took off here. The initiative taken by Central University of Himachal Pradesh is the first step towards developing trained library professionals. There is also need to form professional associations and organizations in order to update professionals in advanced technologies and to address the issues faced by the library professionals in the state.

REFERENCES

1. "Library Scenario in India." *National Mission on Libraries*. Ministry of Culture, Govt. of India, n.d. <http://www.nmlindia.nic.in/pages/display/24>Web. 10 Nov. 2014.
2. Central university of Himachal Pradesh. *Annual Report 2013-14.*

Dharmshala(H.P.): Annual Central university of Himachal Pradesh,Dharmshala(HP), 2014. Print.

3. Malhan, I.V., and G.S. Thakur. *'District Libraries in Himachal Pradesh: A Survey'*. Annals of Library Science and Documentation Vol. 25 No. 1-4 Mar-Dec 1978 (1978): 122.Print.

4. "Himachal Pradesh Facts, information, pictures| Encyclopedia. com articles about Himachal Pradesh." Encyclopedia.com| Free Online Encyclopedia. N.p., n.d. *<http://www.encyclopedia.com/topic/Himachal_Pradesh.aspx> Web. 8 Nov.2014.*

5. "Department of higher education, shimla, himachal pradesh."department of higher education, shimla, himachal pradesh. N.p., n.d. <http://educationhp.org/colleges.html> Web. 10 Nov. 2014.

6. *"Department of higher education, shimla, himachal pradesh."department of higher education, shimla, himachal pradesh. N.*p., n.d.< http://educationhp.org/school.html >Web. 10 Nov. 2014.

7. "Himachal Pradesh Public and Academic Libraries Bill: A Proposed Draft." *Library Legislation in India: Problems and Prospects*. Ed. R. K. Rout. New Delhi: Reliance Publishing House, 1985. 282-293. Print.

8. *"IHBT-Library".Welcome to IHBT- Library (Knowledge Resource Centre). N.p.,n.d <http://library.ihbt.res.in/> Web. 10 Nov. 2014.*

9. "About Our Library."*nrcmushroom.org*. Directorate of Mushroom Research, n.d. <http://www.nrcmushroom.org/html/about_our_library.html >Web. 10 Nov. 2014.

10. *nrcmushroom.org*. Directorate of Mushroom Research, n.d.<http://www.nrcmushroom.org/>. Web. 10 Nov. 2014.

11. "Himachal Pradesh University, India - Library." *Himachal Pradesh University, India - Official Website Home Page*. N.p., n.d.< http://www.hpuniv.nic.in/lib.htm >Web. 10 Nov. 2014.

12. "IIT Mandi." *IIT Mandi*. N.p., n.d. <http://www.iitmandi.ac.in/academics/lib/>. Web. 10 Nov. 2014.

13. "About NITH." *National Institute of Technology Hamirpur (H.P.) - India*. N.p., n.d. <http://www.nith.ac.in/library/index.html> Web. 12 Nov. 2014.

14. *National Institute of Technology Hamirpur (H.P.) – India. N.p., n.d. <http://www.nith.ac.in>* Web. 10 Nov. 2014

15. "Dr. RPGMC Kangra at Tanda (H.P.)." *Dr. Rajendra Prasad*

Government Medical College Kangra at Tanda (H.P.). N.p., n.d. <http://www.rpgmc.ac.in/library.html>. Web. 10 Nov. 2014.

16. *Welcome to IHBT- Library (Knowledge Resource Centre).* N.p., n.d. <http://library.ihbt.res.in/>. Web. 10 Nov. 2014.
17. "Library."*Arni University*. Arni University, Kathgarh, (Indora), Distt Kangra, Himachal Pradesh, n.d. Web. 10 Nov.2014. <http:/ /www.arni.in/Library.html>.
18. "LRC - JUIT."*Home*. Jaypee University of Information Ttechnology, n.d. <http://www.juit.ac.in/lrc/home.php> Web. 10 Nov.2014.
19. "Library Facilities." *Welcome to Maharishi Markandeshwar University - MMU*. Maharishi Markandeshwar University - MMU, n.d. <http://mmumullana.org/library-facilities.html>. Web. 10 Nov. 2014.

11

Library Movement and Development in the State of Jammu & Kashmir

Shabir Ahmad Ganaie
Sr. Assistant Professor
Department of Library and Information Science
University of Kashmir.

1. JAMMU AND KASHMIR : A PROFILE

Jammu and Kashmir is a state in Northern India, It is

located mostly in the Himalayan mountains and shares a border with the states of Himachal Pradesh and Punjab to the south. Jammu and Kashmir has an international border with China in the north and east, and the Line of Control separates it from the Pakistani-controlled territories of Azad Kashmir and Gilgit Baltistan in the west and northwest respectively.

History bears testimony to the fact that the ancient Kashmir has been a great seat of learning and scholarship. The earliest records of rich culture and civilization can be drawn from Nilmatpurana, a 6th century manuscript. History bears testimony to the fact that valley of Kashmir has produced great luminaries like Kalhanna, Abindha Gupta, Sheikh Noor-Din-Noorani, Lal Ded, Habba Khatoon etc in the ancient periods. Their literary contributions are even today very famous among common Kashmiris. With the advent of Islam, Education and Scholarship made strides in the State. The Muslim rulers established schools throughout Kashmir. Zainul-Abideen, popularly known as Budshah, even established a University at his capital Nowshera and also patronized vocational training in Kashmiri handicrafts. The rich literarily heritage of Jammu and Kashmir is the proof for the fertile brains available in this part of the world who had contributed a lot in extending the horizons of knowledge. There are sufficient evidences that libraries in ancient times were associated with temples, patshalas, mosques and like these other religious institutions.

2. PUBLIC LIBRARY MOVEMENT IN JAMMU AND KASHMIR

The Jammu and Kashmir State was consolidated into a political entity in 1846 after the well known treaty of Amritsar between Maharaja Gulab Singh and the British Government. Maharaja Gulab Singh and his successors took keen interest in developing the state of Jammu and Kashmir. As one part of their strategy, they started providing free books to all the Panchayat ghars in the state. Accordingly, Maharaja Ranbir Sigh and Maharaja Pratap Singh established two major public libraries in 1879 and 1898 at Jammu and Srinagar respectively. These two libraries at Jammu and Srinagar are named after the two rulers i.e. Sri Ranbir Singh (SRS) library in Jammu and Sri Pratap Singh (SPS) library in Srinagar. With political awareness among the people of Jammu and Kashmir, people themselves created different book clubs in different parts of the valley.

After 1947, elected government took appropriate measures for upgrading the public library system in the state. One such initiative was the establishment of a separate directorate of libraries and Archives in 1961. This directorate started functioning with great prestige under its first director Prof. S .Bashiruddin , Ex Head , Department of Library and Information Science, University of Kashmir. With the passage of time this directorate witnessed some administrative changes in terms of its nomenclature and its organization. At present it is working as an independent constituent of the government and is named as "The Directorate of Public Libraries and Research". At present the directorate of public libraries and Research is headed by Director Libraries & Research. There are two Deputy Directors at the Divisional level who supervise the functioning of the libraries in their respective Divisions. However, the director of the directorate of public libraries and research is not from the profession of library and information science. The only director from library science background was Prof. Bashir-ud-Din. From small children to aged people irrespective of their caste, creed, color and like these distinguishing features , every section of the society is benefited from the libraries established by the directorate of public libraries and research. Libraries associated with the directorate can be categorized as under:

1. State Central Libraries in Jammu & Kashmir provinces
2. Oriental Research Library
3. City central Libraries
4. District Libraries in all the Districts headquarters. ;

5. Tehsil Libraries;
6. Block Libraries;

There are also reading rooms established by the directorate at different places in the state in order to provide people reading materials. Besides making books on various subjects available to people at public libraries, the reading community is also provided national and local newspapers and magazines to keep them abreast with the latest happenings around the globe. Special Children Corners have been added to Central and District Libraries for the benefit of the younger generation. In order to attract the public towards libraries, directorate of public libraries is organizing different programmes like book exhibitions, seminars, special lectures etc in different parts of the state. . In a recent development, directorate of public libraries and research has launched a website on the internet. Pertinent information about different facets of public libraries in J&K is available on this website. Directorate of public libraries has created a directory of the public libraries existing in the state of Jammu and Kashmir and this directory can be accessed by any one through the website of the directorate.

3. STATUS OF LIBRARY LEGISLATION IN J&K

The state of Jammu and Kashmir has not implemented library legislation till date. However, some efforts were made earlier for implementing library legislation in the state. Mention is to be made of the Randhawa Committee . This committee was formed by the state government in 1975 headed by Dr. M.S. Randhawa, the then Vice Chancellor of Punjab Agriculture University, as Chairman and Prof. Noor-ul- Hassan Khan, the then Head, Department of Library and Information Science, University of Kashmir as one of the members to go into the working of the Directorate of Libraries. The Committee submitted its report on 10th August, 1976. The main recommendations of the Committee focus on implementing library legislation in the state on the pattern of Tamil Nadu. This committee also recommended levying of a library cess of 5 paisa per rupee on property tax and provision of regular grants for promotion and maintenance of standard library services in the state. However recommendations of this committee were not implemented. On the request of governor of J &K state, D.R. Kalia also submitted a report for the improvement of libraries in 1987.

4. ACADEMIC LIBRARIES IN J & K

Education in the state of Jammu and Kashmir has a long history. Several chronicles, travelogues and other historical documents endorsed the view that Kashmir has been a renowned seat of learning in the horary past (Alvi, 2001). Rulers, Maharajas and Emperors who ruled the state contributed each to the educational sectors in one way or the other way. There are evidences that in the pre-independent era there were madrasa , maktabs and patshals in different parts of the state , however, the credit of sowing the seeds of modern education goes to Christian missionaries who took keen interest in spread of modern education in the last quarter of the nineteen century. They established two schools- one for boys and the other for girls in the valley. Later some other educational institutions were also established by them. Gradually the state rulers also began to establish schools on modern lines. During Maharaja Pratap Singh's reign, schools were reorganized. College education in the state was introduced in 1905 with the establishment of prince of Wales college (Now Gandhi Memmorial science college) in Jammu and the Hindu College (Now S.P College) Srinagar (Alvi, 2001). After 1947, state government took measures for strengthening the educational sector in the state. More and more schools were established and a number of colleges were setup in different parts of the state in order to provide opportunity to the citizens to acquire education. A major breakthrough in higher education in the state was the establishment of Jammu and Kashmir University in 1948 which was later split into two full-fledged universities viz.,

(a) University of Kashmir and

(b) University of Jammu

With the passage of time new schools, colleges and universities were established in all the three parts of the state. There are ninety five (95) government run colleges at present in Jammu and Kashmir State (Table 1). Besides these colleges, there is a good number of private colleges operating in different parts of the valley offering different courses like B.Ed, M.Ed, engeenering courses etc.

There are about nine universities at the moment in the state. The universities are:

1. University of Kashmir
2. University of Jammu
3. Central university, Kashmir
4. Central university , Jammu
5. Sheri Kashmir University of Agriculture , Science and Technology, Jammu
6. Sheri Kashmir University of Agriculture , Science and Technology, Srinagar
7. Islamic University of science and technology
8. Baba Gulam Shah Badshah University
9. Mata Vishnu Devi University

Although all academic institutions existing in the state are having libraries but the condition of school libraries is not good as is revealed by the studies conducted in this regard. Majority of these school libraries are lacking balanced collection, professional staff and are also lacking the infrastructure in term of buildings, furniture, and like these items (Sofi, 2011). Libraries attached to the higher educational institutions like colleges and universities are equipped with libraries having better conditions as compared to school libraries. While a few colleges have separate independent buildings, newly created colleges have also established libraries housed in big halls in the main college buildings. Similar is the case with university libraries. Newly established universities have opened libraries with humble beginning with few resources and are marching towards achieving strength in terms of collection, services, resources, staff and like these other items necessary for providing effective and efficient library services to their customers. Brief introduction about some reputed university libraries is given below.

4.1 Allama Iqbal Library, University of Kashmir

The history of Kashmir University Library dates back to 1949 with the inception of "University of Jammu and Kashmir". It was established to cater to the academic and research needs of the scholars, students and teachers of Jammu and Kashmir. In 1975, the Central Library of the University of Kashmir was shifted to its present multistoried building. In 1984, it was renamed as IQBAL LIBRARY and as ALLAMA IQBAL LIBRARY in July 2002. This library (the largest in the state) is presently the Centre of the University Library System, having forty-three Seminar Libraries attached with different Departments, Centres, and the Institutes of the University. The Allama Iqbal Library along with its network of libraries is the largest library system in the state and caters to the academic needs of the large number of University community consisting of faculty members, research scholars, PG and diploma students in various disciplines.

The Allama Iqbal Library has 16 Divisions in well decorated and centrally heated halls managed by well qualified professional staff. The library also provides useful and research oriented services to the reading community in calm, cozy and clean atmosphere. At present, it has a collection of above four lac books. Various local National and International news papers are available to the users on-line for keeping them update. The library is also subscribing one of the leading portal service of India known as J-Gate service where under the content pages, abstract and full text articles (wherever available), appearing in more than eight thousand five hundred reputed scholarly Journals in sciences and social sciences are made available to the users on-line. Xeroxing facility is provided to the readers on the table. The V-SAT and Radio link connectivity installed in the Library provides much needed internet facility to the faculty members, research scholars and PG students. The users are availing this facility through 48 computers installed in its newly established Internet Access Centre.

4.2. Dhanvantri Library, University of Jammu

Library was renamed as Dhanvantri Library, University of Jammu by the Syndicate and the University Council. The nomenclature was changed to give recognition the work of Dhanvantri (1902-1953), in to the freedom movement and the socialist cause in India in general and Jammu and Kashmir in particular besides his contribution to land reforms in the State of Jammu and Kashmir. The University of Jammu Library is one of the most modern RFID Technology enabled library in the region.

This Library is the hub of academic activities. Its four storey building has spacious reading halls and compact stack areas. The Library has a collection of nearly 3.5 lakh volumes. There are 250 current periodicals with back numbers. The Library possesses facilities like photocopiers, LCD projectors, INFLIBNET, CD-ROM databases and inter-connected computer terminals at selected sites. The specialized Jammu and Kashmir section is also there. In addition, the Library is linked to and supported by Departmental Libraries. The University Library is centrally located and constructed on modular plan. It has a total area of about 9,300 square feet which includes a stack area of about 36,000 square feet. The Library has three main reading halls and additional reading areas in the Textbook section, Periodical section, Jammu and Kashmir section, Reference section, Private books reading hall, besides a reading space for newspapers near the exhibition area.

5. SPECIAL LIBRARIES IN J & K

Besides public and academic libraries there are other categories of libraries existing in the state of Jammu and Kashmir attached with different departments. A few of these libraries are as under: The State Central Secretariat houses a library with well organized collection for the use of different administrative units of the government located in the secretariat. This library holds a good number of government related documents.

In the state there are a number of law libraries attached with High Court and another library is attached with the office of Advocate General. There are few other such libraries in lower courts.

These libraries are attached with different government departments like the department of Floriculture, Agriculture, Sericulture, Fisheries, Forest, etc., and are playing a very important role in performing the activities in these departments in a smooth and proper manner. Most of these libraries are managed by the professionals. A few of these libraries have started automation of different housekeeping library operations.

6. LIS EDUCATION IN J&K

The Department of Library and Information Science (University of Kashmir) established in 1970 is committed to the University's mission of teaching, learning, research and community services. By integrating technology with the curriculum, department impart knowledge and skills for Information professionals as well as being actively engaged in innovative projects, conduct seminars, workshops and development of Digital Libraries. Initially, department was conducting course like BLISc and MLISc of one year duration each. However, department is now offering two year integrated MLISc programme . Research Programmes at M.Phil and Ph.D level are also offered by the department .A Bi-annual research journal "Trends in Information Management" is being published regularly since 2005.

Extension services and Training programmes offered during four decades by the department has enabled in successful modernization of libraries particularly in the state. The Department established a *'Digital Repository'* popularly known as "KNOOR" harvests and uploads electronic thesis , dissertations and research contributions of three premier institutes (University of Kashmir, SKIMS and SKUAST) and has recently been inducted in UGC-DRS-I under SAP (2011-16) for the thrust area of Digital Library Research.

6.1. Department of Library and Information Science, University of Jammu

The Department of Library and Information Science (earlier Department of Library Science) was established in 1971 in the Old University Campus and a Certificate course in Library Science was started. In1983-84, B.Lib.Sc. Programme was introduced by the University. From the session 1985-86, the Department also started the M.Lib.Sc. and Ph.D programme in Library Science. In 1998, the Department was shifted to a separate newly constructed wing on the ground floor of the Central Library of University of Jammu.

The newly constructed building has a separate departmental library, lecture halls, faculty rooms and IT laboratory. The Department is recognized as Programme Study Centre of Indira Gandhi National Open University (IGNOU), New Delhi since 1995. In 2008, the nomenclature of the Department was changed from Post Graduate Department of Library Science to Post Graduate Department of Library and Information Science. Thrust areas of research in the Department are Human Resource Management, IT Application to Libraries, Agriculture Information/Knowledge System and Public Library System.

7. LIBRARY ASSOCIATIONS IN J & K

For promoting the cause of libraries and information centers, library associations are playing a very important role.

Thus there are library associations operating at local, regional and national level operating in India. In the state of Jammu and Kashmir there is one state level library organization viz., Jammu and Kashmir Library Association (JAKLA). However the activities of this organization are very few in nature.

8. CONCLUSION

The number of libraries in the state of Jammu and Kashmir belonging to different categories like Public, Academic and Special libraries have increased manifold after 1947. However, due to turmoil in the valley during last twenty years, libraries irrespective of their nature were adversely affected. A number of libraries got turned into ashes and some were being damaged. With the advent of normalcy, both state and central government has taken appropriate steps for strengthening different sectors of the society in order to gain progress and prosperity. Library automation initiatives were taken for automating different activities performed by the libraries. At the moment one can access different resources available in the university libraries like Iqbal library, University of Kashmir remotely through Ezyproxy. Similarly, Directorate of Public libraries and research is has launched its website in order to highlight its activities, operations, services etc to the wider population. Establishment of new colleges and universities with beautiful rich libraries is a sound evidence to the fact that state of Jammu and Kashmir, has met the challenges posed both by unrest in the state and the challenges posed by the revolution brought by information and communication technology. Training in library and information science profession also took a new turn with the starting of different programmes like BLIS,MLIS , M.Phil and Ph.D. These programmes are being successfully carried out by the two universities of the state.

REFERENCES

1. Ahdullah, S M. (1986). Atish-i-Chinar. Srinagar: Ali Mohammed. pp. 48-49

2. Alvi, W.A (2001). Development of libraries in Jammu and Kashmir. In In P.B. Mangia, D.R. Kalia & Neela Jagannathan (Eds). *Library and Information Services in India: states and union territories* (pp. 27-36). New Delhi: Shpra,

3. Bhat, P. (2006). Living Rituals of Nilmat Purana. *Koshur Samachar.* Retrieved on 20th August, 2007 from

4. Jammu & Kashmir.(1976). (Chairman: M.S. Randhwa) Report of the committee on the reorganisation of libraries, research and museums for the Government of J&K (Mimeographed) P19.

5. Jan, R. and Majeed, I. (2009), "Oriental research library of Kashmir: a treasure trove. *Trends in Information Management.* 5(1), pp. 81-95.

6. Sofi, Z.A.(2011). A Survey of Senior Secondary School Libraries in Jammu and Kashmir, India. Library Philosophy and Practice. Retrieved from

   http://www.webpages.uidaho.edu/~mbolin/zahoor.htm

7. Wali, M. L. and Koul, R K. (1969). Library Development in Kashmir. *Herald of Library Science.8* (4)

8. Wani, Z.A.(2006) Public library system in Jammu & Kashmir: An Assessment. *Trends in Information Management.* 2 (2). Retrieveded from ojs.uok.edu.in/ojs/index.php/crdr/article/download/110/99

9. http://www.koausa.org/KoshSam/NilmatPurana.html

12

Library Movement and Development in Jharkhand

Raheeb Thottathil
Librarian, M.U.A College,
Pulikkal, Malappuram, Kerala

1. JHARKAND: A PROFILE

Jharkhand is a state in eastern India. It was carved out of the southern part of Bihar on 15 November 2000. Jharkhand shares its border with the states of Bihar to the north, Uttar Pradesh and Chhattisgarh to the west, Odisha to the south, and West Bengal to the east. It has an area of 79,710 km^2 (30,778 sq mi).

The industrial city, Ranchi, is its capital and Dumka is sub capital, Jamshedpur is the largest and the biggest industrial city of the state, while Dhanbad and Bokaro Steel City is the second & fourth most populous city. The name "Jharkhand" means "The Land of Forests". Jharkhand is famous for its rich mineral resources like Uranium, Mica, Bauxite, Granite, Gold, Silver, Graphite, Magnetite, Dolomite, Fireclay, Quartz, Fieldspar, Coal (32% of India), Iron, Copper (25%of India) etc. Forests and woodlands occupy more than 29% of the state which is amongst the highest in India and the name "Jharkhand" means "The Land of Forests".

2. LIBRARY MOVEMENT AND PUBLIC LIBRARIES IN JHARKHAND

The history and development of libraries in Jharkhand state is the history of libraries in Bihar state, because Bihar is the mother of Jharkhand.

The state of Jharkhand, separated from Bihar, is having 18(eighteen) public libraries established by the state government. These public libraries may be classified into four groups as below:

1. Three State Public Libraries, one each at Ranchi, Chaibasa, Dhanbad and Dumka.
2. One Divisional Library at Hazaribagh;
3. Five District Libraries, one each at Gumla, Lohardaga, Daltonganj and Godda; and
4. Eight Sub-Divisional Libraries, one each at Garhwa, Lahetar, Pakur, Simdega, Chatra, Sahebganj, Saraikela, and Khunti.(Karn).

The library building are, generally, not functional to cater more readers at a time.Furniture is inadequate and water supply system is poor. In short the public library set up in the state is not satisfactory. The lack of public library act has badly affected the development of public libraries in the state.

3. ACADEMIC AND SPECIAL LIBRARIES IN JHARKHAND

Some of the important Academic and special libraries are given below.

3.1. Birla Institute of Technology, Racnhi Library

The BIT Central Library serves as a model of an evolving and dynamic facility in technical learning since 1955. The library, as an established knowledge hub that is conveniently accessible by those associated with the University, has a major contribution in making BIT an internationally top ranked Academic & Research driven institution.

The Library's collection comprises hybrid resources (Print & Electronic) in the filed of science and technology, engineering, pharmacy, management and hotel management. The Library also has a separate Internet section consisting of a number of networked terminals for providing recent and most comprehensive access to online journals, online databases and other online reference resources to the faculty, students and staff under Intranet and Internet environment. The Central library has automated all its routine activities through library software called "LIBSYS".

3.2. Indian School of Mines, Central Library

The Central Library is the heart of Indian School of Mines University, Dhanbad. It is a completely automated library provides services seven days a week, catering information to more than 2000 users belonging to 15 departments and centers. Boasting a rich collection of Earth Science and other branches of engineering and management, the library houses more than 80,000 books, 8000 Ph.D thesis and dissertations, 35,000 bound volumes of Journals and 1200 digital books in the form CD's and DVD's. The library provides access to more than 2000 full text scholarly research journals to its members.

3.3. Xavier Institute of Management Library – XLRI Library

The Library of XLRI came into existence in 1949 when the Institute was established in the Steel City of Jamshedpur, Jharkhand. It was named after late Sir, JehangirGhandy in February 1972. The aim of the Library is to cater to the information needs of our faculty, Research Scholars, Students and itsother Members . It is the heart of the institution and acts as a center for the collection of literature predominantly related to labour relations, management and its allied subjects and intends todevelops a comprehensive collection of information that is useful for teaching, research and learning purpose. User satisfaction is the current day approach to library service. To keep pace with the modern developments in the arena of library, Library has been automated and RFID system has been installed.

3.4. Medical College Library Jamshadhpur

A well-organized library in the college building with rich stock of reading materials can be described as the life line of any academic institution.(over 63000 books). It has been acknowledged as one of the best libraries by even MCI The I library has a very rich collection of more than 63 thousand volumes of Text/Reference books (of many titles in each subject. it regularly subscribes more than 75 National/International Medical Journals covering all the Clinical, Para-Clinical and Pre-Clinical subjects in addition to a long list of WHO periodicals/reports.

3.5. Central Institute of Mining and Fuel Research, CIMFR Library

The Library caters to the information needs of the institute, staff, research institutions & industries. It has more than 35,000 publications covering all disciplines of Science and Technology. The collection comprises printed books, reports, theses, standards, atlases and journal back volumes. The non-book collections include material like micro fiche/ film, and CDROM discs. Our library currently subscribes to more than 100 scholarly journals in sciences and engineering. Under the CSIR E-journal consortium, the library provides On-line access to a large number of full-text journals from various publishers. These databases are accessible on intranet to campus users only. The library provides various services for its members such as - Lending of books and journal back volumes, reservation of books, inter-library loan, document delivery, photocopying , CDROM and Internet services. All the library activities are computerized, including searching of books in the library through a web OPAC using Libsys.

4. LIS EDUCATION IN JHARKHAND

There is no any university department or college which offer any of the Library and Information science course in Jharkhand state.

5. LIS ASSOCIATIONS JHARKHAND

5.1. Jharkhand Information & Library Association (JILA)

Jharkhand Information & Library Association (JILA) was established in 2007 as a non-profit professional registered body with its head quarter at Ranchi. The association (JILA) believes that our libraries and information centres are a great investment in community learning and literacy. They open the doors of opportunity to minds hungry for knowledge and adventure. JILA is therefore committed to the delivery and promotion of high quality library and information services responsive to the needs of the users. It also enables its members/professionals to achieve and maintain the highest professional standards.

The Association has been conducting seminars and workshops time to time. Some of them are – National seminar on Emerging Trends in Libraries & Information Services (ETLIS), National Seminar on Library and Information in Jharkhand organused and National Seminar on "Relevance of Dr. Ranganathan in Present Scenario " in RIMS.

CONCLUSION

Being a separate state, still Jharkhand has to be gained many things for the library development in the state. Even though it has completed 14 years the public library act has not been passed yet. The LIS education in the state is also a dream in the state.

REFERENCE

1. Deshpande, K and B.B. Hungund "What Ails our Public Library System", ILA Bulletin, Vol. 24, No.1&2, 1998.
2. Karn, Sanjay Klumar, *et.al.* Status of State (Public) Libraries in Jharkhand; An Analytical Study. *ILA Bulletin*. XLII(2), Apr.-Jun.,2006. p.25.
3. Kumar, P S G(2011). Library Movement and Library Development in Bihar and Jharkhand. New Delhi, Kaveri Books.
4. Mohammed Taher (2001). Libraries in India's national developmental perspective: a saga of fifty years since independence: New Delhi: Concept publishing.
5. Sharma, S.K (1996). *Public library in India: trends and status.* P.K.Mahapatra (Ed.), Public libraries in developing countries (pp.121-127). New Delhi: Vikash Publishing House.
6. Venkatapaiah (2000) Indian Library Legislation : State Library bills and acts. Delhi, Daya Publishing House.
7. www.jharkhand.gov.in
8. www.en.wikipedia.org
9. *shodhganga.inflibnet.ac.in/bitstream/10603/1204/.../09_chapter*
10. http://www.nmlindia.nic.in

13

Library Movement and Development in Karnataka

Dr. Mehaboobullah. K
Technical Assistant
Kerala University Library
Palayam, Thiruvananthapuram-34, Kerala

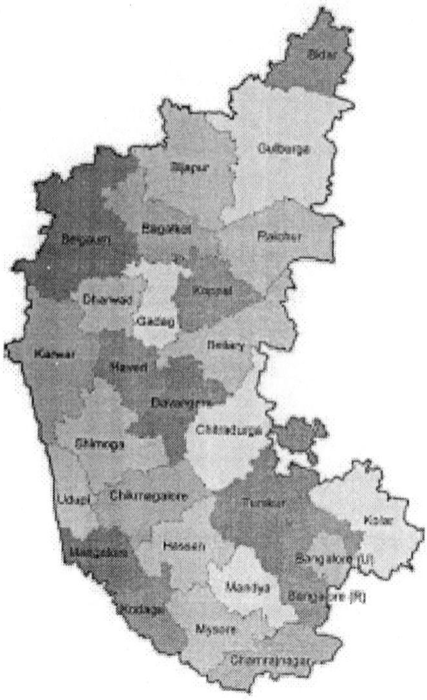

1. KARNATAKA : A PROFILE

Karnataka is a state in South West India. It was formed on 1 November 1956, with the passage of the States Reorganisation Act. Originally known as the State of Mysore, it was renamed Karnataka in 1973. Karnataka is bordered by the Arabian Sea and the Laccadive Sea to the west, Goa to the north west, Maharashtra to the north, Telangana to the North east, Andhra Pradesh to the east, Tamil Nadu to the south east, and Kerala to the south west. The state covers an area of 191,976 square kilometres (74,122 sq mi), or 5.83 per cent of the total geographical area of India. It is the Seventh largest Indian state by area. With 61,130,704 inhabitants at the 2011 census, Karnataka is the eighth largest state by population, comprising 30 districts. Kannada is the most widely spoken and official language of the state. With an antiquity that dates to the paleolithic, Karnataka has been home to some of the most powerful empires of ancient and medieval India. The philosophers and musical bards patronised by these empires launched socio-religious and literary movements which have endured to the present day.

Library movement is a saga of organized growth and development of libraries giving the details of establishment, maintenance and functioning of libraries in a geographical proximity. These aspects viz., establishment, maintenance and functioning make a library a growing organization. No country in the world can progress without providing free public library services to the citizens. It is imperative on the part of the democratic country like India to establish the service institutions like public libraries in order to strengthen the democratization of information and to promote the social, cultural, historical and scientific and technical knowledge in the public at large. Karnataka has a rich tradition in libraries even from its early periods and is one of those few states in the forefront in view of the public libraries system in the country as a whole.

2. PUBLIC LIBRARY MOVEMENT IN KARNATAKA

Public library is largely regarded as the People's University. It has tremendous developments in India from the early period to till date at various stages. Most of the Indian states now have free public library services to develop the people of India at different levels. In Karnataka, the Department of Public Libraries came into existence from 1st November 1966 consequent upon the implementation of Mysore Public Libraries Act, 1965. The act provided for the establishment of the libraries: A State Central Library at Bangalore; Five City Central Libraries; and A District Central Library for each of the 19 Revenue Districts in the State. Thus, the public library movement in Karnataka started with a big bang and a great concern to serve the public in promoting the life long education, and increasing awareness of culture, heritage, etc. of the land in particular and of the world in general. Karnataka public libraries act is indeed a milestone in the library history of the country about its vitality.

At present, Karnataka public library system is one of the most popular and feasible system, as compared to those in the other states in India.

3. KARNATAKA PUBLIC LIBRARIES ACT, 1965

The Karnataka Public libraries Act was passed in 1965. This was the third state public libraries act among Indian states, after Tamilnadu and Andhrapradesh.

The salient features of Karnataka Library public library act is given below.

1. Provision for a state library Authority with Minister-in-charge of Education as chairman

The State Library Authority shall advise the State Government on all matters connected with the administration of this Act, shall be the managing authority for the State Central Library, and shall exercise and perform such powers and duties conferred and entrusted to the said

Authority by this Act, and such other powers and duties as may be prescribed.

2. Provision for creating independent Department of Public Libraries with State Librarian as its head

For the purposes of this Act, a Department of Public Libraries shall be constituted with a Director of Public Libraries as its head and such other officers and servants as the Government may by order specify. Functions of the Department are:-

1. Subject to the control of the State Government, the Department of Public Libraries shall be responsible for the administration of this Act.
2. In particular and without prejudice to the generality of the foregoing power, the Department shall,-
   (a) Superintend and direct all matters relating to all public libraries;
   (b) Promote the establishment of public library service so as to achieve the purposes of this Act;
   (c) Supervise and direct all matters relating to libraries receiving aid from the State Government;
   (d) Maintain State Registers of Libraries and of Librarians;
   (e) Superintend, direct, and deal with the exercise of powers and the performance of duties by Local Library Authorities under this Act;
   (f) Ensure the proper utilisation of the Library Funds and library man-power of the State; (g) Perform such other functions as may be entrusted to the Department by or under the provisions of this Act.
3. Provision for the establishment of State Central Library at the apex of Public Library system in the state.

   The old public library, Bangalore, has been converted as State Central Library in according with Karnataka public Library act. The former State Central Library in

Cubon Park, Bangalore was converted as State Central Reference Library in 1986. Karnataka State Central Library shall be maintained as a reservoir of books and other materials for the proper functioning of the State Library system. In addition to a general library, the State Central Library shall consist of the following sections namely.-

- State Bureau of Copyright Collections;
- State Library for the Blind
- A State Bureau of inter-library loans;
- A State Bibliographical Bureau;
- A State Bureau of Technical Service;

4. Provision for centralised technical processing
5. Constitution for local library authority for cities and districts
6. Provision for setting up of advisory committee for branch and village library services
5. Provision for the levy of library cess

Salient features of library cess in Karnataka is given below:

(a) A library cess in the form of a surcharge on,- (i) tax on lands and buildings; (ii) tax on entry of goods into the local area for consumption, use or sale therein; (iii) tax on vehicles; (iv) tax on professions, trades, calling and employments; shall be levied in the area within the jurisdiction of every City Library Authority under the relevant laws relating to local authorities providing for the levy of such taxes, at the rate of three paise for every rupee of the taxes so levied;

(b) A library cess in the form of a surcharge on tax on lands and buildings shall be levied in the area within the jurisdiction of every District Library Authority, under the relevant laws relating to local authorities providing for the levy of such tax at the rate of three paise for every rupee of the tax so levied.

(c) A City Library Authority or District Library Authority may, with the previous sanction of the State Government , by notification, increase the rate of library cess levied on any item of tax, subject to the condition that the rate shall not exceed six paise for every rupee of the tax levied.

(d) Out of the cess collected by every local authority shall be entitled to retain ten per cent of the amount collected towards the cost of collection and the balance shall be paid to the City Library Authority or the District Library Authority, as the case may be.

At present, Karnataka public library system is one of the most popular and feasible system, as compared to those in the other states in India.

4. PUBLIC LIBRARIES IN THE STATE

4.1. Karnataka State Central Library

The Seshadri Iyer Memorial Hall houses the State Central Library. This library was set up 1915. If history is what you enjoy then this is exactly where you should be since this library offers collections from 0830-1900. The building is situated in the midst of a lovely garden that also has a statue of Sir K. Seshadri Iyer. Constructed entirely in red brick and mortar this monument in Bangalore is also a one stop destination for historians.

The Memorial Hall is a classic European style building supported by Tuscan columns is built in 1915, in honour of Sri K.Seshadri Iyer who was Dewan of Mysore State from 1883 to 1901. The Library is entered through two porticoes at each end of the front, has a lovely rose garden at its frontage decorates and enhances the building. The Memorial Hall is a classic European style building supported by Tuscan columns is built in 1915, in honour of Sri K.Seshadri Iyer who was Dewan of Mysore State from 1883 to 1901. The Library is entered through two porticoes at each end of the front, has a lovely rose garden at its frontage decorates and enhances the building.

5. ACADEMIC LIBRARIES IN THE STATE.

There are a number of university libraries, college libraries and school libraries in the state. The major University libraries are given below.

5.1. Karnataka University of Harvard Library

The Karnataka University Library was established in 1950 along with the university on a small hall of Government Training College for men. Now it has independent building located behind "Gandhi Bhavan" surrounded by beautiful natural greenery. The building has a carpet area of 4030 sq. mtrs. It accommodates about 4 lakhs books in its four stack rooms and around 300 students at a time to read in the reading halls of the library. Library also provides reading facility for physically challenged student. A reading room near the entrance hall of library specially available for physically challenged users.

5.2. Bangalore University Library

Came into existence in the year 1966 by inheriting document collection of about 58000 books and several bound volumes of periodicals held by Central College Library then affiliated to University of Mysore. The Library was shifted to Jnana Bharathi Campus in the year 1975. The present Library Building is built on star modular structure enabling each sections to function independently. The library has a good collection of information resources, which include- 23,726 gifted books, 3,45,068 purchased books, 16290 e-books, 58000 printed bound volumes of journals, 226 current journals and 8000+ e-journals.

5.3. Mysore University Library

University of Mysore is one of the oldest prestigious and foremost centre of higher education in the Country. The motto of the University, as engraved on its emblem "Nothing is Equal to Knowledge". Mysore University library is one of the oldest and largest University Library in the country and Mother of other University Libraries in Karnataka. The Library started functioning in the year 1918. It has a glorious record of 91 years of worthy service with a resource collection 6 Lakhs volumes in its systems today. The inception collection of the library was around 2311 books which was housed in Jubilee building and later moved to Maharaja's college campus and finally the library shifted to new building at Manasagangotri Campus in 1965. The library has rich collection of books, journals, reports, rare materials and archives, with multiple locations and a collection of more than 1.2 million items.

5.4. Mangalore University Library

The Mangalore University Library was established in 1980. It moved to an independent. At present the library has in its Stock 1,92,598 books, 23,085 back volumes apart from Reports, Theses etc., covering a wide variety of subjects. It has a rich collection of about 316 research and general interest journals on a wide range of subjects. It has access to over 4500 Journals in Full text in e-form from UGC-INFONET and Contents pages of 45000 Journals with abstract facility across the globe from inside web Database of British Library Document Supply centre (BLDSC), U.K.

5.5. Gulbarga University Library

Gulbarga University is one of the leading centers of academic excellence caters to the educational needs of the society located in the developing region of Hyderabad Karnataka established in 1980. Gulbarga University Library, a knowledge Center for accessibility developed on modern lines as a prominent Learning Resource Center on sprawling Campus, ideally situated and easily accessible by all the departments and students housing. The University Library, makes sincere efforts to provide user focused services having over 2,27,831 books, subscribes 654 scientific journals, Sixteen CD-ROM databases (Current + Archival), 5800 dissertation/theses and technical reports, microfilm, microfiche, conference papers and rare books. The library received Dr. Padhya Best University Library Award for 2007 instituted by Indian Library Association, New Delhi and recipient of "eINDIA Award 2011" for the Best ICT Enabled University at India's Largest ICT Event during December 2011.

6. PROMINENT SPECIAL LIBRARIES AND INFORMATION CENTRES IN KARNATAKA

Some of the nation's richest libraries are situated in Karnataka and which cater the information requirements of thousands of users from our country and even from abroad.

6.1. J R D Tata Memorial Library

Library of Indian Institute of Science (IISc.) Bangalore, was established in 1911 and it is one of the first three departments started in the Institute. It is regarded as one of the best scientific and technical libraries in India. Apart from the Main Library it has departmental libraries also. In 1995 the library was renamed as "JRD Tata Memorial Library".

The collection of the library which includes books, journals, reports, standards and patents is regarded one of the richest collections in the country, in the field of science and technology. This rich and valuable collection built over nine decades has some of the rare reference materials and several important journals. This vast reservoir of knowledge, on a conservative estimate, is worth over Rs. 400 crores. The annual budget of the library is over Rs. 12.00 crores of which subscription towards periodicals alone is about 11.00 crores. The library currently receives over 1500 periodical titles of which 1210 are subscribed while the remaining titles are received as gratis and on exchange basis. In addition, over 10,000 Journals are accessible online due to INDEST Subscription. The total holdings of the library exceeds 4,11,676.

The library offers services such as Reference Services, Referral Service, User Guidance Service, Cataloguing and

Classification Service, Circulation Service including Inter Library Loan and Document Delivery Service, Weekly display of recent additions of periodicals and books including E-mail distribution of these lists to users on mailing list, Bibliographic Service, Photocopy Service etc. Current awareness service is provided comprising regular display of Photocopy copies of articles published by the Institute faculty and students, in various periodicals that are being received in the library. Under the Corporate Membership Facility (CMF), reference alone facility has been extended to corporate organizations/ industries involved in R&D activities. Currently about 200 organizations/industries are availing this facility.

6.2. Central Food Technological Research Institute(CFTRI) Library, Mysore

Central Food Technological Research Institute(CFTRI), Mysore (a constituent laboratory of Council of Scientific and Industrial Research, New Delhi) came into existence during 1950 with the great vision of its founders, and a network of inspiring as well as dedicated scientists who had a fascination to pursue in-depth research and development in the areas of food science and technology. The Institute has geared up its R&D and impact of the globalisation has given very good dividends with a large number of externally funded projects from national and international agencies

The CFTRI library has been serving the R&D community enabling them to keep track of the technological advances worldwide. The Library has access to global information through several databases, e-Journals through CSIR Consortium of Libraries and high band width Internet/ E-mail connectivity. The services offered include - Current Awareness Service, Document Delivery Service and National and International Database Search Service.

The library has 27189 Books, 373 E-Books (CRC Food net base & others), 43193 Bound Volumes of Periodicals, 12187 Indian Standards/ Specifications and 83633 Patent

Specifications. The library collection has the database of - Food Science and Technology Abstracts (1969-1989, 1990-2006, 2007), Chemical Abstracts (CA) on CD (1997-Current), Chemical Abstracts (CA on web) 1997-current, CA Collective Index (CI on CD) 13th, 14th and 15th, CFTRI Research Papers Database (Citations) 1980+ etc.

6.3. Indian Institute of Management (IIM) Library, Bangalore

IIMB Library is housed in an independent building of 55,000 square feet spread across four floors with a reading area that can accommodate over 400 users. Library collection comprises predominantly literature pertaining to Business, management and allied areas. Its collection development policies and information services are mandated by Institute's teaching; research and training objectives. All house-keeping operations are automated using State - of - the- art - library management system.

The Library has a total collection of- Over 240000 documents (books, back volumes of journals, government publications, technical reports, conference proceedings, non-book materials etc.). access to 72 e-resources and 884 e-books from Elsevier Science, Emerald & Cambridge University press, Subscribes to 2330 print and e-journals, and 27 newspapers. In addition, access to more than 35,000 full text journal titles is available through the databases subscribed by the Library, non-book materials include 4180 CD's, 700 CD's received with books, 420 video cassettes, 577 VCD's and DVD's and 235 Audio cassettes.

6.4. The Karnataka State Archives

The Karnataka State Archives is a treasure of historically important documents. It contains source material relating to the History of Mysore, i.e., establishment of the British Rule in Mysore, French records relating to the correspondence between Hyder Ali - Tippu sultan and the French, and attempts made by the Indian National Congress to out the British from Princely State of Mysore, and Unification Movement, etc. In addition to the above Kannada -Marathi Modi records, and Gazettes from 1866 are available. Most of the records are in English, few are in French, Marathi Modi and in Kannada. Public/Scholars, officers and Officials of Government and Semi Government Organizations avail these records for reference

6.5. Central Power Research Institute (CPRI) Library

CPRI is the power house of the Indian electrical industry. Set up in 1960 by the Government of India, it functions as a centre for applied research in electrical power engineering assisting the electrical industry in product development and quality assurance. CPRI also serves as an independent authority for testing and certification of power equipment. CPRI's governing body includes eminent professionals from industries & utilities, prestigious academic and research institutions & the government. It employs over 300 highly qualified and experienced engineers & scientists besides other supporting staff.

The CPRI Library and information centre, Bangalore was established with the inception of the Institute in the year 1960. This is regarded as one of the best libraries in India in the field of electrical power engineering. The library and Information Centre aims to develop a comprehensive collection of documents that is useful for the research scholars and staff of CPRI in their R & D and testing activities of the Institute and disseminates information to all the clients.

6.6. Indian Statistical Institute Library, Bangalore

Indian Statistical Institute, Bangalore Centre is one among the three important centres of ISI. The ISI Bangalore centre library was established in the year 1976 to meet the academic and research interests of the students, scholar, teachers and others. It has one of the best collection of literature on Statistics, Mathematics, Quality Engineering/

Management and Library & Information Science in India. Presently it subscribes to around 300 international Journals on various subjects. The overall collection of books and reference materials, viz., reports, reprints, directories, encyclopedias, CDs etc., is approximately 23592. At present the library is automated which will enable a better management and easy access of information to users. Very soon the information on library collection will be made available to external users through Internet.

The ISI Bangalore Centre Library has been rendering the following services since its inception in 1978- Computerised Barcode Circulation Service, Documentation Service, Current Awareness Service, Reference Service, Bibliographic Service, Inter-Library loan service, Reprographic service, CD-ROM Services.

6.7. Indian Institute of Astrophysics Library

Indian Institute of Astrophysics is a premier institute devoted to research in astronomy, astrophysics and related physics. The main campus of the Institute is in Koramangala, Bangalore, whereas the Hosakote campus, near Bangalore houses the Centre for Research and Education in Science and Technology (CREST). The main observing facilities of the Institute are located at Gauribidanur, Hanle, Kavalur and Kodaikanal.

The library of Indian Institute of Astrophysics is more than two hundred years old. Since then, the library has been continuously acquiring astronomical literature in the form of books, journals and catalogues, and today it can boast of housing the largest collection in Astronomy in the country. The library has 19,000 volumes of books and approximately 245 active serial titles, the breadth of the collection is exceptional. Special strengths of the collection include materials on observational astronomy and theoretical physics and astrophysics.

6.8. Central Seri cultural Research & Training Institute (CSRTI) Library, Mysore.

Central Seri cultural Research & Training Institute (CSRTI), Mysore, the pioneer research institution in the field of tropical sericulture, was established at Chennapattna in 1961 under the administrative control of Central Silk Board, Ministry of Textiles, Government of India for the overall development of silk industry in the country. During the course of development the Institute was shifted to Mysore the princely city in the year 1963.The centre provides the following information oriented services to its clienteles.

6.9. Centre for Multi-disciplinary Development Research (CMDR) Library, Dharwad

Centre for Multi-disciplinary Development Research (CMDR) is an autonomous social science research institute recognized and financially supported by the Indian Council of Social Science Research (ICSSR), Ministry of Human Resource Development (MHRD), Government of India as well as Government of Karnataka. The Centre for Multi-disciplinary Development Research (CMDR) has been functioning since 1976 at Dharwad as an autonomous non profit research organisation. The Centre has aims to examine the relevance of the received theories in social sciences which have alien origins and form new theories and conceptual frames of greater relevance to Indian conditions.

CDMR library is one of the leading social science research libraries in north Karnataka with a large collection of books, journals, thesis, reports, CDs, working papers and occasional papers of other social science institutes. The collection of the Library is rich and diverse especially in the field of Health Economics, Tobacco, AIDS / HIV, Economics of Education, Environmental Economics, etc. It has a collection of 23585 documents including books, reports, working/occasional papers, etc.

6.10. The Institute for Social and Economic Change (ISEC) Library

The Institute for Social and Economic Change (ISEC) is an All India Institute for Interdisciplinary Research and Training in the Social Sciences, established in 1972 by the late Professor V K R V Rao. It is registered as a Society under the Karnataka Societies Registration Act, 1960, to create a blend of field-oriented empirical research and advances in social science theories leading to better public policy formulation.

The ISEC Library named after Dr. V K R V Rao is one of the major social science resources in India and it serves the students, research scholars, members of the faculty and non- teaching staff of the institute Reprographic and photocopying facilities, E-Journals access service, Internet access service, E-mail service and CD-ROM, Journals Databases access service are provided to the students, research scholars and faculty. The Library has a collection of over 1,21,000 documents including books, bound back-volumes of Journals, reports, etc. The Library has 250 theses, 300 current print journals (Foreign journals 180 and Indian journals 120) and E-Journals in various subjects have been subscribed for the calendar year 2009.

7. LIBRARY ASSOCIATIONS IN KARNATAKA

Karnataka state has some of the prominent library associations which actively involve all professional activities and programmes in the fields of library and information science. Some of the major organisations are discussed here.

7.1. Karnataka State Library Association (KALA)

Karnataka State Library Association (KALA), Bangalore, established in the year 1964 with the aims and objectives to advance knowledge of the principles and practice of Library and Information Science among the library professionals, to initiate, sponsor, undertake, encourage and promote scholarly study and research and consultancy work in the fields of library science and services etc. The Association shall constantly strive to relate its academic work to social needs of the community, and shall focus its research and consultancy work to socially relevant themes. Association organises various lectures, seminars, workshops and other instructional programmes to enhance the knowledge of the library professionals.

The aims and objectives of the Association are :

(a) To advance knowledge of the principles and practice of library and information science

(b) To initiate, sponsor, undertake, encourage and promote scholarly study and research and consultancy work in the fields of library science and services. The Association shall constantly strive to relate its academic work to research and consultancy work to socially relevant themes.

(c) To organise lectures, seminars, workshops and other instructional programmes to further the aforementioned objectives of the Association

(d) To publish books, monographs, occasional papers, journals, bulletins, etc., on topics of interest to professionals as well as lay public relating to library and information services.

(e) To take all lawful action, including legal action in order to protect professional and those areas of public interest affecting, or related to the profession

(f) To make appropriate recommendations to Government and other authorities and organizations for protection of the profession

(g) To subscribe to, become a member of, or otherwise co-operate with any other association having objectives altogether or in part similar the those of the

(h) To do all such other lawful things as are necessary and as advisable for the advancement of its interests .

7.2. Karnataka State College Librarians Association

Karnataka State College Librarians Association was established in 1979 with an objective to improve the service of the college libraries, improve the status and service conditions of library staff, co-operate actively to benefit mutually by the resources available to the libraries, strengthen the financial resources of the college libraries and raise the professional standard of library staff in college libraries. During the span of three decades, significant achievements have been made for the cause of librarianship in Karnataka State to develop the college libraries on par excellence. KSCLA organize six regional workshops on total quality improvement in libraries in different parts of Karnataka. The Registered office of the Association located in Bangalore City.

The aims and objectives of the Association are

(i) to promote fellow feeling, Spirit of National awareness, self help, self reliance and self respect among college librarians;

(ii) to work for improvement in the conditions of service, social status and prospects of the college librarians;

(iii) to protect and safeguard the rights of the college librarians by constitutional methods;

(iv) to provide opportunities for self education and self improvement among college librarians;

(v) to suggest ways and means to improve the conditions of the college libraries;

(vi) to arrange lecturer by eminent persons and conduct seminars by symposiums;

(vii) to publish a professional journal

7.3. Sarada Ranganathan Endowment for Library Science

The SRELS, founded by Dr. S.R. Ranganathan, the father of Indian library science in 1961, is registered as a charitable endowment with government of India. The main objectives of the endowments are:

- To work for improvement of Library and Information services in India
- To train the library and information science personnel in the current development in library and information science field.
- To promote the provision of efficient library and information service
- To apply the research result of library and information studies

For implementing these objectives, the endowment conducts several activities, including the publication of books and journal (SRELS Journal of Information Management), organising workshops, conducting seminars and lectures etc

8. LIBRARY EDUCATION IN KARNATAKA

A course for the training librarians was conducted at Bangalore in the year 1920 under the initiative by the then Dewan of Mysore Sir M. Viswaswaraya was the first official professional training programme for librarians in the state. At present, in Karnataka, the education and training facilities in libraries and information science are offered at various level including certificate course, diploma course, post graduate bachelors degree, masters degree, MPhil and PhD and other continuing educational programmes. The following universities in Karnataka offer masters, MPhil and doctoral level programmes in Library and information science.

1. Kartnataka University
2. Mysore University
3. Banglore University
4. Mangalore University
5. Kuvempu University

Another important institute in Library and information science is Documentation Research and Training Centre (DRTC) which came to established in 1962 with the unstinted efforts of Dr. S.R Ranganathan, known as father of Indian library and information science. Earlier the centre offers a two year training course in Library and information science. After successful completion of the examination, it awards associateship which was recognised by the government of India as equivalent to MLISc awarded by the other universities in the country. Since, 2008-2010, ADIS has been changed to Master of Science in Library and Information Science (MS-LIS) from the Indian Statistical Institute. The centre also serving as an academic and research centre for Research Fellows registered for a PhD in Information Science. DRTC is perhaps, India's only "proper" information school with a very strong research programme. Research at DRTC generally focuses on the application of information technology to library and information science. DRTC is widely considered to be the best research centre in India in the fields of library science and information science. It also has a very strong research programme and a PhD collaboration with the University of Trento, Italy.

9. LIBRARY CONSORTIUM THROUGH BALNET (BANGALORE LIBRARY NETWORK)

BALNET is a registered society for networking the libraries situated in Bangalore city. The main objectives of the BALNET are:

- To promote sharing of resources among the libraries by developing a network of libraries
- Collecting, storing and assembling information and by offering computerised services to the users to co-ordinate efforts
- Developing suitable collection development and reducing un necessary duplication wherever possible

Services of BALNET

1. Developing Union catalogue of books
2. Union list of current periodicals in BALNET libraries

3. Retro-conversion
4. Foreign Exchange service
5. Training and Education
6. Referral service
7. Email/internet service etc

10. CONCLUSION

Karanataka state is one of those few states in the forefront in view of the public libraries system in the country as a whole. The department of public libraries in Karnataka has rendered 45 years of salutary services by installing a network of libraries throughout the state. The department is, by way of offering library facilities striding fast from the capital towards the villages in the direction of evoking an intellectual revolution among the people by instilling in the common man an active interest for reading. Now the government shows an increased interest towards the opening of ICT based rural libraries in all gram punchayts of Karnataka with a profuse of dynamism. It is a milestone, a model and indeed a meritorious point in the very history of libraries in India. Some of the country's rich libraries function in the state of Karnataka. Several Universities conduct different types of education in the field of library and information science from certificate level course to PhD programme.

REFERENCES

1. Central Food Technological Research Institute(CFTRI) Library, Mysore. Retrieved August, 12, 2014 from http://www.cftri.com.
2. Centre for Multi-disciplinary Development Research (CMDR) Library. Retrieved November, 9, 2014 from http://www.cmdr.ac.in/menu_content.aspx?sub_id=33
3. Central Power Research Institute (CPRI) Library. Retrieved August, 13, 2014 from http://www.cpri.in/about-us/departments units/library-and-information-centre.html.
4. DRTC. Retrieved November, 5, 2014 from http://drtc.isibang.ac.in/DRTC/Courses.

5. Indian Institute of Astrophysics Library. Retrieved October, 3, 2014 from http://www.iiap.res.in/lib_collections
6. Indian Institute of Management Bangalore Library. Retrieved September, 24, 2014 from http://www.iimb.ernet.in/library
7. Indian Statistical Institute Library, Bangalore. Retrieved November, 14, 2014 from http://www.isibang.ac.in/~library/
8. Institute for Social and Economic Change (ISEC) Library. Retrieved November, 9, 2014 from http://www.isec.ac.in/library.html#library and documentation
9. Jagdish, M. (1979). *Histories of Libraries and Librarianship in Modern India since* 1850. Delhi: Atma Ram.
10. J R D Tata Memorial Library. Retrieved August, 13, 2014 from http://www.library.iisc.ernet.in/.
11. Karnataka Public Library Act. Retrieved November, 15, 2014 from http://karnatakapubliclibrary.gov.in/pdf/libraryact1965.pdf
12. Karnataka State Archives. Retrieved November, 3, 2014 from http://kannadasiri.kar.nic.in/archives/aboutus.htm
13. Karnataka State College Librarians Association. Retrieved October, 24, 2014 from http://www.karcollegelibrarians.net/htm/constitution.html
14. Karnataka State Library Association (KALA) Retrieved November, 3, 2014 from http://kalaonline.com/node/8
15. Kumar, PSG (2008). *Library Movement and Library development.* B.R Publishing Corporation. New Delhi
16. Kumbar, B. D.(2009). *Growth and development of public library system in India with special reference to Karnataka.* Retrieved November, 3, 2014 from file:///C:/Users/TOSHIBA/Downloads/article-4%20(4).pdf
17. Taher, Mohamed (2001). *Libraries in India's National Developmental perspective.* Concept Publishing Company, New Delhi.

14

Library Movement and Development in Kerala

Dr. Nasirudheen. T
Gr-1 Library Professional Asst.
University of Calicut, Kerala

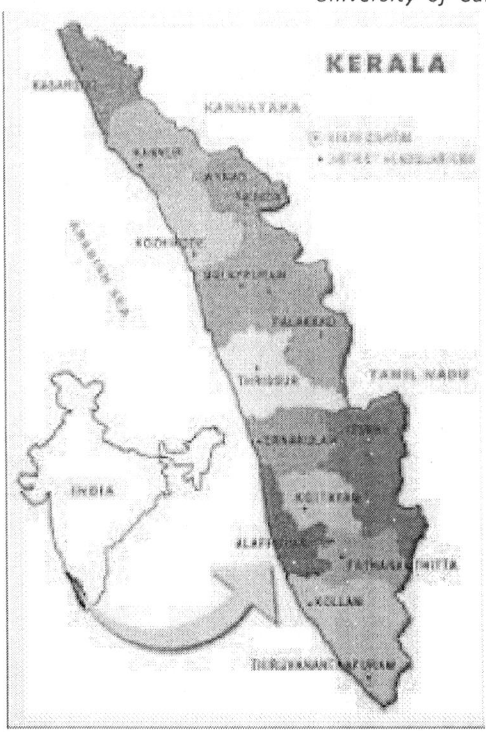

1. KERALA : A PROFILE

Kerala is a state located in southwestern India. Neighbouring states include Karnataka to the north and Tamil Nadu to the south and east; to the west is the Arabian Sea. Besides the state capital Thiruvananthapuram (Trivandrum), the other major cities in Kerala are Kochi (Cochin), Kozhikode (Calicut), Thrissur and Kollam. The principal spoken language is Malayalam.

The state is known for achievements such as near 100% literacy rate, among the highest in India. A survey conducted in 2005 by Transparency International ranked Kerala as the least corrupt state in the country. It is uniquely dependent on remittances from a large Malayali expatriate community based mainly in Persian Gulf countries.

Library movement is a broad term, which includes any endeavor to foster the development of libraries and library services in a country or a state. Library movement in Kerala includes the following areas.

1. Development of public libraries in Kerala
2. Kerala grandha sala sanghom & its contribution
3. Kerala state library legislation.
4. Kerala Library association its contribution
5. Library and Information science education.

2. DEVELOPMENT OF PUBLIC LIBRARIES IN KERALA

Kerala, the southern most state of India is well known for its high level literacy. The birth of public libraries in the state can be traced as early in 1829. Presently there are about 5000 public libraries in the state. Roughly speaking, there is one public library in each ten square kilo meter. A number of reasons can be traced for the existence of such a large number of rural public libraries in the state. The then three constituent parts of Kerala- Travancore, Cochin and Malabar have different streams of public library movements.

2.1. Development of public libraries in Travancore

The early growth of libraries in the erstwhile state of Travancore was, to a great extent, due to the spread of education in this area. The government started direct involvement in education as early as 1817 in Travancore by opening the state–owned schools in vernacular languages. The public library movement in Travancore started with the establishment of Trivandrum public library in 1829. This library was started by the British residents and a few English speaking natives in the city. By 1850s a number of libraries emerged in the state. The establishment of Kottayam public library in 1858 was one of the landmarks in the history of library movement in Travancore state.

During the initial years of 20th century, various types of libraries such as , grand in aid libraries, village libraries and school libraries were established. A number of associations and societies were also established and conducted meetings and seminars for promoting library movement during this period.

2.2. Development of public libraries in Cochin

The early growth of libraries in the state of Kochi was, to a great extent, due to the spread of education in this area. The public library movement in Kochi was started with the establishment of the Ernakulam public library in 1869. The Trichur public library, the other important public library in this state was established in 1873.These two libraries were the landmarks of public library movement in Kochi state.

In 1926, the government of Kochi started to establish village libraries as part of its educational extension activities. The government of Kochi organized separate department of public libraries and appointed a director as the head.

The organized attempts in library movement in Kochi include a number of conferences and meetings of library workers and publication of one quarterly journal. But, unfortunately these attempts could not survive more than one year.

2.3. Development of public libraries in Malabar

Unlike Travancore and Kochi, Malabar was one of the provinces of erstwhile Madras state. The national movement and peasant struggle in Malabar gave birth to the public library movement in this area. Consequently, rural public libraries and reading rooms started to appear in this area. They functioned as the centres of rural mass for reading dailies and periodicals. Thus the rural mass got motivated to fight against imperial and colonial force. The ever first library in the Malabar region was the kozhikode public library which was formed in 1890. Thalasseri Victoria memorial library, which was formed in 1901 by Christian missionaries. Presently this library is known as Azad memorial library. The Kannur public library was formed in 1927.

In 1937, the first Malabar vayanasala sammelanam was conducted at calicut under the chairmanship of K Kelappan. The meeting gave birth 'the Malabar vayanasala sanghom'. In 1952, the local library authority (LLA) was formed for the Malabar district as per the provision of the madras public libraries Act,1948 and kozhikode public library with its 7000 volumes was converted into the district central library under the authority.

3. KERALA GRANDHA SALA SANGHOM

The year 1945 is a mile stone in the history of library movement in Kerala. It was in that year when the representatives of 47 libraries in the erstwhile Travancore met together in the PKM memorial library Alapzha at the initiative of PM Panikar, who was the founder secretary of the library and formed 'All Travancore granda sala sanghom'. The sanghom was renamed as 'Tiru-kochi granda sala sanghom in 1949 with the integration of Travancore and Cochin states.

As on 1949, there were about 350 libraries affiliated to the sanghom. This included the libraries already existed in Travancore, the grant-in-aid libraries, Pachayat libraries and new libraries organized by the sanghom. By 1951, the rural school libraries and the village uplift libraries in Travancore area were also taken by the sanghom. In Kochi area, apart from starting the new libraries and affiliating the already existing libraries, the sanghom also succeeded in making all the government libraries as its members.

In 1956, the state of Kerala was formed, the sanghom extended its activities to Malabar also and renamed as 'Kerala grandha sala sanghom'. About 500 libraries, that had not been getting any grant from the local library authorities in Malabar area, immediately became the members of the sanghom.

The sanghom has been the main channel of the disbursing the government grants among the libraries in the state. It was the sanghom, which brought about a general awareness among people about the relevance of the public library service. The sanghom played a significant role in promoting the cultural, social, and educational life of Kerala through the effective medium of public libraries. Apart from the encouragements and maintenance of public libraries, the sanghom has been showing considerable interest in promoting adult education as well as pre-primary education in the state. Several adult education centers and nursery schools attached to rural libraries have been established at the initiative of Sanghom.

In 1977, the government took over the management of the sanghom and handed over to a control board with the minister of Education as the chairman. By this time there were about 4200 libraries affiliated to sanghom. The Kerala public libraries act, 1989 provides for the merger of sanghom in the state library council with all its assets and liabilities.

4. THE KERALA PUBLIC LIBRARIES ACT, 1989

There has been a long aborted history of attempts made at public library legislation in Kerala. Unfortunately, none of them were successful until 1989 when Kerala public libraries act was passed. The abortive attempts for library legislation for the state of Kerala can be traced since 1948, when S.R Ranganathan drafted a bill for Travancore state at the request of Sir CP Rama swami Ayer, the then divan of the state. Another draft bill again by Ranganathan for Kochi state was prepared at the request of the then educational minister panambally Govinda menon. After the formation of Kerala state, Ranganathan drafted a bill along with thirty year development plan at the request of the then chief minister E.M.S Nambudiripad. But unfortunately all these attempts were aborted.

After the four decades of endeavors, kerala has been provided a legal basis for public library service with the enactment of kerala public libraries act of 1989.

Salient features of the act

Library authority : There is a three tier administrative system for the organization and administration of the public libraries system in the Kerala State. It comprises: 1) Kerala State Library Council 2) District Library Council 3) Taluk Library Union. These duly elected bodies are more democratic in nature and statutory in character. The taluk library union is the base of the hierarchical structure of democratic setup. It is the union of two representatives of each affiliated libraries in taluk. The district library council is formed with 7 elected members of each taluk union and president and secretary of each union in the district. The council also includes the president or any office bearers of the affiliated library in the district head quarters. The state library council is the highest authority. It is formed with one representative of each taluk from district library council. It is the responsibility of state library council to advice government on matters concerned with the establishment and service of public libraries in the state. The state council will coordinate the working of district library council and taluk library union.

Library Finance : The act provides an annual grant not more than 1% of the amount allotted for education in the state budget. So a provision for the financial source of this kind from both cess and budget is the novel feature of this act. This amount will be credited to the state library fund to be maintained by state library council. Apart from this source, contributions and gifts by any other personal body or authority will also be deposited in the state library fund. The act has authorized State library council to levy cess in the form of surcharge in building and property tax at the rate of 5ps per every rupee. The cess will be collected by panchayat or municipal council as the case may be and transfer to the state library council.

5. PUBLIC LIBRARIES IN KERALA

There is a well established public library system in Kerala. The state central library known as the thiruvananthapuram Public library, which is directly run by Govt. of Kerala. There are district libraries (14) and municipal and panchayat libraries. The major public libraries in the state are – Thiruvananthapuram public library, Kottayam public library,Thrissur public library, Kerala sahitya academy library- Thrissur and Kozhikode public library.

5.1. Thiruvananthapuram public library (State Central Library)

The State Central Library is one of the oldest Libraries in India. It was established in the year 1829 A.D during the reign of His Highness Sree Swathi Thirunal Maharaja of Travancore. The work of starting and organising the Library was entrusted to Col. Edward Cadogan, the then British Resident who was the grand son of Sir Hans Sloan, the founder of the British Museum. He was the first president of the Trivandrum Public Library committee. The successors of His Highness Sree Swathi Thirunal and the British Resident Col. Cadogan took active interest in the advancement and progress of the Library. At that time only a privileged class who were called to attend the Durbar of His Highness the Maharaja was allowed admission to the Library. The Library was then known as "Trivandrum People's Library".

In the year 1898 AD the assets of Trivandrum People's Library were transferred to the administrative control of Government on condition that "a suitable building should be erected for housing the Library for the benefit of the Public and that Government should undertake its maintenance in a suitable manner under such regulations as the Government may deem fit from time to time". In 1898 this institution was opened to the public. His Highness Sree Moolam Thirunal took a special interest in the development of this library. He ordered the construction of a beautiful building for housing the library in 1900. AD the present building of architectural beauty in the Gothic style was put up in Trivandrum City in commemoration of the Diamond Jubilee of Her Majesty Queen Victoria. In the year 1938 A.D the administration of the Trivandrum Public Library was handed over to University of Travancore. In 1948 by a resolution of the State Legislature, the State Government was directed to take over the administration of the Library from the University. In the year 1958, the Trivandrum Public Library was declared as 'State Central Library'. Subsequently in the year 1988 the library was given the status of a minor department under the administrative control of Higher Education Department with the State Librarian as Head of the Department. In the year 1992 Government declared Malayalam as the official language of this department.

5.2. Kottayam public library

Kottayam Public Library was established in 1882 and has completed 130 years of valuable service to the public of Kottayam town and surrounding areas. During the long period of its existence, the Library has grown from a " Reading Room" in a small 2- room building to the present 3-units, with the main Library and Administrative office at Shastri Road, reading rooms in the heart of the town near the Gandhi Statue at Thirunakkara and the Children's Library & Jawahar Balbhavan west of Thirunakkara Temple.

Kottayam Public Library has the distinction of being

the first Library to be established and run by the public in Kerala and also of being the second largest public Library in Kerala, the largest being Trivandrum Public Library owned by the Government. There are more than one and a half lakh books in the Library for lending and for reference. Periodicals such as newspapers and magazines in Malayalam and English are also available in the reading rooms. Kottayam public library is one of the oldest public libraries in India. It is located at Kottayam city. It was established in 1882.

5.3. Thrissur public library

It was in 1873, A. Sankarayya, the famous Diwan of Cochin convened a meeting of a handful of 21 youths and discussed how to help the reading public of Thrissur.

Books and a few periodicals were what is today called the print media but, they were much beyond the reach of even the elite of the society. The meeting took a far reaching decision to start a reading room in the small town, housing in a public building where the St. Mary's college library stands today. History tells us that it turned out to be a honeycomb for the headers - who were of course very few in numbers. The visitors of the Reading Room were limited to a few journals and books of the old type and it is continued to serve the people for six and half decades in the same premises, growing gradually and feeling strongly the inconveniences of an old building.

It was in 1938 that the, the Maharaja of Cochin embarked on the regal Thrissur Town Hall. As soon as it was completed, he ordered to shift the Reading Room to the facades of the Town Hall, the most beautiful edifice even today, situated in the middle of a 4 -acre square compound, easily the land mark of the town. The King generously contributed money and materials, for the shifting - 1200 rupees and plenty of wood from the forest land.

6. ACADEMIC LIBRARIES

There is a good academic library system in Kerala.

There are well established University libraries, college libraries and school libraries in the state. The major university libraries are listed below.

6.1. University libraries in the state

Both general universities and special universities are there in Keala. The general universities are – Kerala University, University of Calicut, Mahathma Gandhi University, Kannur Univrsity, Malayalam University, Kochin University of Science and Technology, Sanskrit University and Central Univesity of Kerala. The special universities are, , Fisheries University, Kerala Agricultural University, Kerala veterinary University, , National University of Advanced legal studies, Kerala Health University and Kerala Kala Mandalam (deemed University). Along with these Universities there are Aligarh Muslim University off campus (Malappuram) and IFLU off campus (Malappuram). Eventhough there are this much Universities the well established university libraries are a few. The important among them are give below.

6.1.1. Kerala University Library

The Kerala University Library (KUL), established in 1942, is the oldest and biggest university library in Kerala and is situated adjacent to the University Senate Hall campus in the Thiruvananthapuram city. It stocks over 3,50,000 books (growing at 5000 titles annually) and subscribes to nearly 500 journals/ periodicals/ magazines. It also offers digital information services such as UGC Infonet. Among its special collections, the Kerala Studies is a unique one. The special collections also include Women's Studies, Government Publications, General Biographies, UN and World Bank Publications, bound volumes of newspapers and journals and rare books. It is the only library in Kerala which serves as a depository of UN and World Bank publications. The library is currently in the process of digitizing its rare collections.

The University in Travancore, founded in 1937 had at

its disposal the Trivandrum Public Library until a separate library was started in the present Arts College building. This was soon shifted to the eastern side of the University College (which was then under direct control of the University), in 1946. The present building was constructed with UGC assistance of 10 lakhs and started functioning in September 1962. Prof. K. A. Isaac, a student of Prof. S. R. Ranganathan, was appointed as the Full time librarian in 1959. He continued to lead the library until 1980 when Sri K.C. John succeeded him. Prof Ranganathan's influence on the Kerala University Library is still extant in the form of usage of colon system of cataloging devised by him.

The Kerala University Library is complemented with a number of specialised Department Libraries and also Campus Library at Karyavattom and Study Centre Libraries at Alappuzha, Kollam and Pandalam. The University Institutes of Technology (UITs), University Teacher Education Centres (UTECs), and University College of Engineering (UCE) also have specialized libraries.

6.1.2. Calicut University Library (CHMK Library)

The Calicut University Library, established in 1971 and later renamed after *C. H. Mohammed Koya*, (the former Minister for Education, Government of Kerala), is one of the important academic libraries in the state. The library is situated at the main campus at Thenhippalam on the side of the NH17 and is 23 Kilometers away from the historic Calicut City.

It plays an important role in the provision of information to the academic community in the Malabar region. It has a collection of about ninety five thousand books and subscribes to 218 Journals and 10 Newspapers. Library follows the Anglo American cataloguing Rules II (with slight modifications) for Cataloguing and Dewey Decimal Scheme of Classification for the classification of books. It has the distinction of being the first fully automated University Library in the state of Kerala. Presently library is working with KOHA open source software. CHMK Library has facilitated reading materials to visually challenged users through its ICT centre.

6.1.3. Mahathma Gandhi University Library

The Mahatma Gandhi University Library is situated in the main campus of the University at Athirampuzha, 14 kms away from Kottayam town, on the top of the Priyadarshini hills. The University library was started in 1989 under the supervision of Special Officer Prof. K A Isaac, former University Librarian and Prof. & Head, Dept of Library & Information Science, University of Kerala. Sri K Ravindran Asari took over charge of the University Library in 1991. Under his leadership, the library system built up the required Information and Communication Technology infrastructure to facilitate access to relevant internal and external sources of information to academic community of the University. The Library Introduced various services on modern lines.

6.1.4. Kochin University Library

Kochin University Library was established in 1977, the University Library is fully automated and one of the best scientific and technical libraries in the country. It has built up a balanced and rich collection on all branches of Science and Technology, as well as books of general interest in various subject fields. The KOHA FOSS package, a user-friendly library management software that supports all in-house activities of the library is installed here. The bibliographic records of books, journals and theses in the Library can be accessed globally through WebOPAC(http:// opac.cusat.ac.in.). The Library provides campus-wide IP-enabled access to online journals under the UGC- INFONET DIGITAL Library Consortia and INDEST Consortia, under which electronic full text access is provided to scholarly literature of all major areas of learning like IEEE digital library, Science Direct, ACS, RSC, Nature, IOP, Springer etc.

6.1.5. Kerala Agricultural University Library

The Kerala Agricultural University is entrusted with the triple functions of producing trained personnel, carrying out research and extension activities in agricultural sector. Information is a valuable resource and important constituent that determines the quality of education, research and extension activities. Kerala Agricultural University Library and Information System (KAULIS) is envisaged for the collection, organisation and dissemination of information on agriculture which includes Crop and Animal Production, Fisheries, Forestry, Nutrition and Rural Development. The KAULIS consists of the Central Library, College Libraries in 10 constituent colleges and Research Station Libraries.

The unit for Library and Information Services was established in 1995 at the Kerala Agricultural University as per the provisions of the Kerala Agricultural University Act of 1971. Kerala Agricultural University Library and Information System (KAULIS) was formally inaugurated by the then Honourable Minister for Agriculture Sri. Krishnan Kaniyamparambil on 24th of December, 1998.

Along with university libraries there are some sound college libraries. Some of them are Faoork College Library (kozhikode), Maharajas College Library – Ernakulam and Victoria college library Palakad.

7. SPECIAL LIBRARIES IN THE STATE.

Some of the major special libraries in the state are given here.

7.1. Kerala Forest Research Institute (KFRI)

Kerala Forest Research Institute (KFRI) is a multi-disciplinary team of experts conducting research on tropical forests and forestry. This Institute has contributed significantly to research in tropical forestry and biodiversity conservation over the past three decades of its existence. Founded in 1975, Institute is envisioned as a Centre of Excellence in Tropical Forestry to provide scientific support for decision making on matters related to forestry, with particular emphasis on conservation, sustainable utilization and scientific management of natural resources. KFRI became a part of the Kerala State Council for Science, Technology and Environment (KSCSTE) along with five other R&D Centres of the State, when the KSCSTE was constituted in 2002.

KFRI Library-functions as a full-fledged resource centre on tropical forestry and as a special repository of literature on teak, bamboo and rattan. It also functions as national level Bamboo Information Centre.

KFRI library with a core collection of 16,000 books and 9,000 back volumes of journals on forestry caters to the information requirements of scientists and research scholars of the Institute and elsewhere. The library subscription to 90 international and national journals and electronic bibliographic databases. The collection includes many valuable reference books, doctoral theses and back volumes of periodicals and databases in CD-ROMs.

7.2. Vikram Sara Bhai Space Centre (VSSC)

VSSC at Thiruvananthapuram is the major center of ISRO, where the design and development activities of satellite launch vehicles and sounding rockets are carried out and made ready for launch operations. The centre pursues research and development activities for associated technologies such as launch vehicle design, propellants, solid propulsion technology, aerodynamics, aero structural and aero thermal aspects, avionics, polymers and composites, guidance, control, and simulation, computer and information, mechanical engineering, aerospace mechanisms, vehicle integration and testing, space ordnance, chemicals and materials. The centre has a sound library with the collections of its specialization.

7.3. Centre for Water Resources Development and Management (CWRDM)

Centre for Water Resources Development and Management (CWRDM) was established as an autonomous research organisation by the Government of Kerala, under its Science and Technology Policy in February 1978. The Centre originally established at Thiruvananthapuram was shifted to the present 35 ha-campus at Calicut in 1979.

The Division has a good collection of publications on water resources and allied areas. It includes around 10500 books, 60 current periodicals, 4200 back volumes and 3400 reprints and CWRDM publications and reports. It provides lending, reference, bibliographic news clipping and photocopying services. Reference and photocopying services are extended to outsiders including trainees, researchers and students from other institutions

7.4. Indian Institute of Management- Kozhikode (IIMK)

IIMK library has become one of the finest and best in class management information centers in the country, complemented with state-of-art technology supports to the users. It is a cornerstone that supports learning, teaching, and research activities. With a variety of knowledge and information resources, facilities, and latest information and communication technologies available in this library. In addition to print materials, the library offers thousands of electronics books, journals, magazines, videos, cases, newspapers and many more. You can access these resources anytime from anywhere in the campus.

7.5. Media Libraries

Along with these special libraries, there are more than 20 media libraries (channel libraries), News paper libraries and AIR libraries. The news paper libraries are – Malayala Manoram News paper library, Mathrubhumi News paper library, Madhyamam News paper library, Kerala Koumudi News paper library, Thejas News paper library, Deshabhimani

News paper library, Chandrika News paper library, Siraj News paper library and Deepika News paper library etc. The prominent channel libraries are – Asianet channel library, Surya channel library, Manorama channel library, Idnia vision channel library, Kairali channel library, Mediaone channel library, Amrita channel library, Jeevan channel library, Matrhubhumi, Jaihind channel library etc.

8. LIBRARY ASSOCIATIONS AND ORGANISATIONS IN KERALA.

Kerala library professionals organization(KELPRO) and Kerala Library association (KLA) are the two important library associations in the state. Kerala academic librarians' association, Kerala assembly librarians association are also functioning in kerala.

8.1. Kerala Library association (KLA)

Library associations have their own role in the library movement of our state. The objective of a library association is to strengthen and expand the library movement in a country or a state. These objectives are fulfilled by conducting local, zonal, national, international workshops, seminars, meetings and discussions. The kerala library association is a professional body Of librarians in kerala. It was registered under societies act in 1971. The office of the association is located at Trivndrum.

Since its inception, KLA has been able to represent the interests of the qualified librarians working in different libraries, always with due foresight and objectivity, keeping in view the proper development of the libraries and library services in the state. For creating necessary public opinion in matters of policy related to library and library service in the state, the Association has so far held several seminars and conferences to help the Government discuss and formulate policies relating to different aspects of library service. The achievements of KLA spanning over a period of three decades of steady progress is well reflected in the developmental history of library movement in Kerala. The Association has played a pivotal role in the scientific management and quality improvement of Library and Information System (LIS) in the State.

The role played by KLA in various Reforms Committees and Commissions especially in the academic sector needs special mention, the most important among them being the VP Joy Committee Report on College libraries and School Libraries. The discussion held with the Commission on School Education in Kerala headed by Dr.U.R. Ananthamoorthy and proposals made by KLA were well understood and appreciated. A major programme launched by the Association in the recent past is the undertaking of Project works to re-organize and modernize libraries in various parts of the state.

Objectives of KLA

a. To unite all libraries in Kerala by holding conferences and meetings for the discussion of questions affecting the library profession and matters affecting libraries.

b. To promote library movement and improvement in library services.

c. To promote appropriate library legislation in the state.

d. To promote the better administration of libraries.

e. To promote library science education and the improvement in the training of librarians in Kerala.

f. To promote and encourage bibliographical study and research.

g. To promote the establishment of libraries, documentation and information centres in Kerala.

h. To publish information of service or interest to the members of the Association or for the promotion of the objects of the Association.

i. To promote whatever may tend to the improvement of the position and qualifications of the librarians.

j. To affiliate to the Association, other associations in Kerala with similar objects.

k. To co-operate with other State, National, International and other organizations with similar objects.

The Major activities of KLA are,

1. **Professional Development Programmes, such** as-
   (a) Developing Policies and Guidelines in consultation with Regional, National and International Professional Bodies in LIS.
   (b) Prof. K.A. Isaac Commemoration Lecture in every year.
   (c) KLA Gold Medals for BLISc & MLISc Toppers from all the three Universities of Kerala.
   (d) Prof C.A. Augustine Holy Cross Endowments.
   (e) Seminars and Workshops at International, National and Regional levels.
   (f) Workshops on LIS software/ technologies/tools.
   (g) UGC-NET Coaching Programmes.
   (h) Skill Development Programmes for Researchers, Faculty and Students.
   (i) National Library Week, Librarians' Day and Reading Day celebrations.
   (j) Career Orientation Programmes for LIS students.
   (k) Lectures, Talks and Sensitization Programmes on recent developments in LIS.
2. Representing and Lobbying for favorable Policy decisions from the Govt. for the overall Professional well being of the Members working in different Sectors.
3. Collaborative activities with other National and International Professional Associations, Govt Organizations, NGOs and Sponsoring Agencies.
4. Consultancy, Planning and Implementation Library Modernization Projects.

5. Publication of a Quarterly Newsletter, Books, Seminar Proceedings , Reports and Brochures.

8.2. Kerala library professionals organization (KELPRO)

Kelpro has also their own contribution in the library movement of the state. It is a pioneer organization of its kind in kerala and which was formed in 1992. Kelpro has succeeded in giving proper guidance in observing the new dimensions in the field of library and information service in the state.

Objectives or KELPRO

1. To promote communication, co-operation & unity among librarians.
2. To conduct, seminars, lectures, short term courses & workshops for members.
3. To bring out publications
4. To offer consultancy services to libraries & information centres.
5. To undertake research projects.
6. To represent the profession in discussions & negotiations with the government and other policy making bodies.

8.3. Kerala Academic Librarians' Association

Kerala Academic Librarians' Association is a professional association of librarians working in colleges and universities of Kerala. The associations was started in 1979 at kochin.The journal " Academic Librarian" was the publication of the association.

8.4. Kerala Assembly Library staff association (KALSA)

It is an association of the librarians of the Kerala legislature secretariate, Thiruvananthapuram.

9. LIBRARY AND INFORMATION SCIENCE EDUCATION IN THE STATE

There is a well established library science education system in the country. There are CLISc, BLISc, MLISc, Mphil and PhD courses in the state. The university which are providing LIS course are – Kerala university-Thiruvananthapura, (MLISc – 2 year integrated , Mpil and PhD), Calicut University- Thenjipalam, Malappuram (MLISc-2 year integrated, Mphil and PhD), Mahathma Gandhi University- Kottayam (BLISc- 1 year , MLISc- 1 year and PhD) and Kannur University- Kannur (MLISc- 2 year integrated and PhD).Department of Library sicnece Kerala University is the oldest department in the state. The Dept. of Library and Information Science started in 1961. The dept. provides learning opportunities and undertakes research projects in concept and techniques related to diverse areas in LIS. It also undertakes a number of continuing education programmes such as Refresher courses, workshops etc. The Department of Library and Information Science at the Calicut University was established as a full-fledged department of study and research in 1985.

Along with these university departments-Ettumanoorappan College, Ettumanoor Kottayam Government College (GC), Nedumangad Trivandrum Mahathma Gandhi Education Foundation (MGEF), Alappuzha Mar Thoma College for Women, Perumbavoor MES College for Advanced Studies (MESCAS), Edathala Kuriakose Elias College (K E College), Kottayam Regional Institute of Engineering (RIE), Trivandrum St. Berchmans College (SB College), Changanassery Divine College of Management Studies (DCMS), Cochin Rajagiri College of Social Science and Farook College Calicut provides BLISc or MLISc courses. In addition to these, State central library, Kerala Grantha sala sangom and IHRD also give certificate course in library and information science

10. CONCLUSION

Kerala, the highest literate state of India has presently a strong public library system. The state achieved this envious position by different streams such as- government interfering, the public library act of 1989 and the role of library associations like kerala library association and kerala grandha sala sanghom. Even though the density of public libraries in the state is very high, the condition of majority of these libraries is not satisfactory. The majority of these libraries function with old building, old furniture, old book collection and old technology. All these are to be developed efficiently and effectively for the better public library service in the state.

REFERENCE

1. John, Pa, and Nair, VKG. public library movement in Kerala. souvenir- 25th all India library conference,1979.
2. Kumar, PSG. Library movement and library development in Kerala & Lakshadweep, BR Publishers, New Delhi.
3. Mohammed Taher (2001). Libraries in India's national developmental perspective: a saga of fifty years since independence: New Delhi: Concept publishing.
4. Venkatapia, Indian library legislation: state library bills and acts, Daya publishing house, New Delhi.
5. www.kfri.res.in
6. www.keralauniversity.ac.in/
7. www.universityofcalicut.info
8. www.kannuruniversity.ac.in
9. www.ssus.ac.in
10. www.kfri.org
11. www.cpcri.gov.in
12. *https://www.iimk.ac.in*

15

Library Movement and Development in Madhya Pradesh

Mahjabeen Aydeed
Research Scholar,
Department of Library and Information Science
University of Calicut –Kerala

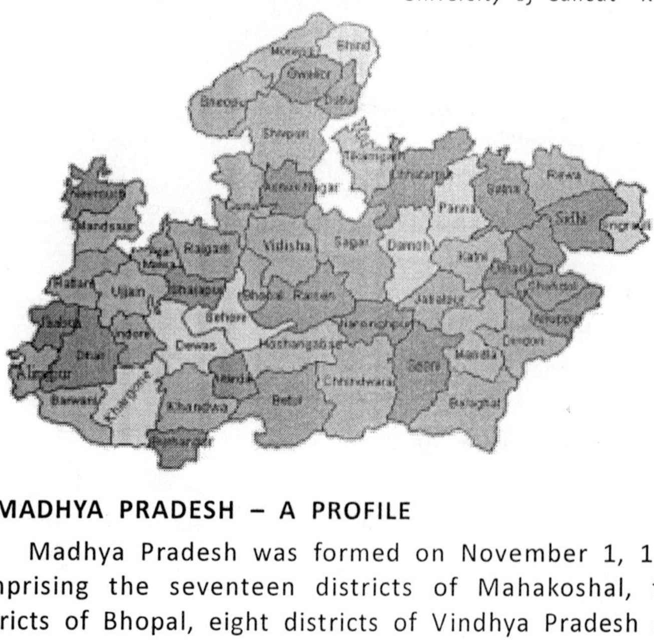

1. MADHYA PRADESH – A PROFILE

Madhya Pradesh was formed on November 1, 1956 comprising the seventeen districts of Mahakoshal, two districts of Bhopal, eight districts of Vindhya Pradesh and sixteen districts of Madhya Bharat. At the time of its formation, the state had 43 districts. Subsequently, two large districts were bifurcated. Sixteen more districts were formed in the year 1998. The Chhattisgarh region, comprising of 16 districts, was separated to form a new state as per the provisions of Madhya Pradesh Reorganization Act, 2000 and recognized present State of Madhya Pradesh came into existence on 1st November 2000. Again three new districts i.e. Burhanpur, Ashoknagar and Anooppur were formed in the year 2003. The total geographical area of the state is now 308 thousand sq. kms. Madhya Pradesh, a state in the central India is nicknamed as the "heart of India" due to its geographical location. It is the second largest state in the India by area and borders the states of Uttar Pradesh to the northeast, Chhattisgarh to the southeast, Maharashtra to the south, Gujarat to the west, and Rajasthan to the northwest.

2. DEVELOPMENT OF PUBLIC LIBRARIES IN MADHYA PRADESH

The development of the public libraries in Madhya Pradesh can be explained in two parts, as follows:

1. Public libraries before independence; and
2. Public libraries after independence.

2.1. Public libraries before independence

A major part of the Madhya Pradesh was under princely rule before independence of India. The State comprised of several small provinces, during pre-independence period. No appreciable library development had taken place in princely states except for the setting up of a few libraries by the public in the capital towns and few big towns of the state. There are big collections of books in the royal palaces of Maharajas. The Majaharaja of Indore, Gwalior, Rewa, Dewas, Dhar, Panna, Nagod and Datiya had big collection of books. The personal collection of MaulviLiyaqat Hussain in Bhopal and Sukhasampat RaiBhandari in Bhanpura were also very valuable. Dr.Hari

Singh Gaur of Sagar had very good collection of books. He donated a lot of books from his own collection to the Sagar University. The books were made available to the members of royal families and their friends.

The notable libraries in the four component provinces were as follows

1. Vindhya Pradesh area : Venkat Vindhya Sadan, Rewa
2. Madhya Bharat area : Indore Public Library, Indore; Hindi SahityaSamiti, Indore; Yuvraj Library, Ujjain; Public Library, Dhar; Madhav Library, Central Public Library and Hindi SahityaSamiti Library (Lashkar) .
3. Mahakoshal Area : Central library, Jabalpur; Public library, Nagpur.
4. Bhopal area: - Hamidiya State library, Bhopal; Indore Public Library, Indore was established in 1854; Madhav Library, Lashkar in 1899; and Hamidiya State Library of Bhopal in 1909 (now known as Maulana Azad Central library). These are the oldest libraries. Library of Hindi Shanty Semite which was inaugurated by Mahatma Gandhi had good collection of Hindi literature.

2.2. Public libraries after independence

The present Madhya Pradesh is a state formed out of four units namely - Bhopal, Vindhya Pradesh, Mahakoshal, and Madhya Bharat. Library movement became faster after independence of India. Different types of libraries were established during the first five year plan. Four central libraries were established under a government of India scheme for establishment and expansion of a network of libraries in the country during the first five year plan period. Each of these regions had its own established at the different district headquarters of Mahakoshal, Vindhya Pradesh, Bhopal, and Madhya Bharat regions. This scheme provided for the establishment of a state central library at the seat of the capital, and district libraries at district headquarters of each district. To provide library service in the interior villages, book/deposit centers were to be opened at convenient places and these centers were to be served with books by district libraries through mobile vans, fourteen district libraries in Mahakoshal region were provided with jeeps for this purpose. The district libraries were to serve as nucleus of the entire scheme. The fifth Central library at Indore was established in 1964. The Barmendra library at Nagod (Satna) was taken over by the government in 1973. Although there are five regional libraries at Bhopal, Gwalior, Indore, Jabalpur, and Rewa, there is still no central library in the state. A committee was constituted by the State in 1958 under the Chairmanship of Shri M.G. Kamikar, I.A.S.,the then commissioner of Bhopal Division to present a report on the development of Maulana Azad Central Library, Bhopal as State Central Library for the state. The committee submitted its report to the government in 1958. The report was later on published by the government but no further action appears to have been taken on it. During Sixth Five Year Plan (1980-85), 19 district libraries were established in the State. No efforts were made in respect of the establishment of new public libraries after 1980-85.

After India's independence, Madhya Pradesh state was created with Nagpur as its capital: this state included the southern parts of the present-day Madhya Pradesh and north-eastern portion of today's Maharashtra. In 1956, this state was reorganized and its parts were combined with the states of Madhya Bharat, Vindhya Pradesh and Bhopal to form the new Madhya Pradesh state with Bhopal as its capital; the Marathi-speaking Vidarbha region was removed and merged with the then Bombay State. This state was the largest in India by area until 2000, when its southeastern Chhattisgarh region was made a separate state.

The State of Madhya Pradesh was formed on 1st November 1956 with Bhopal as the state capital. It consists of 48 districts and has an area of 308,346 sq. km. Besides the libraries maintained by voluntary organizations for a fairly long time, the government of Madhya Pradesh maintains

Regional and District Libraries and assists the libraries at the Gram Panchayat level. The people of this State recognized the importance of library legislation long back. The draft Library Bill prepared by Dr. Ranganathan for the then Central Province was submitted to Shri S. V. Gokhale, the then Education Minister in 1946. But no action resulted out of it. In 1968 the Seventeenth All India Library Conference was organized at Indore. The issue of the Library Bill was discussed in this conference, and it was resolved that the Madhya Pradesh Library Association would take up the issue of library legislation. As a result of this Dr. G. D. Bhargava and Shri V.S. Moghe drafted a Library Bill and presented it, through the Association, to the Education Minister, Shri Jagadishnarain Avasthi. The Bill was processed in various departments, but could not yield results. The Association is still pursuing the matter in the Assembly.

The various libraries in the state are under the control and supervision of either (a) The Director of Public Instruction, or (b) The Panchayat and Social Welfare Department of the government. So far as urban libraries are concerned, they are under the overall control of Directorate of Public Instruction. The regional and district libraries come in this category) There are 49 libraries (5 regional and 44 district) in the State. These libraries provide library services for urban area.

The libraries in rural and tribal area are looked after by the directorate of Panchayat and Social Welfare. These libraries provide library service" to the rural and tribal area; all there are four types of libraries in Madhya Pradesh:

(a) Libraries under the Directorate of Public Instruction

(b) Libraries under the Directorate of Panchayat and Social Welfare

(c) Public Libraries managed by Local self Govt. i.e. Nagar Nigam, Nagar Palika etc.

(d) Libraries under Directorate of Information & Publicity.

3. PUBLIC LIBRARY SCENARIO IN MADHYA PRADESH

The different types of public libraries are depicted in the table below. These public libraries are governed by two different departments- Directorate of public instruction and E-libraries under Sarve Shiksha Mission.

The state has 1 State Central Library in the State capital of Bhopal, 04 Divisional Central Libraries, 36 District Public Libraries, 50 E libraries established under the General Information Access Network (GIAN) project by the SarveShiksha Mission in Madhya Pradesh, 381 Branch Libraries, 13985 Delivery Stations, 507 Rural libraries under the Panchayat and Social Welfare Department and 47, 100 Rural libraries Under the Sarve Shiksha Mission.

At present in Madhya Pradesh there are 51 districts, but only 36 district public libraries are in a working condition, so government should take a further step to establish remaining 15 district public libraries in the state.

The rural and tribal library services are looked after by Director, Panchayat and Social Welfare of the state. This is so because social education is a part of education as in other constituent states. The Directorate of Panchayat and Social Welfare provides library services to the rural and tribal area under three schemes as follows:

1. Village library scheme;
2. Village reading room scheme; and
3. Grant-in-aid scheme for registered societies.

The draft public library bill envisages a structure for the libraries in the state.

The bills were acted in 1946, 1950, 1958, 1959, 1968, 1970, 1978 and in 1990. The Historic Public Library Act of Madhya Pradesh was passed in 2013.

4. ACADEMIC AND SPECIAL LIBRARIES IN MADHYA PRADESH

There are conventional universities, central university,

deemed universities and private universities in the state. The major academic libraries have been listed below.

4.1. Rani DurgawatiVishwavidyalaya (RDV) Library, Jabalpur (1956)

Rani Durgavati University also known as University of Jabalpur is a public university in Jabalpur. It was named after the queen Rani Durgavati. The university was constituted and established on 12 June 1956 under the Jabalpur University Act, 1956. University library was established in the foundation year of Rani Durgavti University. There is huge collection of various types reading materials in the library.

4.2. Vikram University, Ujjain (1957) Library

Vikram University was established in Ujjain on the 1st of March, 1957. The University library is well stocked with over 1, 60,856 print books and 4800 back sets of periodicals, 26 news- papers and more than 80 electronic media like CDs/DVDs. The library house industry relevant reports, standards, annual reports, magazines, newsletters, etc.. The library and e-resource center plays a proactive role to ensure that the information resources are acquired and organised to meet the present and future needs of its users.

4.3. JiwajiVishwavidyalaya (JV) Library, Gwalior (1963)

Jiwaji University in Gwalior came into existence on May 23, 1964. It was a generous contribution of Scindia family, in particular Kailashwasi Maharaja ShrimantJiwajiRaoScindia and late RajmataShrimatiVijayarajeScindia. The institution was christened after the name of KailashwasiShrimantJiwajirao Scindia as a standing memorial to his personal. The University has a central library which has a collection of over 1,40,000 books and about 8000 bound volumes of research journals. It also contains a section of unpublished theses.

4.4. JawaharLal Nehru KrishiVishwavidyalaya (JNKV) Library, Jabalpur (1963)

Jawaharlal Nehru KrishiVishwaVidyalaya (JNKVV), an agricultural university which was named after the architect of modern India, Pt. Jawaharlal Nehru was started by the Government of India based on the recommendations of Radha Krishnan commission on October 2, 1964.The Central Library of Jawaharlal Nehru KrishiVishwaVidyalaya, a home of one of the largest and richest collection of learning resources in the country on agriculture and allied sciences.

4.5. Devi AhilyaVishwavidyalaya (DAV) Libraries, Indore (1964)

Devi Ahilya University established in 1964 was also called Indore University is a university operated by the state of Madhya Pradesh at Indore, India, named after Devi Ahilya BaiHolkar belonging to the Holkar dynasty of the Marathas. The Library of the university was established in 1964 and it is one of the first Departments started in the University. It is regarded as one of the best library in the Malwa region of MP. Apart from the Central library the university has strong departmental libraries also. The library provides a portal called EJ- Server which act as a single platform and it provides easy and fast access to various E-Resources.

4.6. Awadesh Pratap Singh University, Library Rewa (1968)

The Awadesh Pratap Singh University has been named after the captain Awadhesh Pratap Singh, a distinguished son of the soil and a freedom fighter. The University was established on the 20th July 1968 and got UGC recognition in February 1972. The APS University is a teaching-cum-affiliating University with its jurisdiction over 65 colleges situated in the districts of Rewa, Satna, Sidhi, Shahdol, Umariya and Singrauli. The university has a central library which contains around 75000 books.Besides books, the library contains short research papers, Ph.D thesis etc.

4.7. Barkatullah University, Library Bhopal (1970)

Barkatullah University, formerly known as Bhopal University was established in 1970 in the capital city of Madhya Pradesh. In 1988, it was rechristened as the Barkatullah Vishwavidyalaya, in the living memory of the great freedom fighter, Prof. Barkatullah. The territorial jurisdiction of the university extends to the eight districts of Bhopal, Sehore, Vidisha, Raisen, Hoshangabad, Harda, Betul, and Rajgrah. There are more than one hundred seventy colleges affiliated to the University. The University has a well-established library comprising of nearly 75000 books, more than 5700 thesis, 3000 Research magazine and 60 Sankrit MSS.

4.8. Mahatma Gandhi Chitratakoot Gramodaya Vishwavidyalaya Library, Chitrakoot(1991)

Mahatma Gandhi Chitrakoot Gramoday University (MGCGV) was established by Rashtrarishi Nanaji Deshmukh on February 12, 1991. Named after Mahatma Gandhi, this university aims at providing higher education mainly to people living in rural areas with emphasis on preparing man power devoted to up liftment of poor and down-trodden. The University has a sophisticated (e-library) central library. It has 47890 text and reference books, 1200 video-cassettes, 100 audio-cassettes and 1000 CD-ROMs.

4.9. Makhanlal Chaturvedi Rashtriya Patrakarita National University of Journalism, Bhopal (1991)

Makhanlal Chaturvedi Rashtriya Patrakarita Vishwavidyalaya, Bhopal, named after a renowned freedom fighter, poet and journalist was formally inaugurated by Dr. Shankar Dayal Sharma, the then Vice President of India, on 16th January, 1991. The University has a well-organized Library and documentation Unit. The Library has more than ten thousands books on different subjects.

4.10. M. P. Bhoj (open) University, Bhopal. (1991)

Madhya Pradesh Bhoj (Open) University was formed in 1991 under an act by the state legislature. It is named to honour the Illustrious King Raja Bhoj Deva, the most illustrious of the Parmar rulers of Malwa, who established the famous university at Dhar for Sanskrit studies. This University aims to The university has a well-equipped library or resource center.

4.11. Maharishi Mahesh Yogi Vedic Vishwavidyalaya, Jabalpur. (1995)

Maharishi Mahesh Yogi Vedic University, also known as Maharishi Mahesh Yogi Vedic Vishwavidyalayais an accredited, public university located in Katni, Madhya Pradesh, India. It is a part of the Maharishi Educational System and was established by the state legislature in 1995. The University head office is situated at Brahmsthan of India, Village-Karaundi, District-Katni, and Madhya Pradesh. This Vedic University has a central library to cater to the needs of the student community.

4.13. Rajiv Gandhi Proudyogiki Vishwavidyalaya (RGPV) Library, Bhopal (1998)

Rajiv Gandhi Proudyogiki Vishwavidyalaya was established in the year 1998, by Madhya Pradesh Vidhan Sabha Act 13, 1998 as a center of excellence in the arena of technical education, research and innovations. Under its umbrella there are 05 UTD's, 219 affiliated Engineering Colleges, 87 Pharmacy Colleges, 80 MCA Colleges and 05 Architecture colleges imparting graduate level instructions running around 21 under graduate level courses, 85 Polytechnic institutions. The Library of Rajiv Gandhi Technical University is equipped with books, periodicals, national and international journals, CD-ROMS, covering all aspects of academic studies and research material.

4.14. Maulana Azad National Institute of Technology (MANIT) Library, Bhopal (Deemed, 2002)

The Maulana Azad National Institute of Technology, Bhopal, Madhya Pradesh, one of the first eight Regional Engineering Colleges started in the country, was inaugurated on 4th September 1960. The institute has been named after Maulana Abul Kalam Azad, a renowned educationist, scholar and academician of India. The Government of India, Ministry of Human Resources Development, New Delhi has upgraded the institute as Maulana Azad National Institute of Technology (MANIT) along with a status of Deemed University with effect from 26th June 2002.

4.15. Dr. Harisingh Gour Vishwavidyalaya (HSGV) Library, Sagar (1946)

Jawaharlal Nehru Library of Dr. Hari Singh Gour Vishwavidyalaya Sagar (Central University) is the oldest and largest University library situated in Sagar District of Madhya Pradesh. The library has more than 3.0 lakhs books and bound journals in its collection besides a good collection of rare manuscripts and reference books.

4.16. The Indira Gandhi National Tribal University, Amarkantak, Madhya Pradesh (2008)

The Indira Gandhi National Tribal University came into existence on July 2008. The jurisdiction of the University extends to the whole country and it is fully funded by the Central Government through the University Grant Commission. The university caters to the tribal's long cherished dream of higher education. The University Library of Indira Gandhi National Tribal University is a center of information for the academic community of the University and is expected to be developed into a hub of knowledge to all the academic community and a gateway to national and global knowledge.

5. LIBRARY ASSOCIATIONS IN MADHYA PRADESH

5.1. Madhya Pradesh Library Association

When Dr. S.R. Ranganathan visited Vikram University, Ujjain, as a visiting professor in the teaching department of Library science in 1957, he formed the Madhya Pradesh Library Association. In view of the successive failures of putting library movement on firm basis in the state, Ranganathan persuaded the then governor of M.P. Shri, H.V.Patsarkar to become the president of M.P.L.A. Under his Presidend ship, the M.P.L.A started active work. Necessary data were collected and assembled to work out a Library development plan for M.P. It was a difficult task as the state had just then been formed by amalgamating areas taken from different administrations. However a draft library bill was prepared, approved by the M.P.L.A and forwarded to the care of the government. In 1968, the Seventeenth All India Library Conference was held under the auspices of the University of Indore. At this conference the need for library act in the state was reiterated through the resolutions. M.P.L.A was authorized to take concrete steps in this direction. Consequent to this, in 1970, Bhargava and V. S. Moghe prepared a draft public libraries bill for M.P.

5.2. Madhya Pradesh College Librarians Association is the another important body which keeping in line with regional needs,

5.3. Indore Library Association emerged also emerged. It did promote the public of regional language material, including the quarterly serial, Pustakalaya Sandesh stated in 1967.

6. LIS EDUCATION IN MADHYA PRADESH

In Madhya pradesh there are a number of institutions offer LIS courses. Devi Ahalya Viswa vidyalaya offer BLISC, MLISc, Mphil, PhD and PGDLAN courses. Jivaju University also offers these courses except PGDLAN. The other universities offer PG and Mphil in library science are -

Makhanlal Chaturvedi Rashtriya Patrakarita Vishwavidyalaya, Rani Durgavati Vishwavidyalaya and Vikram University Ujjain. The following universities provide BLISc and MLISc courses only - AEC Training College And Centre, Dr Harisingh Gaur university Vishwavidyalaya, Govt. MLB Arts & Commerce Autonomous College, Awadhesh Pratap Singh University, Mahatma Gandhi Chitrakoot Gramodaya Vishwavidyalaya, Along with these universities - Madhya Pradesh Bhoj Open University, Dr. Harisingh Gour Vishwavidyalaya Sagar (DHGV-IDE) and Awadhesh Pratap Singh University offer both BLISc and MLISc in distance mode.

REFERENCES

1. Barua, B. P. (1994). Raja Ram Mohan Library Foundation and Library Movement in India. *39th All India Library Conference, Delhi, Indian Library Association*.
2. Bhargava, G.D. (1986). Public library movement in Madhya Pradesh: retrospect and prospect.In Rout, R.K. (Ed.), *Library legislation in India: problems and prospect* (pp. 325-335). New Delhi: Reliance publishing house.
3. Deshpande,K and B.B. Hungund "What Ails our Public Library System", ILA Bulletin, Vol. 24, No.1&2, 1998.
4. Kumar, PSG (2009). Library Movement and Library Development in Gujarat, Dadra and Nagar Haveli and Daman and Diu. New Delhi, B.R Oublishing Coroporation.
5. Mohammed Taher (2001). *Libraries in India's national developmental perspective: a saga of fifty years since independence*: New Delhi: Concept publishing.
6. Ramakant Sharma (2013).A critical study of public library services in Madhya Pradesh: model plan for resource sharing and networking. Unpublished doctoral dissertation, Guru Ghasidas University, Madhya Pradesh. pp.14-16, Accessed from http://shodhganga.inflibnet.ac.in/bitstream/10603/12662/9/09_chapter%204.pdf
7. Venkatapaiah (2000) Indian Library Legislation : State Library bills and acts. Delhi, Daya Publishing House.
8. Sharma, S.K (1996). *Public library in India: trends and status.* P.K.Mahapatra (Ed.), Public libraries in developing countries (pp.121-127). New Delhi: Vikash Publishing House.

16

Library Movement and Development in Maharashtra

Dr. Shashank Sonaji Sonwane
Assistant Professor
Department of Library and Information Science
Dr. Babasaheb Ambedkar Marathwada University,
Aurangabad, Maharashtra

1. MAHARASHTRA: A PROFILE

The separation of the then bilingual Bombay State has given birth to two separate states, viz. Gujarat and Maharashtra, on 1st May 1960, under the Bombay

Reorganization Act, 1960 with the predominant Marathi speaking areas of Hyderabad (Marathwada) and Madhya Pradesh (Vidharbha) and most of the districts of the former Bombay state constituted the new state Maharashtra. The Metropolitan city Bombay (now Mumbai) remained the capital of Maharashtra State.

The state covers an area of 3,07,710 sq. km (118,809 sq mi). Previously it was divided into four administrative divisions, viz. Bombay, Pune, Nagpur and Aurangabad (popularly known as Marathwada). Recently it has been divided into six administrative divisions, viz. Konkan, Nasik, Pune, Aurangabad, Amravati and Nagpur. In all the six divisions have been divided into 35 districts and further divided into 109 sub-divisions of the districts and 357 talukas (Govt. of Maharashtra, 2014a).

According to the 2011 census, the total population of the state is 112,374,333 (9.28% of India's population) of which male and female are 58,242,056 and 54,131,277 respectively (Govt. of India, 2014a). The literacy rate in Maharashtra rose to 83.2%. Of this male literacy stood at 89.82% and female literacy 75.48%. The total number of literate people in Maharashtra stood at 81,554,290 of whom 45,257,584 were male and 36,296,706 were female. (Govt. of India, 2014b). The Official language is Marathi, the mother tongue of majority people in the state (The Bombay Hight Court, 1965). The state is rich in literature, about 1500 books are published per year in Marathi language.

2. LIBRARY MOVEMENT IN MAHARASHTRA

The first landmark in the history of library movement was made with the establishment of literary society of Bombay in 1804. Development of public libraries in the state was started before the British rule in India with the collection of manuscripts. Bombay Royal Asiatic Society at Bombay open with library in 1804 is treated as the first library of the state. This was established exclusive for the Europeans mostly of higher income group residing at other civil and military stations at Surat, Pune, and Baroda etc. Thus from 1804-1830 libraries meant exclusively for the Europeans were established, in this period most of the libraries established in Maharashtra.

As a sharp reaction towards the policy of the literary society of Bombay regarding the non-admission to Indian members and its high amount of subscription fee, the Bombay Central Library was established in 1830. Numbers of libraries by the end of 1880 were established in various parts of the state. The period from 1881-1921 is marked by important landmarks as libraries of Marathi books.

The library established in 1930 occupies a sphere of its own being only institution of its kind in the Labour Area of Bombay. In 1935 a fresh effort was made to infuse life in the library activities by establishing the Pune Granthalaya Sangh. In 1939 the first popular Ministry of the Bombay Government appointed the library development committee with A. A. Fyzee as the chairman, to consider the desirability of establishing a network in the province.

The Committee constituted in 1939 and submitted its report in 1940. The recommendations of the Committee could not be implemented upto 1947 because of the Second World War. After the independence, the then Government of Bombay province decided for development of public libraries to implement the recommendations of the Fyzee Committee.

The Fyzee Committee recommended that the Government should encourage local initiative by recognizing private libraries and give them financial aid on the conditions that the libraries allow free use of the books and reading material to the nonpaying members in the locality within the premises of the library. The Committee also recommended the establishment of one State Central Library at Mumbai and one Regional Library at Pune. According to the recommendations of this committee the functions of Central Library were entrusted to the Asiatic Society of Bombay in 1947. In 1950, the Trust Deed was executed between the then Bombay provincial Government and Asiatic Society of Bombay for this purpose. During this period the Regional Library was also established at Pune.

The committee further recommended that one District Library and one Taluka Library at each district and taluka places should be recognized. The formula of financial grants to these libraries was determined on the category of public library and the limit which was based on admissible expenditure incurred by concerned libraries in the previous year. The work of inspection and supervision of these libraries was being done by Curator of Libraries, who was working under the control of the Directorate of Education. This situation continued upto 1967. The working and development of these public libraries recognized under the Fyzee Committee Report could not give sufficient service and attention on account of inadequate funds for their progress. This situation was considered by the library association, library activists, political leaders, in the field of libraries and they pressed Government for the introduction of library legislation in the State (Vaishnav, 1994).

3. MAHARASHTRA PUBLIC LIBRARIES ACT, 1967

The workers in library movement in Marathwada were pressing hard to the Government for adopting Library Legislation. The workers in the field of Library politics and sociology along with the Library Associations built up a pressure on the Government to enact a Public Library Law in the State.

The Government reacted to this pressure and introduced an official bill in early 1967 to the State Legislature by the then Education Minister, Mr. M. D. Chaudhary. It was passed by Legislative Assembly on 27th November, 1967 at its Nagpur Session, with the amendment of 'not less than Rs. 25 laks'; instead of the words 'not more than Rs. 25 lakhs'. The amendments were passed on 28th November, 1967 and the act was implemented with effect from 1st May, 1968.

The salient features of the Act

Following are the salient features of the Maharashtra Public Library Act, 1967:

1. Establishment of a separate Department of libraries for planning, maintenance, organization and development of Public Libraries in the State;
2. Establishment of the State Central Library for the whole State and Divisional Library in each division, financed and managed by the Government;
3. Establishment of the State Library Council to advise Government on all matters related to the Library development;
4. Establishment of District Library Committee for each district for advising Govt. on all matters concerned with the public libraries in the district;
5. Government is responsible for providing an amount of not less than Rs. 25 lakhs every year for the development of public libraries. The administrative expenditure is in addition to the above amount;
6. There is no provision of library cess in the Act.

Reactions of the experts to the act were not very encouraging. They considered it as retrograde, weak and ineffective piece of legislation. However, Dr. Ranganathan commented that something is better than nothing (Vaishnav, 1994).

Enactment of the Act

With the Enactment of Maharashtra Public Libraries Act, 1967 the directorate of the libraries was set up in the state of Maharashtra on 2nd May 1968. Under the directorate upto 31st March 2009 one state central library, 6 divisional libraries, 20 District Libraries and one reference library and 6 offices of Asstt. Director of Libraries & Head Quarter of Directorate thus 35 offices are established.

The Director of Libraries is the Head of the Department and he has been entrusted with certain functions under Superintendence, direction and control of the State

Government. He is responsible for planning, maintenance, organization and development of Public Libraries and Library system in the State. He is assisted by the Divisional/ Asstt. Directors working at the Divisional Head Quarters. These (6) Asstt. Directors are responsible for supervision, inspection and technical guidance for the recognized public libraries. They have been allotted with the staff viz. Inspectors and Sr. Clerks.

The Director is assisted by one Dy. Director and one Asstt. Director at head office. Dy. Director looks after establishment so also, the work of Book Selection Committee and preparation of bibliographies. He is expected to give technical guidance to the Divisional Libraries. The State Central Library, established at Mumbai and the Divisional Libraries established at Pune and Nagpur, are under the control of Class I Officers. They have been given the additional responsibilities of receiving, processing and preserving the books received under the Press and Registration of Books Act, 1867. They are also at the apex of the Inter-Library loan system in the state and division respectively (Government of Maharashtra, 2014b).

4. PUBLIC LIBRARY SCENARIO IN THE STATE

The basic principle of Maharashtra Public Libraries Act 1967 is that, the voluntary organizations should come forward to establish new Public Libraries for the purpose of grant-in-aid in the State. Since, the implementation of the Act, the development of public libraries in the State has taken a momentum.

The Directorate of Libraries is established on 2nd May, 1968 under the provisions of this Act. The State Central Library which was temporarily worked by Asiatic Library since 1947 was separated from Asiatic Society on 1st July, 1994 and being worked fully by Directorate of libraries, 6 Divisional Libraries, 20 District Libraries, and one Reference Library is established in the State. New 10 District libraries will be established in 2009-10 Besides, 9624 Public Libraries for the purpose of grant-in-aid are recognized in the State. Of which 496 are belonging to Gram panchayats. Besides 162 sub centres of these libraries, so also 35 Research Institutions are recognized for the purpose of grant-in-aid in the State.

4.1. State Central Library, Mumbai

The Library development in Maharashtra is based on the recommendations of a Fyzee Committee, appointed by the then Government of Bombay province, for the development of libraries in the State. The Committee constituted in 1939 and submitted its report in 1940. The recommendations of the Committee could not be implemented up to 1947 because of the Second World War. After the independence, the then Government of Bombay province decided for development of public libraries to implement the recommendations of the Fyzee Committee.

The Fyzee Committee recommended that the Government should encourage local initiative by recognizing private libraries and give them financial aid on the conditions that the libraries allow free use of the books and reading material to the nonpaying members in the locality within the premises of the library. The Committee also recommended the establishment of one State Central Library at Mumbai and one Regional Library at Pune. According to the recommendations of this committee the functions of Central Library were entrusted to the Asiatic Society of Bombay in 1947. In 1950, the Trust Deed was executed between the then Bombay provincial Government and Asiatic Society of Bombay for this purpose. During this period the Regional Library was also established at Pune.

The committee further recommended that one District Library and one Taluka Library at each district and taluka places should be recognized. The formula of financial grants to these libraries was determined on the category of public library and the limit which was based on admissible expenditure incurred by concerned libraries in the previous year. The work of inspection and supervision of these libraries was being done by Curator of Libraries, who was working under the control of then Directorate of Education. This situation continued upto 1967. The working and development of these public libraries recognized under the Fyzee Committee Report could not give sufficient service and attention on account of inadequate funds for their progress. This situation was considered by the library association, library activists, political leaders, in the field of libraries and they pressed Government for the introduction of library legislation in the State.

The Directorate of Libraries is comparatively a new Directorate concerned with the public library development in the State. In fact, public library development is a new subject. The public library is expected to perform various functions. In a democratic society the public library is much more important than other institutions of formal education. Governments role in this respect is of supervisory and that of rendering financial aid. Public Library service is a new social service and has to be looked after carefully till it get established and accepted by all. The Maharashtra Public Libraries Act envisages development of library service with the help of non-official public libraries. To run the State Central Library and the Six Divisional Libraries and District libraries is the responsibility of the State Government. Director is making efforts to develop the services within the framed rules of the Act and the financial resources available.

The Central library is expected to perform the functions as under-

(a) Acquisition, maintenance and preservation of books and periodicals received under the Press and Registration of Books Act, 1867;

(b) One of the four public depository libraries in the country designed under the Delivery of Books (public libraries) Act, 1954 and as such receives all the books, periodicals and newspapers published in the whole country.

(c) To serve the general public as a reference library for all the books, periodicals and newspapers received under the two Acts (State and Central) stated above;

(d) To maintain a collection of rare and costly books so as to be in a position to supplement the resources of the divisional libraries in the state;

(e) To coordinate the resources of the divisional libraries in the state;

(f) Inter library loan among the libraries under the library system and educational institutions etc.;

(g) Reference service on the premises and by correspondence;

(h) Bibliographical work such as compilation and publishing of bibliographies of books printed and published in the state and other bibliographies for the use of reading for public, scholars and research workers;

(i) To further the library movement in the state and to guide it whenever necessary etc.

In 1955, the Government of India notified the Central library as a National Depository library under the Delivery of Books (Public libraries) Act, 1954 and books started coming in from December 1955. This decision of the Government of India was not with the prior approval of or even advice to the society.

As this added responsibility involved heavy administrative and financial responsibilities a committee (Prof. Niharranjan Ray) was appoionted by the Government of India in 1976 to study and report on the needs and requirements of Central Library. The committee recommended that–

1. The Central Library should be freed from the Asiatic Society of Bombay and the State Government should establish the State Central Library for the whole State under the provisions of Maharashtra Public Librareis Act, 1967;

2. A separate new building for the State Central Library should be constructed at Vidyanagari, Kalina Campus, Santacruz, Mumbai. The financial assistance for erecting a new building may be sought from the Central Government.

As per the recommendation of Prof. Niharranjan Ray Committee the functions of Central Library were taken over by the Government and established the State Central Library under the provision of Maharashtra Public Libraries Act, 1967, w.e.f. 1.07.1994. (Government of Maharashtra, 2014b).

4.2. Asiatic Library

The Asiatic society of Mumbai was born on Nov. 26, 1804 as the literary society of Bombay. Aimed at 'Promoting useful knowledge, particularly such as is now immediately connected with India'. It defined its scope formally as the encouragement of oriental arts, sciences and literature. The Asiatic society forms part of the network of institutions created by the British to generate, systematize and disseminate knowledge of India and the orient a vast body of information learning and knowledge that came to be known as indology.

The library of the Asiatic Society built up its vast and valuable collections over two centuries, by purchasing and acquiring books through donations from other institutions, associations and individuals. In 1826, the literary society of Bombay merged with the Royal Asiatic society of Great Britain and Ireland to become its Bombay branch. Post independence, it became a separate entity; The Asiatic Society of Bombay. In 2002, it renamed itself as The Asiatic Society of Mumbai.

The personalities intimately connected with the society in its early years included administration, jurists, educationists and missionaries, several of whom were scholars as wells many were active and influential in public life, engaging with issues of social reforms & nationalism. Some were also philanthropists who donated money and their collections of rare books, manuscripts and antiquities to the society. The society originally located in Government house in Parel moved in 1930 into the Town Hall building which was still being build. The town hall was thus, from its very inception not only the civic nucleus of British Bombay, but also a centre for learning and knowledge.

The Town hall was build when Bombay was still a fortified settlement and the East India company's territory, with its growing trade interest, had to be defended from attacks, its scale and design were meant to convey the message of might and authority. After the mid nineteen century, British imperial power was consolidated and the port walls were dismantled. In that phase, with burgeoning commercial prosperity as well, Bombay underwent an architectural and institutional restructuring.

Today, the area is dotted with skyscrapers. It is an important business district with many bank and offices. Yet, along side the din and bustle of 21st century traffic, the imprint of colonial geography, architecture and institutions is palpable. The Town hall and the Asiatic society are an organic part of this landscape (Government of Maharashtra, 2014b).

5. ACADEMIC LIBRARIES IN MAHARASHTRA

5.1. University Libraries in Maharashtra

University libraries which were considered to be the part of an ivory tower till a few decades ago have now become practical instruments and supposed to render meaningful services to the teachers, researchers and students. After independence reconstruction of national education was realized as the prime concern and improvements in standards of higher education was another important requirement for competitive and qualitative advancement. So to maintain the standards of teaching, research and extension, the national apex body lime UGC was created under an Act of Parliament in 1956.

The important university libraries are given below.

5.1.1. University of Mumbai – Library

The University of Mumbai (Bombay) was established in 1857. In August, 1864, Premchand Roychand, a merchant prince of Bombay, offered to the University a donation of Rs. 2,00,000 "towards the erection of a university library which may be an ornament to the city, and by becoming a storehouse of t he learned works, not only of the past but of many generations to come, may be the means of promoting the high ends of the University." Two months later this gift was followed by another gift of Rs. 2,00,000 from the same donor for a clocktower in connection with the library to perpetuate the memory of his mother Mrs. Rajabai. The foundation-stone of the library and the Rajabai Clock tower was laid on March 1, 1869, and the work was completed in November 1878. It was formally opened to readers on February 27, 1880, after a conversazione by the Chancellor.

5.1.2. Tata Institute of Social Science (TISS) Mumbai-Library

TISS Library established along with the institute way back in 1936 is one of the leading social science libraries in the country. The library was named as **"Sir Dorabji Tata Memorial Library"** on **3rd May, 2002** in the memory of late Sir Dorabjii Tata. It is geared to meet the academic and research information needs of the user community. It provides a conducive environment for intellectual enquiry by providing user-focused services to obtain and evaluate scholarly information and knowledge. Since the library specializes in the field of applied social sciences, it has become most sought after library for the social scientists in India.

5.1.3. SYPMBIOSIS International University Library

The University has 20 libraries across all its campuses. The collections at all the Libraries are the result of more than forty years of continuing commitment by librarians, faculty, students, and private donors to build one of the best libraries in India. The library directly supports the Research and instructional needs of the University, while also serving as a custodian of culture and discovery. The collection of more than 2 lac books, supports current University Programmes and those areas of Research which will be needed by future scholars. Library is one of the core foundation upon which a student's education is built and form the cornerstone of University Research efforts. Students and all other library users are encouraged to give their suggestions for purchasing any books.

5.1.4. Indian Institute of Science Education and Research(IISER) LIBRARY - PUNE

IISER Pune Library is a creative and innovative partner in teaching, learning and research activities which in turn contributes to the achievement of the institute's mission to become a science university of highest caliber with state of the art research and high quality education. Library has undergone a sea of transformation, not only with doubling of books but also providing online access to all premier journals as well as full-text & bibliographic databases available in the field of science and allied subjects. Efforts are being put to apply ICT in all possible operations and services of library to improve its service quality.

6. LIS EDUCATION IN MAHARASHTRA

The subject of LIS is relatively a younger one compared to those like Chemistry, Physics, Literature, and Philosophy. In Maharashtra it is taught as short term certificate level to postgraduate research degree level. The universities offering LIS in Maharashtra are: University of Mumbai., SNDT Women's University, Mumbai., Pune University, Pune,Dr. Babasaheb Ambedkar Marathwada University, (BAMU), Aurangabad, Rashtrasant Tukdoji Maharaj Nagpur University, Shivaji University, Kolhapur, Sant Gadge Baba Amravati University, Swami Ram, Teerth Marathwada University, (SRTMU) Nanded, North Maharashtra University, Jalgaon,

Tilak Maharashtra Vidyapeeth, Pune, Bharati Vidyapith Deemed University, Pune, Yashvantrao Chavan Maharashtra Open University, (YCMOU), Nashik and IGNOU Regional Centres.

6.1. Department of Library Science, University of Mumbai, Mumbai

Training in Librarianship in Mumbai University was started in 1943, when a Diploma in Librarianship was instituted by the University Library. In 1964, a full-fledged Department of Library Science was established and the Diploma Course was converted into the Degree Course (B.Lib.Sc.) with some changes in the syllabus. The Master's Course leading to the M.Lib.Sc. degree was introduced in 1968/69. In 1995, the Ph.D. programme of the Department was revived (University of Mumbai, 2014).

6.2. Department of Library and Information Science, SNDT Women's University, Mumbai

A pioneering tradition has characterized the School ever since its founding in 1961 as a constituent unit of the SNDT Women's University. The School began by offering a Post-Graduate Diploma programme in Librarianship. Presently they are offering Ph.D. in Library & Information Science , Master of Library & Information Science (M.L.I.Sc) and Bachelor of Library & Information Science (B.L.I.Sc.).

6.3. Department of Library and Information Science, RTMN University, Nagpur

The Department of Library and Information Science, Rashtrasant Tukadoji Maharaj Nagpur University, Nagpur is one of the oldest department of Library Science in the country. This department was started on 20 August 1956 and had a history of fifty years. Starting in the year 1956 with a diploma course in Library and Information Science it has come a long way upgrading the diploma to BLISc, starting MLISC of one year course (1984) and MLISc (Integrated two years course) as per UGC guide lines in the year 2003. The department also has to its credit Ph. D. program from 1987 onwards.

6.4. Department of Library and Information Science, University of Pune, Pune

Training in Library Science was instituted at the University in 1958 and the first Diploma Course in Library Science was introduced in1958-59. Diploma Course was converted into the Bachelors Degree in 1965. The Department of Library and Information Science was established under the faculty of Mental Moral And Social Sciences in 1978 and two years integrated M.L.I.Sc course was introduced from 2002. The department is also conducting M.Phil. and Ph. D programmes (Universityof Pune, 2014).

6.5. Department of Library and Information Science, Dr. Babasaheb Ambedkar Marathwada University, Aurangabad.

Dr. Babasaheb Ambedkar Marathwada University introduced the Post Graduate Diploma in Library Science Course during June 1968. From the year 2002 the University introduced 2-year integrated MLISc course with semester pattern. From June 2006, the department has introduced special subjects (cafeteria) in the curriculum to develop knowledge on the latest techniques of information storage, transfer and retrieval; help to acquire necessary skills in handling, accessing and application of electronic resources, tools and media; and help to know the latest developments in the Information Technology. From June 2008, the department has introduced M. Phil – LIS . Presently they are offering PhD. also.

7. LIBRARY ASSOCIATIONS IN MAHARASHTRA

For promoting the cause of libraries and information centers, library associations are playing a very important role. Thus there are library associations operating at local, regional and national level operating in India. In the state of Maharashtra the following are the Library Associations;

- **BUACLA** : Bombay (Mumbai) University Affiliated College Librarians Association
- **PULISAA** : Pune University Library & Information Science Alumni Association, Department of Library and Information Science, Jayakar Library, University of Pune, Pune—411007 http://pulisaa.googlepages.com Email : pulisaa@gmail.com
- **NUACLA** : Nagpur University Affiliated Colleges Librarians Association.
- **BAMULISAA** : Dr. Babasaheb Ambedkar Marathwada University Library and Information Science Alumni Association, Department of Library and Information Science, Dr. B.A.M.U., Aurangabad.
- Library and Information Professionals Study Circle, Amravati
- Vidarbha Library Association[VLA]
- Khandesh Library Association [KLA]
- Maharashtra Librarians Association (Public Libraries)

8. CONCLUSION

Public libraries have always been the door to learning for a great majority of the populations that they serve. They are knowledge centres and contribute to lifelong learning. For Maharashtra, there are bumps in the road that leads to the goal of having an institution to serve the masses, which is even more imperative in the present information society, in a nation where 40 percent of the population is living below the poverty line. A massive investment in public libraries is needed to make them true information resource centres for the layman.

The transition of libraries from information centres to resources centres in a knowledge-based society is a noteworthy phenomenon of the 21st century. The advances in ICT has intensified the expectations from librarians. The performance of future librarians will be dictated by how efficiently the library services will be designed and disseminated. Attitude towards service, social sensitivity, time management, communication ability, curiosity and desire to perform well, will be the personal characteristics that will be detrimental in measuring effectiveness of a librarian.

Library Science schools have to take a cognizance of such emerging trends and needs of the knowledge-based society and prepare an action plan on collaborative basis. The present syllabi would possibly need frequent restructuring with computer-supported training, online/ web-based learning to suit the environment. The LIS departments affiliated to universities in Maharashtra have taken a positive note of the changing scenario, which is an encouraging scene.

REFERENCES

1. The Bombay High Court. (1965). "The Maharashtra Official Languages ACT". http://bombayhighcourt.nic.in/libweb/acts/1965.05.pdf (accessed on 21 June 2014)
2. Census of India. (2011). "Literacy ratio in state". http://www.census2011.co.in/literacy.php (accessed on 27 June 2014).
3. Gokhale Pratibha. (2010). Library and Information Science Education in Maharashtra: A Perspective. DESIDOC Journal of Library & Information Technology, Vol. 30, No. 5, September 2010, pp. 48-55
4. Government of India (2014a) . Ministry of Home Affairs. "Census of India – Socio-cultural aspects".http://censusindia.gov.in/Census_Data_2001/Census_Data_Online/Social_and_cultural/Religion.aspx (accessed on 20 June 2014)
5. Government of India. (2014b)."Maharashtra Population Census data 2011". Census 2011. http://www.census2011.co.in/census/state/maharashtra.html (accessed on 21 June 2014)
6. Government of Maharashtra. (2014a). District department. "Talukas of Maharashtra". https://www.maharashtra.gov.in/english/mahInfo/state.php (accessed on 20 June 2014)
7. Government of Maharashtra. (2014b). Directorate of Library. http://dolmaharashtra.org.in/ (accessed on 20 June 2014)
8. RTMN University. (2014). Department of Library and Information Science. http://www.nagpuruniversity.org/links/faculty_of_social_science.htm (accessed on 12 July 2014)

9. SNDT University. (2014). Department of Library and Information Science. http://libraryinfosc.sndt.ac.in/default.htm (accessed on 12 July 2014)

10. Sonwane S.S. and Vaishnav A. A. (2009). *Milestones in LIS Education at Dr. Babasaheb Ambedkar Marathwada University, Aurangabad*. In: National Seminar on "Library and Information Services in Changing Era", organized by Department of Library and Information Science and Jaykar Library, Pune, held at University of Pune, Pune during January 22nd – 23rd , 2009. Pg. 405- 412.

11. University of Mumbai. (2014). Department of Library Science http://www.mu.ac.in/arts/library_science/profile.html (accessed on 12 July 2014)

12. Universityof Pune. (2014). Department of Library and Information Science. http://www.unipune.ac.in/dept/mental_moral_and_social_science/library_and_information_science/default.htm (accessed on 12 July 2014)

13. Vaishnav, A. A. (1994). Public Library Services in Maharashtra. In: Public Library Services in India. Edited by L.N. Verma and U.K. Agarwal, Himanshu Publications, Delhi. Pg 127-134.

17

Library Movement and Development in North East India

Dr. Manoj Kumar Sinha
Associate Professor and Head of the Department
Department of Library and Information Science,
(Swami Vivekananda School of Library Sciences)
Assam University, Silchar-788 011

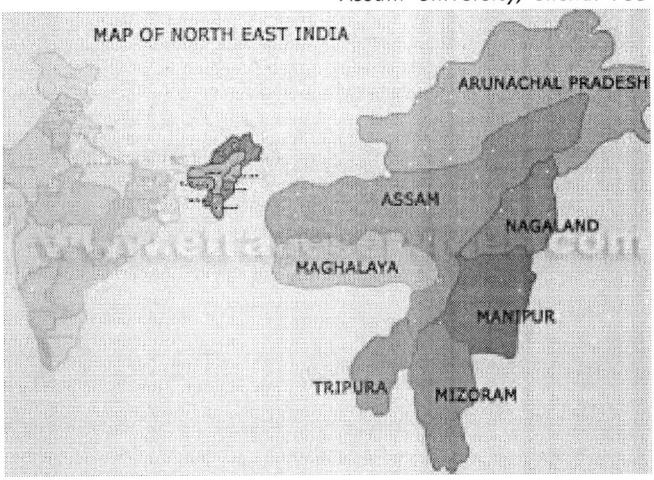

1. NORTH EAST: A PROFILE

North Eastern Region (N E Region) of India has attracted attention of the government of India since two decades for overall development of the region. The North

Eastern States comprise of seven states which is popularly known as seven sisters and recently in 2001 the eight States "*Sikkim*' has been included in the North Eastern Region. These states are viz., Arunachal Pradesh, Assam, Manipur, Meghalaya, Mizoram, Nagaland, Sikkim, and Tripura. This is a review paper which highlights the present status of Academic, Public and Special Libraries in North Eastern States in general and Assam in particular. Since last two decades many developments have been taken place especially in special/ technical and academic libraries in the region. The growth and development in public libraries including rural libraries are not in tune with academic and special libraries. In this paper an attempt has been taken to put the development in the areas of libraries of North East India in general and Assam in particular in brief. It is not possible to include all the details of library services, infrastructure in this paper owing to limitation of time and space. But this will give glimpses of the status of libraries in this region.

2. PUBLIC LIBRARY SYSTEM IN NORTH EAST INDIA

The seven North Eastern States are earlier known as "Seven Sisters" But in 2000, the Sikkim has been included in the North Eastern States. But the development of library science profession and library system is very poor. At the professional level some library associations like Assam Library Association, Guwahati Library Association, and Manipur Library Association etc. are available and they are working for the enactment of library legislation in the remaining states of North East India. But still more has to be done for the development of the libraries located in the North East.

Public Library System in North East India in general and Assam in particular has not been in a good position. Out of eight states only three states of North East India Manipur, Mizoram and Arunachal Pradesh have passed the Public Libraries Act in 1988 ,1993 and 2009 respectively. But the implementation of library legislation is not as desired at the time of passing the Public Libraries Acts in these three states. Remaining States are trying to enact the Public Libraries Act in their respective states. In Assam efforts are going on from the Govt. of Assam side and also on the pursuance of the local LIS professional bodies like Assam Library Association, Assam College Library Association, Guwahati Library Association and Civil Society of Assam for the enactment of Library Legislation, but till date this has not been materialized. If the Public Libraries Acts is passed, then many posts for library and information professionals would have been created. So there is an urgent need for the enactment of Library Legislation not only in Assam but also in remaining states of North East India where Library Legislation/ Public Library Act has yet to be enacted which would definitely opens up new avenues for the development of the public libraries in urban and rural areas of North East India in general and Assam in particular.

3. LIBRARY LEGISLATION

Out of eight states only three states of North East India Manipur, Mizoram and Arunachal Pradesh have passed the Public Libraries Act in 1988 ,1993 and 2009 respectively. But the implementation of library legislation is not as desired at the time of passing the Public Libraries Acts in these three states. Remaining States are trying to enact the Public Libraries Act in their respective states. In Assam efforts are going on from the Govt. of Assam side and also on the pursuance of the local LIS professional bodies like Assam Library Association, Assam College Library Association, Guwahati Library Association and Civil Society of Assam for the enactment of Library Legislation, but till date this has not been materialized.

3.1. Manipur

Manipur is the sixth state in an independent India that has enacted Public Libraries Act in 1988. The preamble stated the objectives of this Acts as, "An Act to provide the establishment and maintenance of Public Libraries in the State of Manipur and matters connected therewith". Salient features of this Act are given hereunder:

1. Constitution of a State Library Committee, to advise the State Government on all matters arising under this Act and to exercise and perform such other powers and duties as may be prescribed.
2. Constitution of a separate Department of Public Libraries under the Director, as its head.
3. Constitution of District Library Authority for each district to supervise library services in the area of its jurisdiction.
4. Provision to constitute Executive Committee and Sub-Committees of District Library Authority to inquire into and report or advice on any matters, which it may refer to them.
5. Constitution of Library fund formed mainly with the contribution of the State Government.

3.2. Mizoram

Mizoram is the ninth state of India to have library legislation. Preamble of this Act stated its objective as, "An Act to provide for the establishment, maintenance anddevelopment of comprehensive public libraries system in the State of Mizoram". Important features of this Act are:

1. Constitution of State Library Council to advise the Government on all matters relating to libraries and also in regard to promotion and development of libraries in the State;
2. Constitution of the Department of Public Libraries to control and supervise the public library system in the State;
3. Constitution of State Library, District Library, Sub-Divisional Library and Village Libraries;
4. Provision of grant-in-aid to recognized libraries;

5. No library cess. All expenses shall be made from the Government funds. Mizoram Public Library Scenario is discussed at the next chapter in detail.

4. ACADEMIC LIBRARIES IN THE NORTH EAST

Here are the major academic libraries in the North East area.

4.1. Arunachal University Library

The University will maintain an e-library and e-classrooms wherein students would be able to log in and pursue their concerns anytime from any corner of the world right away. All the construction works are underway for the same and the University is also in the process of procuring books and e-books for the libraries.

4.2. Assam University Library

Assami University Library was started with the establishment of the University in the year 1994 as a central facility for meeting information requirements of the academic community of the university. The central library of Assam Univesity was shifted to its new permanent central library cum computer centre in January 2006 and renamed as Rabindra Library. The new building has a total plinth area of 38,700 sq.ft. the main function of library includes collection and development of knowledge resources, technical processing, organization, retrieval and dissemination to the academic community.

4.3. Tezpur University Library

The Central Library, Tezpur University was established in 1994 along with the establishment of the University. The library holds 65873 volumes of print documents and subscribed 630 titles of current journals (print 128, online 502). The UGC-Infonet Consortia of INFLIBNET Center is providing access facility to 9081 (including 525 on perpetual basis) e-journals and seven databases. Central Library also gets online access of 926 e-journals through DelCon

Consortium. The library also holds more than 1800 CDs scattering to different thought contents. Library users can access book database, theses database, journal database, e-journals and other e-resources from any terminal within the University campus.

4.4. Manipur University Library

The Manipur University Library is located at the centre of the University Campus. It has a four storey building with a floor area of 3200 sq.m. It is the heart of self education for the students, teachers and staff of the University. It is also a Referral Library of the state. It is used as information centre by more than 3000 registered members consisting of 2170 P.G. Students, 702 Research Scholars, 191 Teachers and 483 Non-Teaching staff. Many outsiders also come to the library in search of information. Since the inception of the library in 1972, it has been playing a vital role in preservation and conservation of the documents pertinent with the university community.

The library has a collection of more than 1,61,000 books and subscribes to more than 200 printed journals. Manipur University Library is in the forefront of library automation and networking in the North East India. The library became a node of INFLIBNET since 1993.

4.5. North East Hill University, Shillong Library

The North-Eastern Hill University (NEHU) Library, which started with a collection of 600 books in 1973, is now a premier university library of the North-Eastern Region of India with a collection of over 2.3 lakh volumes of books and bound periodicals supplemented by the enormous information resources now available through the UGC-INFONET Consortium and the links to global information resources and services provided on its webpage. The NEHU Central Library is now equipped with high-end computers and other electronic and audio-visual equipment to provide seamless in-house and online services. Following the

University Grants Commission's selection of North-Eastern Hill University as a "University with Potential for Excellence", the NEHU Library has launched a major effort to provide the best services through internal reorganisation, optimisation of available resources, launching of innovative services, and by taking the initiative to reach out to the user community through various programmes.

4.6. Mizoram University Library

Central Library, Mizoram University has continuously been witnessing noteworthy development in various spheres. Growth may be seen in its holdings, users and application of technology. The collection by March, 2014 included 95,818 number of books, 213 Thesis, 123 M.PhilDissertations, 269 Master Degree Dissertations/Project Work and 10,776 numbers of Bound Volumes of Journals.The Library at present subscribes to 226 Journals, 48 General periodicals and 14 dailies (English: 5, Mizo: 8, Hindi: 1).

4.7. Nagaland University Kohima Library

When the erstwhile center for postgraduate studies NEHU Nagaland Campus, at Kohima merged with Nagaland University, on 6th.Sept. 1994, the Library had only 19475 volumes of books. The Library thus started with a very small collection. The Nagaland University Central Library, Kohima, started its collections of books when the University received the statutory recognition and within a short span the collection has grown up to 44,534 volumes of books. It has build up reasonably very useful collection of books. Currently the library subscribes to 24 International and National Journals.

4.8. Tripura University Library

The Central Library of Tripura University came into being in 1987 with an initial collection of 18780 books and documents, taken from the erstwhile Calcutta University Post Graduate Centre (CUPGC). The University maintains the library especially in 28 major and inter-disciplinary subjects. It serves the students, research scholars, faculty members and participants of the various programs and also other organizations through the inter-library loan system and public consultation. Over the years, the Central Library has developed a lot and may claim to be one of the richest higher educational libraries in the State. The Central Library acts as a crucial resources and learning centre of the University to meet the information needs of its clientele for the growth and overall development of the University. The collection and dissemination of data and information and the creation and sharing of knowledge are the success of the central Library in the present era of learning.

5. LIBRARY ASSOCIATIONS IN NORTH EASTERN STATES / ASSAM

There are many Library Association in Assam which are working towards the development of Library and Information services and professionals in Assam. These Library Associations are Assam Library Association (ALA), Assam College Library Association (ACLA), Sadau Asom Gramya Puthibharal Santha, Guwahati Library Association which are working towards overall development of the Library professionals and library services. Details of these Associations are given below:

5.1. Assam Library Association

The Assam Library Association (Asom Puthibharal Sangha) was started in the year 1938 mainly by the personal enthusiasm of Shri Kumudeswar Borthakur (1893-1966), a man who devoted his life for the growth and development of libraries in Assam. He was fully assisted in the matter of public library services by Ayadhya Prasad Goswami, Benudhar Sarma, Tankeswar Chutia, Tirthnath Sarma, Suren Bharali, Purna Goswami, Harendra Nath Baruah, Lokapriya Gopinath Bardoloi and other political and social workers. By establishing this Association, Assam became the 8th State in country in establishing state level library association.

Functions and Activities of Assam Library Association : As per the report available in Web Site of Assam Library Association, it has been performing the following functions and activities.

- Making People Aware for Library Movement in the State
- Organization of Rural Libraries
- Preparation of Draft Public Library Act
- To Start Certificate Course in LIS
- Publications
- To Organise Seminars, Conferences, Workshops and Training
- To Organise Librarian's Day Celebration
- To arrange Felicitation to LIS Professionals

5.2. Assam College Librarians' Association (ACLA)

The Assam College Librarians' Association is a premier association committed to the cause of College Library Movement and Development in Assam. The Assam College Librarians' Association is the state level association which represents those who work in or advocate for College Libraries of Assam. It is fighting for the academic and Social status of the college librarians in Assam and also for the development of the Library profession in Assam. ACLA has provided a wide variety of services and programs to its members and others in the library community since its formation in 1973.

5.3. Sadau Asom Gramya Puthibharal Santha

Sadhu Asom Gramya Puthibharal Santha came into being on 27th January, 1985 in a public meeting held at the District Library Auditorium with a spontaneous decision by the representatives of village libraries and Social Workers, is a non-political, non- communal State Level Voluntary Organization. Sri Putul Ch. Bora was the founder President of the Santha while Sri Balladev Sarmah is the General

Secretary since its birth till date. The Nagaon Zilla Puthibharal Santha since has taken a leading role for establishing Sadhu Asom Gramya Puthibharal Santha. The Santha has attained 25 years of functioning. Accordingly Santha has celebrated silver Jubilee Year with a year long Programmed with a inaugural celebration held on 20th, 21st and 22nd March / 09 at Santha's head quarter at Nagaon and closing function of the Silver Jubilee year will be held during the month of Dec, 2010 at Sonitpur District.

5.4. Manipur Library Association (MALA)

The Manipur Library Association which was earlier formed in 1975 had a short life. The present Manipur Library Association (MALA) was established on 24th May 1987. The present MALA has been taking sole responsibility for the overall development and movement of the library in the state. The main objectives of the association are to create a congenial library atmosphere throughout the state and to encourage the library movement for achieving the goal. Since its inception in 1987, MALA has been involving in a number of activities related to the library movement and promotion in Manipur. Some of them are listed below:

- Drafting and passing of Manipur Public Libraries Bill 1988 (Bill was passed on 1stAugust 1988);
- Publishing of a Quarterly Journal entitled Librarygee Eehou (Library Movement) since April - June 1988. But this journal cannot be published regularly;
- Imparting of Library Training Course to the public mainly to the youths of the voluntary organisations;
- Holding Annual Conferences and Seminars under the sponsorship of RRRLF, Kolkata;
- Celebrating Library Day, National Library Weeks etc.;
- Organising symposia, essay competitions, debating competitions, book exhibitions, mass rallies for the cause of the library movement; 48

- Organising Library Awareness Programmes from time to time

6. LIS EDUCATION IN NORTH EAST INDIA

In North Eastern Region of India, out of eight LIS Schools offering LIS courses, Assam State is having three universities offering LIS courses viz. DLIS, Guahati University, Guwahati; Centre of Library and Information Science Studies (CLISS), Dibrugarh ; DLIS, Assam University, Silchar. North Eastern Hill University (NEHU) has been established in the year 1985 and the DLIS has been established in the same year. Manipur University, Imphal was established in the year 1980 and it started LIS course in the year 1986. Mizoram University was established in 1994 and DLIS has been started in 2002. In Tripura University and Sikkim University, Ram Thakur College and D.S. College have introduced One year Bachelor of Library and Information Science Course in 2010-11 and 2004 respectively. In Nagaland University and Tezpur University, Library and Information Science Course has not been offered.

6.1. Assam

6.1.1. Gauhati University, Guwahati

One-year BLIS was introduced by the University Library in 1966. Initially it was started as an evening course, headed by the then University Librarian Jogeswar Sarama. The University introduced MLIS since 1979. University's Department of LIS started independent functioning since 1 August 1983. The name of the department was changed as the Department of Library and Information Science on 1 January 1985 and it started functioning as a full-time day department. Both BLIS and MLIS became full-time day courses changing their nomenclature to BLIS and MLIS. In 1987, PhD programme was also introduced. From 2001-02, two year (four semester) integrated MLIS, programme has also been introduced

6.1.2. Dibrugarh University, Dibrugarh

The Centre for Library and Information Science Studies (CLISS), Dibrugarh University was established in January 2005 with a view to impart education and practical training in library and information services. A one-year BLIS programme also introduced with intake of 24 (20+4 endowment) students. In 2007, one-year (two semester) MLIS programme was introduced with intake of 20 (15+2 endowment+3 deputation) students.

6.1.3. Assam University, Silchar

Department of Library Science' was established by Assam University in 2009. But recently it has been renamed as the Department of Library and Information Science. The department has introduced MLIS course. This is a PG full-time day course of two-year consisting of four semesters with intake of 25 students. This department was initially started under School of Information Science. This department is at present under separate School of Studies named as Swami Vivekananda School of Library Sciences. The name of Dean of this school is Prof. Sumanash Dutta, Department of Economics , Assam University, Silchar since January 2013.

6.2. Manipur

Manipur University was established on 5 June 1980 at the old historic Langthabal Palace of Canchipur, Imphal, the capital city of Manipur. It was converted into a Central University on 13 October 2005. It is the only University in the state which has library science training programme. The Department of Library and Information Science was established on 2 April 1986 and started offering one-year PG programme in BLIS in response to the demand for training human resources in the field particularly for the state of Manipur. Intake was limited to 40. Subsequently, MLIS was introduced in 2004 with an intake of 6. Since academic session 2006-07, these two have been replaced by a two-year integrated MLIS programme with 20 seats with the provision for 5 seats against lateral entry at the 3rd Semester25. In addition, it has introduced PhD programme since 1987.

6.3. Meghalaya

Meghalaya was created as an autonomous state within the state of Assam on 2nd April 1970 and got fullfledged statehood on 21 January 1972. The Northeastern Hill University is the only University of the state to promote higher education in this hill region. The Department of LIS was established in 1985 with a new approach to Library and Information Science education in the country. The Department introduced for the first time in the country a two-year integrated programme leading to MLIS. There are 25 seats of which 20 seats are reserved for the students from Meghalaya. In addition, Department also has PhD programme 26, 27.

6.4. Mizoram

Mizoram is a new name given to the mountainous region earlier known as the Lushai hills, a district of Assam. In 1972 it became a Union Territory. In 1987, it got full-fledged statehood. Soon after this, Mizoram witnessed revolution in library activities. These include establishment and development of number of libraries. Due to high literacy rate and reading habits of the masses, the libraries are constantly getting recognition from all walks of life. Since its inception, Mizoram University introduced BLISc in 2002. In 2003, MLIS of one-year duration was introduced29. However, these two courses have been replaced by two-year integrated MLISc since July 2005. The Department has also introduced PhD since 2005. In 2007, M Phil was introduced which is the first of its kind in NE states.

6.5. Sikkim

DS College, Gangtok, started BLIS in 2004. Earlier this college was affiliated the North Bengal University, West

Bengal. But with the establishment of the Sikkim University, the College was automatically affiliated to Sikkim University, which is a Central University.

6.6. Tripura

Tripura was integrated with Indian Union in October 1949 and became a Union Territory in November 1956. In 1972 it was elevated to the status of a full-fledged state. A full-fledged University namely Tripura University started functioning in 1987. The University has recently started (2010-11 session) a BLIS course in Ramthakur College, one of its affiliate. Total intake is limited to 30. Minimum qualification is graduation with honours in any discipline32. LIS Education has not started yet in Arunachal Pradesh and Nagaland.

7. CONCLUSION

Considerable progress has been made in the college, university, and technical libraries of Assam in particular and North East India in general. But the condition of public libraries are in deplorable condition. Out of eight states, only three states viz., Manipur, Mizoram and Arunachal Pradesh have enacted Library Legislation in their states and other states are trying to get it enacted. The states where Library Legislation has been enacted, the provisions of the library legislation or Library Act have not been implemented properly. There is an urgent need for implementing the provisions of the legislation to give library facilities to the rural masses.

If we look into the development of academic libraries and special libraries/technical libraries, the development is satisfactory. Adequate ICT infrastructure has been developed in theses libraries with provisions of access to Internet and e-resources which have been made available under UGC-INFONET and N-LIST Programme. If we through light in LIS Education and Research in North Eastern States, it is satisfactory to note that eight universities / colleges have been offering LIS courses at different level. Research Programmes have also gaining momentum in Gauhati University, Guwahati; NEHU, Shillong, Manipur University, Imphal; Mizoram University, Aizawl and Addam Uniersity, Silchar. The Central Universities located at Arunchal Pradesh, Nagaland ,Tripura and Sikkim have not started the Integrated MLIS courses in universities. Although in Sikkim and Tripura have introduced the BLISc, courses at college level.

As far as Library Association is concerned, Assam and Manipur states are having Library Association. In Assam, Assam Library Association, Guwahati Library Association and Assam College Library Association are actively working whereas in Manipur, MALA (Manipur Library Association) has been working for the development of library professionals and public library system in Manipur. Other states might be having Library Association at local level but may not be popular at regional level.

At last it may be concluded that the North Eastern States are having more potential for LIS profession to grow and there is a better prospects for job opportunities and employment if the library legislation is enacted in each states and more jobs are created for the employment of the local LIS professionals looking for job elsewhere in rest of India. With the financial assistance and support from the INFLIBNET, the college and university libraries have developed their libraries and able to provide online resources to their library users for academic and research purposes. The future of LIS education and research, LIS profession is bright and would attract the young generations from across the disciplines to adopt library profession.

REFERENCE

1. Agarwal, S.P.(1929).Development of Library Services in India, Concept Pub. Company, New Delhi, 1929.
2. Assam Library Association (http://www.ala.net.in/p/about-us.html) (Date of Visit: 04/12/2013).Augustine, C.A. – 'Public Library System in India'

3. Barthakur. K. (1964). Sodou Assom Library Sangha (All Assam Library Association). ALA Souvenir, 8th Annual Conference, 1964.

4. Bhattacharjee, Sudip , Sinha, Manoj Kumar and Bhattacharjee, Sucheta (2014). Awareness on Cloud and Mobile Technology Based Services Among Central University Library Users of North East India : A Case Study. *Asian Journal of Multidisciplinary Studies*, 2(3), March 2014, 118-123. (ISSN : 2321-8819)

5. Das, Utpal (1997). Fifty Years Without a Library Policy, The Assam Tribune, 12th August, 1997.

6. Directorate of Library Services, Assam – Statistics on Public Libraries in Assam, 2010-11.

7. Ekbote, G.R., Public Library System, Hyderabad, Ekbote Brothers, 1987.Functions and Activities of Assam Library Association (http://www.ala.net.in/p/activities.html) (Date of Visit: 04/12/ 2013).

8. Goswami, Bhupen (1987). Library Legislation and Library Association in Assam, The Sentinel, 5th February,1987.

9. Goswami, Ram (1964). Organisation and Development of Library Services in Assam; Souvenir, 8th Annual Conference, Assam Library Association, Guwahati, 1964.

10. Granthar Itihash' – Dr. Hari Charan Das, Aranya Prakash (1998). Reflection of Rural Information in leading newspapers of Assam: A Critical Study' by Dr. Hari Charan Das, Orang Press Club, 2007.

11. Mukherjee, S.K. (1969) Development of Libraries and Library Science in India World Press, Calcutta.

12. Neog, M. Libraries and Library Movement Souvenir, 8th Conference, Assam Library Association.

13. Singh, Sanjay Kumar. 2009. LIS Schools in NER with reference to Gauhati University. *In*: Digitisation and Networking of Library and Information centres in North East India : Proceedings of the National Seminar held in Guwahati, January 9-10, 2009 (*Eds*:Narendra Lahkar and Sanjay Kumar Singh), Department of Librar and Information Science, Gauhati University, Guwahati.

18

Library Movement and Development in Odisha

Prof. Pushpanjali Jena
Professor & Head, P.G Dept. of Library and Information Science
Utkal University, Bhubaneswar-751004
Nilaranjan Barik
Asst. Librarian
KIIT University, Bhubaneswar-751024

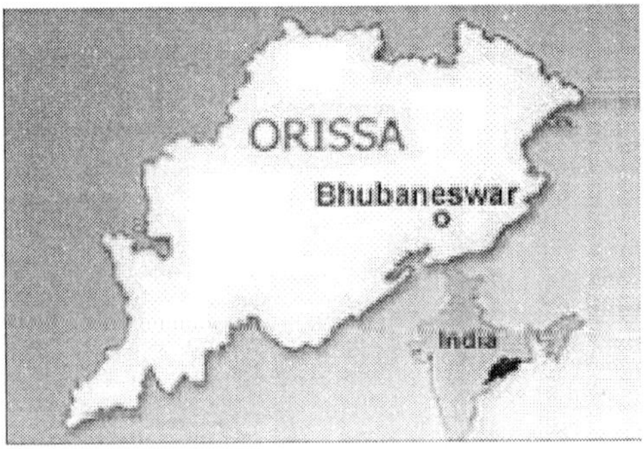

1. ODISHA : A PROFILE

Odisha (formerly known as Orissais an Indian state on the subcontinent's eastern part. It is surrounded by the Indian states of West Bengal to the north-east, Jharkhand to the north, Chhattisgarh to the west and north-west and Andhra Pradesh to the south.Odisha also has approx 480 km of coastline stretched across Bay of Bengal on its east. It is the modern name of the ancient kingdom of Kalinga, which was invaded by the Mauryan Emperor Ashoka in 261 BCE resulting in the bloody Kalinga War. The modern state of Orissa was established on 1 April 1936, as a province in British India and consisted predominantly of Oriya speakers. 1 April is therefore celebrated as Utkala Dibasa (foundation day of Odisha). The region is also known as Utkala when mentioned in India's national anthem, "Jana Gana Mana". Cuttack remained the capital of the state for over eight centuries until 13 April 1948 when Bhubaneswar was officially declared as the new state capital, a position it still holds.

Odisha is the 9th largest state by area in India, and the 11th largest by population. Oriya (officially spelled Odia) is the official and most widely spoken language, spoken by three quarters of the population.

2. LIBRARY MOVEMENT IN ODISHA

Public Library System in Odisha state has its origin from the very ancient period when Odisha was called as Udra, Kalinga or Kosala. In the pre-historic days as there were no formal libraries, the pillar inscriptions and other monuments were the open place public libraries of its kind. Later 'Bhagbata Tungi' or 'Bhagbata Matha' were recognized as a public place where 'The Bhagabata Geeta', 'Puranas' 'Manuscripts' and other reading materials were read and stored. Every evening the old men and women, house wives and children of the village were gathered in such 'Tungi' and 'Matha' to hear the Bhagabata Geeta and Purana stories. From time to time from ancient time to present day society, the public library system has changed its form and size.

In Pre-Independence era public library were setup by some liberal kings and rulers. Also some nationalistic attitude & influential people of the soil have contributed their role in forming and developing public library system in the state. Diamond Jubilee Library at Kendrapara and Baripada, 'Ramakrishna Mission Math' at Bhubaneswar were the prominent examples during that time.

The development of public library system in Odisha can be seen in to two main period i.e., 1) Pre-Independence Period and 2) Post-Independence Period. As in Pre-Independence period some liberal rulers and eminent personalities of the soil lead the public library movement in the state, similarly in Post-Independence era both the state Govt. and India Govt. enacted laws and commissions for development and growth of public library system in the state.

2.1. Pre-Independence Period (Upto 1936)

While tracing the history and development of public library system in the state, it has been unfortunately observed that the public and the masses of Odisha have never evinced interest towards library development due to lack of education, appreciation and awareness. Development of public libraries in Odisha was very much suffered, because of the fact that different regions of the state were under the administrative control of the presidency of

Bengal and Madras. Odisha as separate state had no existence till 1936. Unified rules were followed for the establishment and administration of the presidencies.

Most of the officials of the presidency were Bengalis, Telugu and Tamils who had no interest for Odias. In those periods establishment of libraries in Odisha did not get due consideration and patronage of the British administration.

2.1.1. Royal Patronage Libraries

As such most of the libraries in different areas of Odia speaking tracks were attached to palaces of the Maharajas, Ruling Chiefs, Zamindars, Feudals, heads of the religious institutions as a symbol of aristocracy and status. These libraries were never meant for dissemination of knowledge to the masses and therefore those were opened to a selected few. Thus one may observe that libraries got royal patronage not for the sake of education, social and economic benefits of the people but for the royal pride and prestige of the royal people. People working in those libraries were performing custodial function only and therefore there was no opportunity for common masses.

2.1.2. Establishment of Palace Libraries

This attitude of the royal families resulted in emergence of palace library at Paralakemundi, Baripada, Bolangir, Bamanda, Badagada, Kanika, Talcher, Dharakot, Madhupur, Athgarah Hindole, Jayapur and other places of Odisha state.

2.1.3. Liberal Education

With introduction of liberal education and local Self government by the Britishers some educated and eminent persons of Odisha state thought of starting public libraries in their respective areas by the end of 19th and beginning of 20th century. Such attempts were given rise to establishment of public libraries in different parts of the states. Diamond Jubilee Library at Kendrapara in 1897 and at Baripada in 1898 are the burning examples of this kind. Few other libraries were Sriram Chandra Pathagar Baripada, Utkal Sahitya Samaja Pathagar Cuttack, Public Library Berhampur, Sachidananda Pathagar Deogarh, Raghunath Pathagar Puri, Sobhagya Manjari Pathagar Nayagarh, Anchalika Pathagar Chikiti, Jayakrushna Bahinipati Pathagar Rambha, Raghunath Pathagar Balipadar, Public Library Khalikote, Upendra Bhanj Pathagar Tanarada, Kanakamanjari Pathagar Kabisurya Nagar, Banchhanidhi Pathagar & Sri Aurobindo Sangahalaya at Nayagarh etc. These libraries were oldest in their existence prior to formation of the state of Odisha in the year 1936.

2.2. Post Independence Period (After 1936)

With the establishment of Odisha as a separate state in 1936 and after its reorganization in 1956, the public library movement received due importance in the state.

2.2.1. Enactment of Library Law (1938)

Governor of the then Odisha in the year 1938, for the first time desired to enact library laws similar to the state of

Baroda. Sri Biswanath Das, the then Prime Minister of Odisha deputed Prof. Rama Mahapatra and Prof. Laxminaryan Sahu to study the library system at Baroda state and submit a report. But before submitting the report government collapsed in the 1939.

2.2.2. Utkal Library Association (1944)

Subsequently in the year 1944 Utkal Library Association formed as a mouth piece of library movement in the state to raise slogans, pressurize government and make the people library consciousness. But lack of political will was the main stumbling block for receiving any patronage and supports from the subsequent government for the library development. Though the politicians and social workers like Dr. H. K. Mahatab Dr. Radhanath Rath, Laxminaryan Sahu, Krupasindhu Narendra Dev, Kabi Shyam Sundar Mishra, Sradhakar Supakar, Dandapani Mishra, Balakrushna Kar, S. Mahapatra. Pabitra Mohan Pradhan, Lingaraj Mishra and others were very much associated with the association. They failed to bring any visible change in the public library scenario of the state. Perhaps the time was not favorable for development of public library system in the state.

2.2.3. Odisha Grama Panchayat Act. (1948)

It was in the year 1948 with the enactment of Odisha Grama Panchayat Act., the government of Odisha thought of establishment of Village Libraries, but there seems to be no sincere effort made by the government to establish such type of Panchyat Libraries or Village Libraries in the rural areas.

2.2.4. Establishment of Utkal University (1943)

By 27 November 1943 Utkal University was established. As a result a lot of pressure for establishment of libraries in the state was built up. With the recommendation of K. P. Sinha Committee on Public Libraries, the Government of India decided to establish a state central library in each state capital in 1959 and accordingly grants were received in

Odisha to establish State Central Library by constructing a huge building.

2.2.5. Harekrushna Mahatab State Library (1959)

The State Library of Odisha was set up during the 1st Five Year Plan of the Govt. of India in 1959 with a majestic building of around 16000sq. ft. carpet area, enshrined within a beautiful land of 3 acres in a prime location of capital city of Bhubaneswar. Later in the year 1987 it was reorganized and renamed in memory of Dr. Harekrushna Mahatab, the builder of modern Odisha as "Harekrushna Mahatab State Library". It is the apex public library in the state.

2.2.6. All India Library Conference (1975)

It was in the year 1975 the All India Library Conference was held at Bhubaneswar under the president ship of Sri D. R. Kalia the then president of Indian Library Association (ILA). It was in the conference the local participants demanded shifting of DPI office to elsewhere. Prof. D. R. Kalia met Sri Jadunath Das Mahapatra and Sri Akbar Ali Khan the then minister of Education and Governor of Odisha respectively and got assurance for shifting of the DPI's office elsewhere. This took ten years to find an alternate accommodation for the DPI's office and it was only in December 1985 due to firm decision and intervention of Sri J. B. Patnaik, Ex-Chief Minister of Odisha who was very much known for libraries development in Odisha.

2.2.7. Odisha Public Library Legislation Act. (2001)

Odisha Public Library Act-2001 was passed by the Odisha State Legislature with the assent of State Governor in the year 2002. The Act constitutes so many recommendations and law to promote fund and develop the public library system in Odisha state. The legislation advocates for the power and functions of the state public library and formation of different district libraries, municipality libraries, block level libraries etc.

3. ODISHA PUBLIC LIBRARY LEGISLATION ACT. (2001)

Odisha Public Library Act-2001 was passed by the Odisha State Legislature with the assent of State Governor and published vide Odisha Gazette Ext. No 368 and dt. 11. 03. 2002. The Act constitutes so many recommendations and law to promote fund and develop the public library system in Odisha state. The legislation advocates for the power and functions of the state public library and formation of different district libraries, municipality libraries, block level libraries etc. The Act. was constituted under twenty principles or pillars, which includes; i) Short title and commencement, ii) Definition, iii) Constitution of Odisha Public Library Council, iv) Constitution of Odisha Public Library Authority, v) Power and functions of Library Authority, vi) Power and functions of Chairperson and working Chairperson of Library Authority, vii) Constitution of Directorate, viii) Power and functions of Director, ix) State Library, x) District and City Libraries, xi) Constitution of District Library Committee, xii) Odisha Public Library Fund, xiii) Accounts and Audit, xiv) Reports and Returns, xv) Inspection of Public Libraries, xvi) Annual Report, xvii) Transfer of Management and Amalgamation of Public Libraries, xviii)Vacancies etc. not to invalidate, proceedings, xix) Power to make rules and xx) Power to remove difficulties.

The major principles of the Odisha Public Library Legislation Act. (2001), which advocates for public library system in Odisha can be outlined here;

State Library *(under clause 9)* **1)** The State Library shall be headed by the Director of Public Libraries who shall be not below the rank of a Class-I Officer. 2) The State Library shall function as a reference library and not as a lending library in respect of the books therein except in cases of inter-library loans.

District and City Libraries *(under clause 10)* **1)** The Government may, by notification establish a District Library in the headquarters of every district and, for the purpose of this section, a District Library established by Government prior to the commencement of this Act, shall be deemed to be a District Library established under this Act. 2) Where the population of any- city, town or any other urban area is two lakhs or more, the Government may, by notification establish in that area a City Library or declare an existing library, which is established by it, to be a City Library, not withstanding that a District Library already exists in the concerned district.

3. PUBLIC LIBRARY STRUCTURE AND VISIBILITY IN ODISHA

The structure of public library system in Odisha is a hierarchical structure. The state library is the head and apex of all public library system in the state. Figure-1 depicts the hierarchical structure of public library system in the state where as Figure-2 shows the statistical visibility of public libraries in the state of Odisha. Amongst the 30 districts in the state only 17 districts are having Districts Libraries, 1 City Library in Bhubaneswar capital, 5 number of Ex-District Board Libraries, 1 Sub Divisional Library, 12 numbers of Municipality/ NAC Libraries, 314 numbers of Block Level Libraries, 12 numbers of Grantee Libraries, 65 numbers of Information Centers, 3 numbers of Aided Libraries and 4 number of Memorial Libraries.

4.1. Harekrushna Mahtab State Library (HKM State Library)

The concept of Harekrushna Mahtab State Library was conceived during 1st Five Year Plan under the advice of Government of India and was completed in 1959 with a majestic building of around 16000 sq.ft. Carpet area, enshrined within a beautiful land of 3 acres in a prime location of Capital City of Bhubaneswar. In 1967, it was named as Gandhi Bhawan commemorating birth centenary of Mahatma Gandhi, the father of the nation. The State Library was located in this building, but in a corner only. In 1987 it was renovated and entire space of the four storeyed building was utilized for the functioning of two Libraries i.e. State Library for the entire State of Orissa and another Public Library for Bhubaneswar City.

In 1987, Government decided to rename the State Library and the Public Library as Harekrushna Mahtab State Library (in memory of Dr. Harekrushna Mahtab, the builder of modern Orissa) and the Bhubaneswar Public Library respectively. The former is a Reference Library and lending of books are not permitted whereas the latter is a Lending Library for the public of Bhubaneswar City. These two Libraries have managed to function over the limited space. Total readers seats available are about 350 against the present demands of 600-700 readers per day. The library has total1, 44,000 book collection, 56 maganzines 6000 and registered members

4.2. Sambalpur Public Library

The Sambalpur Public Library will not only preserve knowledge but also to act as an agency for making knowledge available to the people. As per the UNESCO guidelines, the Library will adopt scientific techniques for its maintenance and operation. The library will also hold seminars, debates and discussions from time to time to disseminate its objectives and update information for all sections of the society. Thus, the main function of the Library will be the collection and preservation of knowledge for its dissemination to all. It will act as soul-raiser and up-lifter and strengthen knowledge industry of Odisha in 21st century. Efforts will also be made to transmit reading materials through Cable with linkage for the benefit of out-station readers throughout Odisha. Thus the Library will not only perform its traditional role of a storehouse of knowledge and preserver of value but it will also be an information transmission node and reach its readers at their door steps. As automation of a library is most relevant, mechanization of the Library housekeeping operations will be made by computerization. The Library will also adopt an integrated approach to the whole system as found in most of the advanced libraries of the world. The Library will meet the new challenges with proper planning to development research activities for qualitative development besides providing library services and facilities to the readers. The Library will also launch a floating library to reach the readers at their door steps so as to promote the reading habits and become better equipped for the needs of this knowledge century.

4.3. Odisha State Museum

The museum libraries are also very instrumental in the public library movement and development of the Odisha state. Odisha State Museum comprises records of ancient cultural history, classic literature to present day society of Odisha state. The museum libraries are built in its museum surroundings to preserve, document and promote the rich cultural history of the state. The origin of Odisha State Museum can be traced back to 1932, when some historian and professors, like William Jones, Ghanashyam Das, N. C. Banarjee and Dr Harekrushna Mahatab established a museum in Revenshaw College, Cuttack. Later the museum was shifted to Bhubaneswar and given the status of State Museum by the government of Odisha. The museum consists of documents and resources in various disciplines such as Archaeology, Epigraphy, Numismatics, Armory, Mining, Geology, Natural History, Arts & Crafts, Contempory Art, Patta Painting, Anthropology and Palmleaf Manuscripts etc.

4.4. The National Museum of Natural History

The Regional Museum of Natural History, Bhubaneswar is the 3rd regional museum in the Eastern Region of the country established in the year 2004, under the ministry of Environment and Forests, Govt. of India, New Delhi. As a National Institution, the National Museum of Natural History is functioning for the entire country in respect of creating environment awareness and promoting conservation education. The museum offers an exciting opportunity for hands on and minds on activity to interact about the harmony of plants and animals and their inter relationship in nature. The museum showcase the vibrant biodiversity of Odisha, the North East and the Andaman and Nicobar Islands depicting their richness and making people aware of the natural heritage of the state.

4.5. Tribal Research Institute Museum:

The Tribal Research Institute Museum, Bhubaneswar is a tribal cultural center of Odisha state. It has preserved more than 2000 culturally significant and fascinating tribal artifacts and art objects. There are five Tribal Huts of the Santal, Juang, Gadaba, Saora and Kandha made in the traditional style to promote, preserve, document and display their rich traditional art and craft objects. The museum library has a wide collection of computerized survey data, research reports, monographs, books etc.

5. ACADEMIC AND SPECIAL LIBRARIES IN ODISHA

Prominent academic and special libraries in the state have been given below.

5.1. Central University of Orissa, Koraput Library

The Library has 13075 nos of books in its collection. Central Library is subscribing 74 nos of print Journals/ Magazines and 8000 nos of E-Journals through UGC-Infonet Digital Library Consortium Programme being provided by INFLIBNET Centre, Ahmedabad. The Library provides access of JSTOR, Oxford University Press, Taylor & Francis, Springer, Project Muse, Wiley-Blackwell Publishing, Cambridge University Press, & other E-Journals within short period of time. The Library is also subscribing 18 Newspapers (07 Oriya daily + 10 English daily, including one Employment News) for the students.

5.2. Utkal University Library

The UTKAL University Library was established in 1946. The Library of the Utkal University is named as "PARIJA LIBRARY" in the memory of late Dr. Pranakrishna Parija, the first Vice-Chancellor of the University and Scientist of international repute. There are 237695 Nos. of books in the Library. Besides 1572 Books and Theses have been received as donations. 236 nos. of journals, both Indian and foreign, have been subscribed and 3673 nos. of Manuscripts are available in the Library.

5.3. Ravenshaw University Library Kanika Library and Ravenshaw Knowledge Centre (RKC)

Kanika Library, the biggest and oldest library in the State and the central library of Ravenshaw University which is very close to the hearts of Oriya intellectuals, is all set for upgradation at par with reputed university libraries of the country. Kanika Library, located in an area of 9,000 sq ft was opened in the year 1922 by Lt Governor of Bihar and Orissa. Maharaja of Kanika Sri Rajendra Narayan Bhanjadeo had generously donated Rs. 55,000 for its construction, which stands today as a beautiful piece of architecture. In his honour the library was christened as Kanika Library, and now prompt steps are being taken to revive its lost glory. Kanika Library already boasts of more than two lakh books and journals, and grand plans are being made to update the library with more books and international journals. Moreover, digitization of old books and rare manuscripts are being done and uploaded on the web server so that they will not easily perish.

5.4. Sambalpur University Library

The library was established in the year 1970, Prof. B.Behera Central Library houses a wide range of resources, which Includes about 122523 books, about 4500 subscriptions to e-journals subscribed under the UGC-INFONET e-journal consortium programme, 13 newspapers, 14, 323 bound volume and 1988 theses besides 260 CDs.

5.5. National Institute of Technology (NIT),Rourkela Library

Biju Patnaik Central Library is the central library of the National Institute of Technology Rourkela. The Library. BPCL has started functioning since 1965. At present, the library holds about 65,000 books and 18,000 back volumes of periodicals. Apart from the online journals and standards provided by INDEST-AICTE consortium, the library has purchased license to access more than 2000 online science and technology research journals to support local research activity. The BPCL is automated with integrated library software package called Libsys – LSmart and modernized with latest Radio Frequency Identification (RFID) based automation system that facilitates self check-in, self check-out and automatic security system.

5.6. Berhampur University Library (R.P Padhy Library)

The University R.P. Padhi Library came into existence in the year 1968. Over the years it has considerably grown in size both in terms of its membership as well as in its holdings and services. At present there are 1,28, 000 books/7752 rare and antique books and 830 back volumes of Journals. The Library also subscribes to 117 current journals, 42 magazines, around 8000 e- Journals through UGC Infonet, 1797 Ph.D Thesis and 20 news papers. Its membership extends mainly to students, scholars, teachers and employees of the University.

5.7. Orissa University of Agriculture and technology Library

The Central Library of the University was formed by integrating the Libraries existing in the Constituent Colleges. The Central Library has 90,781 lakhs volumes of books, 133 foreign and Indian subscribed journals, 3374 theses and dissertations as well as Annual and Technical reports (8243) of different Universities and institutions.

5.8. Veer Surendra Sai University of Technology Library

The University Library is the largest technical library of the State. The library has started functioning in its newly constructed building since July, 1997. The total acquisition of the Library is more than 70,000 volumes including Photostat and microfilms. About 70% of the total collection is of Engineering disciplines and balance 30% is of Science,

Humanities and General reference type. The library has one microfilm reader for reading microfilms.

5.9. XIMB – Bubaneswar Library

The library has an excellent collection of books and journals on management and related subjects.Besides the print materials, the library provides access to electronic databases such as EBSCO Publishing (Business Source Complete), ProQuest, ELSEVIER, JSTOR, ISI Emerging Markets Databases, CMIE database, ACM Digital Library, IEEE Computer Society, Bloomberg Terminal and so on. While EBSCO Publishing covers nearly 6000 journals, ISI Emerging Markets provide detailed information about Indian Business and Industry. CMIE gives information about 26000 companies. Library is also having Annual Report database, which covers information on nearly 6000 companies.

5.10. Central Institute of Plastics Engineering and Technology Library

The collection includes some rare books on Plastics. The Total number of books in the libraries at all the centres is around 40,000. Journals relevant to the Curriculum of all the courses offered at CIPET are available at all libraries in order to keep the students abreast with the latest technological developments in the relevant field of study. Online with the latest advancement in the Information Technology, Digital library is also established at CIPET Centres, wherein the students can have access to the electronic books, journals and institutional repositories. Specialised services like CAS is also in the process of implementation for the benefit of the students.

5.11. National Institute of Science Education and Research - NISER Library

The NISER library is located adjacent to IOP library. Library is growing rapidly and is expected to expand into an outstanding library within the next few years. The members of NISER can also use the books, journals and other facilities of IOP's excellent library. Currently, NISER library houses around 15,000 books in the disciplines of Biology, Chemistry, Mathematics, Physics, Computer Science, Humanities and other interdisciplinary areas. Journals: Currently, NISER library houses around 2,500 journals in the disciplines of Biology, Chemistry, Mathematics, Physics, Computer Science, Humanities and other interdisciplinary areas mostly in electronic version.

6. LIBRARY ASSOCIATIONS IN ODISHA

6.1. Utkal Library Association

Utkal Library Association was formed in 1944. But it is not functioning presently. The association has a great role in the development of library movement in Odisha state. The association was constantly pressing the government of Odisha to bring out the library legislation. In 1974 Mr. A Tripathy, on behalf of the Utkal Library Association submitted a draft library bill for consideration of the government. Again after the state level conference of working libraries organized by Utkal Library Association held at Bhubaneswar, smt Umrani Patra MLA president of association submitted a draft act in Orissa legislative assembly. Inshort the ultimate mind and hands of the Orissa Library Act was Utkal Library Association.

7. LIS EDUCATION IN ODISHA.

The Odisha state has a well set up education system for Library and Information Science. Here not only teaching department of Universities, but also some colleges offer this course. But research facilities are seen only in two universities in the state.

7.1. University Teaching Departments

North Orissa University and SMIT, Berhampur University provides BLISc courses. Utkal Unviersity, Sambalpur University, SMIT, Berhampur University offer MLISc courses. Only Sambalpur University and Utkal

University offer M.Phil and Ph.D. course in Library and Information Science.

7.2. Colleges

Asian Workers Development Institute, Rourkela, Sailabala Womens' College, Cuttack and Pandit Nilakantha College of Library Science, Bhubaneswar conduct BLISc and only Pandit Nilakantha College of Library Science Bhubaneswar conducts MLISc course.

7.3. Distance facility

North Orissa University, Biju Pattanaik Computer Academy (BPCA), Bomikhal, Bhubaneswar, SMIT, Berhampur University conducts BLISc in distance mode and Sambalpur University and SMIT, Berhampur University conduct PGDLAN courses in distance mode.

8. CONCLUSION

As so many commissions and programs have been initiated by both the government of Odisha and India for development of public library system, still there are no eye catching development and growth of public library system in the state. Some districts and blocks are there with no district library and block library till date. So, there is need of more and more establishment of public libraries in the state to meet the 21st centuries' information need.

REFERENCES

1. Barua, B. P. (1994). Raja Ram Mohan Library Foundation and Library Movement in India. *39th All India Library Conference, Delhi, Indian Library Association.*
2. Chatoopadhyay, D. P. (1998). Chattopadhyay Committee on NPLIS. *CLIS Observer* 15(1-2), 12.
3. Jayaswal, P.K. (1990). Librarianship and Bureaucratic Organization: A study in the Sociology of Library profession in India, Taj Press, Delhi, page-54
4. Paikray, Braja (2011). Dasarathi Pattanaik- The Father of Library Movement in Orissa. *Orissa Review*, Sept- October, 80-81.

5. Panda, B D. (1993). *Handbook of Public Library System*. New Delhi: Anmol.

6. Rao, K. Ramakrishna (1961). Library Development in India. *The Library Quarterly*, XXXI (2) April, 135-153.

7. Wani, Zahid Ashraf (2008). Development of Public Libraries in India. Library Philosophy and Practice (e-journal), Paper 165, http://www.webpages.uidaho.edu/~ mbolin /wani.pdf

8. http://kamaldelhi.webs.com/documents/RRLF.pdf

9. http://hkmsl.gov.in/librariesorissa.htm

10. http://nmnh.nic.in/Bhubaneswar.htm

11. http://orissamuseum.nic.in/

12. http://knowledgecommission.gov.in/downloads/documents/nkc_maths.pdf

13. http://lislinks.com/group/raja-rammohun-roy-library-foundation-rrrlf

14. http://www.orissa.gov.in/law/acts/pdf_files/2001/OPLA_2001.pdf

19

Library Movement and Development in Punjab

Baldev Singh
Dy. Librarian,
Lovely Professional University, Jalandhar, Punjab

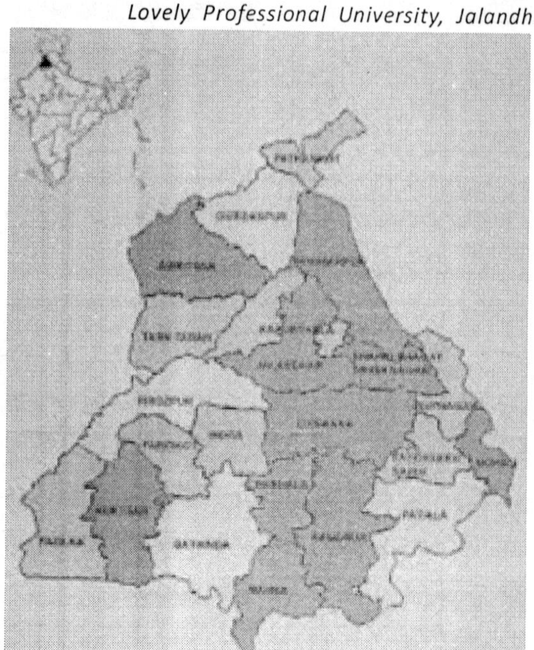

1. PUNJAB: A PROFILE

Punjab is located in North-western part of India. Four different states boundaries are attached with Punjab and

Pakistan is in its western region. Punjab's capital is Chandigarh, which is Union territory and Haryana's capital also. Land of Punjab is very fertile and so main occupation of people in the state is agriculture. Mostly people live in village and speak Punjabi which is also official language of Punjab written in Gurumukhi script. Punjab is also very famous for their industrial product too. There are various industries in the state such as textile, fertilizers, bicycle, science instruments manufacturing, sugar mills, coca-cola etc. Total population of the state is 2,77,04,236, which is distributed in twenty two districts. Punjab has very well education system at all levels from primary to higher. The literacy rate in Punjab at present is seventy five percent, in which male literacy is slightly high than the female. Punjab government always tries to increase the literacy rate in the state.

2. HISTORY OF LIBRARY MOVEMENT

In India, Punjab is the state which suffered a lot due to partition of Indo-Pak. After partition Punjab is divided in two parts-Eastern Punjab and Western Punjab. As a result of this many marvelous and famous libraries went to Western Punjab which is now the part of Pakistan. In 1884 Government of India establish Punjab Public Library which was the second largest library of the country is also now the part of Pakistan. Punjab Public library played a very significant role in the library movement in Punjab. Government of Punjab, local/religious bodies and philanthropist also gave their contribution in the development of library movement in the state. S. Dayal Singh Majithia and S Ganga Ram are famous philanthropists and called the 'Humanitarian of Punjab'. S Dayal Singh and S Ganga Ram established Public library (1896) and Commercial Public Library (1923) respectively in the state. Both these libraries have rich collection of reading materials.

In 1921 Lala Lajpat Rai's Lok Sewak Mandal established a Public library in Lahore which rehabilitated at Chandigarh after partition with its rich political collection. It was the year 1878 when first municipal library was come into exist in Ludhiana and after that many others established. Gram Panchayats gave their contribution to start village library or reading rooms in every village. Under the Gram Panchayat Act 1953, it was the duty of Gram Panchayat to establish library and reading rooms with their limited funds. Some public libraries and reading rooms also established and maintained by the local bodies in big towns and villages. Mostly all Gurudawaras (Sikh's temple) have their own library and reading rooms with religious and other rare reading materials. Development society, Singh Sabha Society, Arya Samaj society, Bhai Vir Singh and some other societies and missionaries gave their contribution for the educational development in the state through libraries.

3. STATUS OF PUBLIC LIBRARIES IN THE STATE

In the absence of library legislation Directorate of Public Instruction (DPI) is handling the public library system in Punjab with the help of assistant director of current affairs. At present Punjab have one central state library, fourteen district libraries, 107 municipal libraries, 2304 rural libraries and approximately more than 8000 reading rooms. Work of construction of district libraries in Barnala, Ludhiana, Moga, Mukatsar, Nawanshahar, Fazilika, Tarn Taran and Pathankot district almost in the last stage.

Amritsar Zila Parishad maintains three district board libraries. Pandit Moti Lal Nehru Municipal is the largest library housed in spacious building in the district established in beginning of twentieth century. It contains about 30,000 books on various subjects. There are some private libraries too as Sri Guru Ram Das Library, Swantantra Nand Library and Marwari Pustkalya available in the district. Faridkot district library (1980) is comes under the control of Punjab education department. It has a large collection of reading materials. Some rare and valuable books are also available in the library. During 1992-93, some other public libraries in the district were Baba Farid library, Lal Lajpat Rai library, Dhudike and Desh Bhagat Yaadgari library. Library movement in Fatehgarh district is not very old, district library established in 1995. Some private organization, NGOs, schools and colleges in the district organized and maintained libraries with excellent collection. The collection of Fatehgarh Sahib District library is more than 25,000 reading materials, 32 periodical, 11 daily newspapers and 12 weekly/monthly magazines. District library Gurdaspur established in 1966 comes under the control of Patiala State central library. All the libraries in the district have good collection. Dainik Prathna Sabha managed a library in Batala called Prathna Pustkalya, established in 1946 in Moti Bazar and transferred to new building in 1951 in Kila Mandi.

Hohiarpur district library (July, 1971) comes under the control of education department. People of Hoshiarpur district have very good reading and learning habits. They love to visit library. Library in this district plays an important role for the educational as well as cultural development. Along with the district some other noticeable libraries in the district are Lachhman Dass Municipal library, Doctor Harbhajan Singh library. These libraries are famous for their collection and services. Jalandhar district library came into existence in 1957. This library at present has a big collection of more than one lac reading materials including books, periodical, magazines etc. It subscribes ten daily newspapers also. Kapurthala district library (July 1971) called Guru Nanak district library. It has large collection of books on various subjects and languages with daily newspapers and weekly/monthly magazines and periodicals. Beside this other noticeable libraries are Shri Sanatan Dharam Sabha library, Gurudwara Sri Ber Sahib library also available for the book lovers in the district. Every municipality in the district maintains library and reading rooms for public use.

Ludhiana public library came into existence in 1878 by the efforts of G.E.Wakefield worked as Deputy Commissioner and Municipal Committee President of

Ludhiana. Only one private library in the district is Shri Atma Ram Jain library which known for their collection and exemplary services. District library Mansa (December, 1995) comes under the control of Education department, other well known libraries in the districts are: Sant Harchand Singh Longowal Municipal library, Mansa; Nagar council library, Budhlada and Sardar Amolak Singh Yaadgari library, Joga. In the Muktsar district there is no district library. But all the municipal council in the district viz., Muktsar, Malaut and Gidderbaha maintain library and reading rooms. Apart from these Dashmesh Public library and Mata Sunder Kaur Memorial libraries are also providing their services in the district. Nawanshahar Municipal library established in 1948, two other prominent libraries in the district are Sant Bab Sewa Singh library, Naura (November 1982); Dr. Ambedkar Municipal committee library, Banga (April 2001).

Musafir Memorial Library Patiala is known as Central State Library of Punjab, was founded in 1955 and opened for the public in 23 July 1956. The library was named in the honour of late Giani Gurmukh Singh Musafir, literary Chief Minister of Punjab. This library provides free service to the people with nominal security. Reference section of this library has got very rich collections of rare and historical books and manuscripts. Research scholar from all over India take advantages of valuable material available in this section. A picture gallery is also attached with this library. This library is known as a centre of cultural activities as an auditorium with seating capacity of 800 audiences, also the part of this library. There is also a lecture hall with more than 250 seating capacity. Nabha district library came into existence in 1946 and maintains by Punjab education department. This library has more than 50000 books of different subjects and languages. Some rare and valuable material is also available in the library which composed/written in English, Sanskrit, Persian and Gurumukhi. Rupnagar district library came into existence during 1970-71 under the control of Punjab education department. It has large collection of reading materials around fifty four thousands. One another old but small library in district is Nehru Yovak Kendra library which established in 1973. Sangrur District library was set up by Maharaja Ranbir Singh and the only public library in the district. There are many languages books available in the library as English, Urdu, Persian, Hindi, Gurumukhi and Sanskrit. 'Ajanta cave painting', 'Prince of Wales, Great Wars (First and Second), Imperial Coronation Darbar, Historical record of Imperial visit of India, Princes and Chiefs of India, Encyclopaedia Britanica etc are the names of some rare and valuable books available in this library. In December 1962 this library came under the control of Director of Public Instruction, Punjab.

3.1. NRIs contribution in Library development

Punjab's people known for their hardworking nature and strong determination. Many people from the state after hard struggle well settled in different developed countries. These NRIs come to Punjab time to time and give their contribution for the development of their native village/ state/country. They know the importance of education as well as library for human development. They donate large amount for the construction and maintenance of library in the state frequently. Some of the main contribution by these NRIs' are such as Dr. Jagtar Singh a retired librarian from USA donate twenty six lakhs to start a mobile library and also construct a library building; Joginder Singh Kalsi and Suresh Chander Kapil from Canada donated more than twelve lakh for the furnishing of library building and subscription of books for the library, a computer centre also added to the library with their contribution; Baldev Dhaliwal an engineer from USA also set up a library with computer centre in the state recently; one another NRI Surinder Binepal also construct a public library with twenty lakhs; and who can forget the contribution of Mr. Joginder Singh Ramdev who is the founder of SATKAL trust. He is a philanthropist and contributes many things for the development of library profession. He donated twenty lakhs for the development of library profession through Satinder Kaur Ramdev Memorial Trust for Advancement of Librarianship" (SATKAL).

4. LIBRARY LEGISLATION IN PUNJAB

There is no need to explain the importance of library legislation, but its importance increases more when we talk about Punjab which has rich historical and cultural values. Moreover, RRRLF provides matching grants under different schemes for the development of public library system in the country. It will be worthwhile to mention here that these grants are not being availed fully by Punjab government because there is no library legislation here. It is thinkable that such developed state like Punjab, which is very far advance in every sphere of life from the other states has no library legislation till date. But it does not mean that no efforts have been taken in this regards. Many conferences and seminars had been conducted by various associations to enact the library legislation in the state. One such association is Punjab Library Association, which had been done and is currently doing many efforts to enact the library legislation in state. This association had been making attempt since 1948, when Mr. Trehan submitted a memorandum to the government for enacting Punjab Public Library act. Local government of Punjab took action in 1964 after the initiation approach of Punjab Library Association, but these efforts not enough to passed library act. In 1968 a fresh draft of Public library bill submitted to the Central library committee, but again due to some financial constraints it could not passed. In 1989 the association revised with new enthusiasm and in November 1991, it organized a seminar to set a network of public library system supported by public up to block and village level. In 2006, a draft bill called 'Punjab Public library and Information bill' prepared for the enactment of library legislation. The major contents in this bill were composition and establishment of state library advisory board, a separate state library directorate, one state central library at apex level and work as a depository library for the state, coordination in urban, town and rural libraries, create a separate state library fund for the smooth functioning of public library system, government should have the authority to make rule and regulations under the act.

5. MAJOR ACADEMIC LIBRARIES IN THE STATE

5.1. Punjab University Library, Patiala

There is marvelous number of academic libraries in the state at school, college and university levels. All the libraries have their own importance at every level, but university library plays a significant role for the research and development purpose. Punjabi University Patiala library, is one such library has a spacious modern building with large collection around 5 lakhs volumes; subscribe more than six hundred journals (national and international) printed and online. Library kept open from 360 days of a year from 8:15 morning to 8:15 till night. A special library called Dr. Ganda Singh Punjabi reference library also added in which a rich collection of Punjabi language, culture, historical books/ manuscripts available there, which are very useful for the research scholars.

5.2. Lovely Professional University Library, Jalandhar

Lovely Professional University (LPU) grew so rapidly within a short period of time that no other university in India do so till date. LPU is largest university in India in term of number of students in a single campus. It is the result of great vision of Mr. Ashok Mittal (Chancellor of LPU) whose motive and aim to transforming India through transforming education. LPU has a high class international infrastructure and how it can behind in the library context. LPU has a largest library building in the state with nine storey full air conditioned and with all advance facilities like Wi-Fi, apple lab, automated circulation system, RFID, CCTV cameras at every corner of the library with full back up, online database, card punching system at the entrance gate of the library and many more. Central library of LPU called Dr. Vijay Gupta library, named after Ex-Vice-chancellor of the university. There are more than four thousands seating capacity in the library at a time. It opens twenty four hours in a day and closed only three days in a whole year: 2nd October, 26th January and 15th August.

5.3. Guru Nanak Dev University Library, Amritsar

Guru Nanak Dev University has been accredited five stars by National Accreditation Committee. University has won many awards in different fields in education as well as sports and other activities. Library of the University is also well know library in the state with five storey pyramid shaped building called Bhai Gurdas Library, named after great Sikh scholar. The library was founded in March, 1970. Library opens for the whole years except Republic and Independence Day. Library subscribes hundreds of national, foreign and online journals for its clienteles. It has taken the membership of Developing Library Network (DELNET), Delhi and INFormation LIBrary NETwork (INFLIBNET) UGC-Infonet e-journal consortium programme. Library has a separate air conditioned reading hall which open twenty four hours for the library users. There is a digital section in the library of GNDU which preserve the historical manuscripts and M.Phil, PhDs theses in CDs form. Library almost finished his work of microfilming the manuscripts and rare materials.

6. MAJOR SPECIAL LIBRARIES IN THE STATE

Different subject specific libraries situated in different parts of Punjab, Description some of them is as under:

6.1. Medical library

Christian Medical College Ludhiana was the first medical school for women in Asia. It was found by Dame Edith Mary Brown. Christian Medical college library is one of the oldest medical libraries in the state which was set up in 1956. Mr. Eric Massey appointed as the first librarian. The library provides various medical literatures to its user with some other recreational materials like fiction, general knowledge books, biographies, magazines and poetry books. Library provides printed as well as non-printed materials to the users. It opens fourteen hours a day. One another medical library in the state is Baba Farid University of Health Science Library, Faridkot. This library is known for its e-resource and services. The library has rich collection of online journal and databases.

6.2. Agriculture library

Only one major agriculture library of the district is Punjab Agriculture University Ludhiana's library along with departmental libraries in various universities of Punjab. This library played a significant role to bring the green-revolution in 1960s-70s in the state. Library was set up with very small collection of two hundred books only in 1959. But now it has very rich collections with five storey building full of reading materials related to agriculture and allied subjects. Name of the central library of the university is Mohinder Singh Randhawa Library with 760 seating capacity in its five reading halls. The library services available not only for the students of this university but for the others non-members and research scholar can also use its resources to a limited extent. Number of Agriculture scholar and scientist from all over India visit this frequently. As we know main occupation of the people in Punjab is agriculture, so the importance of this library automatically increased many folds.

6.3. Law Library

Rajiv Gandhi National university of Law, Patiala has a prominent place in the field of law. University has a fully Wi-Fi and air conditioned library. The library has more than twenty two thousand volumes covering general and special subjects; it subscribes eighty Law Journals and about 25 magazines. This library is an exemplary in the field of law and known for its rich collection and services.

6.4. Sports Library

Netaji Subhash Institute of Sports (NIS), Patiala is one of the famous and well known sports centre in India. Many international and national camps of different sports regularly are held by this centre. NIS has a large sports library with excellent physical education material. Most of the research scholars in sports in Indian as well as other Asian countries and who are interested in sports visit this library to satisfy their requirements. It subscribes best set of Journals from national and international publishers. The library also runs bi-monthly documentation service in eighteen sports disciplines both in English and Hindi. The library is regularly resource sharing with friendly countries.

6.5. Science and Engineering Libraries

There are many institutes in the field of science and engineering in Punjab state those helpful to bring revolution in industry sector. Ludhiana is the main hub for the textile industry in the northern region. Some of the well known libraries in the field of science and technology in the state are Punjab Technical University Library, Dr B R Ambedkar National Institute of Technology's library, Sant Longowal Institute of Engineering Technology's library, Thapar Institute of Engineering Technology's library, DAV Institute of Engineering and Technology's library etc. All these universities/institutes has a well established library with application of information and communication technology, automation, online public access catalogue, various online database and e-resources, facilities of audio-visual materials. These institutes are contributing a lot in the field of engineering in the state with such advanced library facilities. A NGO name Punjab Digital library is in the process of conservation and preservation of Punjab cultural heritage since 2003. It stored significant materials about Sikhism and Punjabi culture in digital form and provide online since August 2009 with funded help from Nanakshahi Trust. This digital library includes the manuscripts of Khalsa Diwan,

Shiromani Gurudhwara Parbhandhak Committee, Delhi Sikh Gurudwara Management Committed and manuscripts of Kurukshetra University library.

7. LIS EDUCATION IN THE STATE

There are only three Universities and One Govt. Polytechnics (For women only) in the state providing the education in the field of Library and Information Science at different level. Polytechnics College for women in Jalandhar provides two years Diploma in Library and Information Science. It includes also the six months training in some libraries with project report by the students. At the university level all the three universities have approximately same syllabus. It was 1962 when the Library and Information Science department establish in Punjabi University, Patiala. Guru Nanak Dev University, Amritsar and Punjabi University Patiala provide the Diploma in Library and Information Science, Bachelor Library and Information Science, Master in Library and Information Science and Ph. D, Whereas Lovely Professional University, Jalandhar only provides Diploma, Bachelor, AND Master degrees in Library and Information Science. There is no university in the Punjab which provides M.Phil Degree in the field of Library and Information Science. All these universities organize the conferences, seminars and workshops time to time in the field of library science for the development of library profession.

8. LIBRARY ASSOCIATIONS IN THE STATE

8.1. Punjab Library Association (PLA)

Punjab Library Association (PLA) is one of the earliest library associations formed in India. Its roots can be traced back in th pre-independnce era to the year 1916. This year Dr. A.C. Woolner, Honorary University Librarian, Punjab University, Lahore took inititive to form **PLA**. Another first of this PLA was the publication of a manual entitled Punjab Library Primer in the year 1916. This manual was published by PLA to give practical training to the new entrants to the profession which was still in its infacncy in India. Other firsts of PLA include starting of a first journal in library science in India entitled 'Modern Librarian' in 1930. Later the journal was taken over by the Indian Library Association. Dewey College of Librarianship was also started by PLA in 1937. Partition of Punjab in 1947 caused a severe blow to the rich libraries in Punjab, the library community, and the PLA.

PLA was rehabilitated at the first book festival of Shimla (then Simla) in 1948. It shifted its headquarters to Chandigarh in 1952. PLA remained very active during 1950's, 1960's, and early 1970's. It organised seminars, brought awareness among people towards libraries, organised book festival and national library week, published quality literature (books and journals), championed the cause of libraries and library staff, and conducted certificate course in library science. A court case against PLA election held in 1974 caused the second severe blow to this association. As a resut of the court case and the deteriorating political atmosphere, it remained inactive for about a decade and a half. The enterprising punjabi spirit again demonstrated its strngth when a group of librarians met in January 1989 to enroll new members for PLA.The political atmosphere in the state was very bad, and terrorism had still not faded away. Even in such conditions, as a result of the January 1989 meeting and enrollment of new members, elections were held in May 1989 and the PLA was rejuvenated. Today the rejuvenated PLA is an active association of library professionals in the state with a rich legacy for guidance, and a forward looking attitude for meeting its objectives.

9. CONCLUSION

Punjab govt. is very much concerned about library legislation in the state since independence but some obstacles come in its way every time. A central library committee was set up in 1950 by the govt. for the coordination and maintenance of library services by various department and other legal bodies. Randhawa plan could only be implemented with the efforts of this committee. Under this plan a network of libraries has been set up at village and town level. Since last two years, Public library and information are trying to implement a draft bill called 'Shabad Parkash Punjab Public Library and information services bill 2011'. It is estimated that to implement this bill will require one hundred forty six crore rupees and ten years. It can be predicted that after a few days, strong library legislation will be in the Punjab state and it is very compulsory for give the right direction to the youth of Punjab, who are addicted towards drugs. Drug abuse is a very serious problem and is spreading at very rapid rate in Punjab. More than seventy percent of total male population use intoxicant or other advance drugs in addition to alcohol. Most of these people are either illiterate or have very low education qualification. To remove this and make them literate and productive for the society their leisure time must be utilize in some creative and fruitful activities such as reading and learning books from the library. It will helpful to make informative and good citizen for the society.

REFERENCES

1. Census of India (2011). Retrieved from *http://www.census2011.co.in/census/state/punjab.html*
2. Christian Medical college library, Ludhiana. Retrieved from *http://en.wikipedia.org/wiki/ Christian_Medical_College_Ludhiana*
3. David, Donald G, Jr (1989). Status of library history in India: a report of an Informal survey and a selective bibliographic essay. Journal of Library and Information Science, 14(2), pp.98-114.
4. Department of Revenue, rehabilitation and Disaster Management (2008). Retrieved from *http://punjabrevenue.nic.in/gaz ptl18.htm*
5.
6. Dinesh Kumar, Arjun and Bose, Sharmila (2010). *Libraries in Punjab: a history of public library.* Retrieved from *http:www.apnaorg.com/research-papers/arjun-1/*

7. Guru Nanak Dev University Library, Amritsar. Retrieved from *http:// www.library.gndu.ac.in/*
8. Jatinder Preet (2013, February 23). *NRIs open libraries in Punjab.* The Sunday Guardian. Retrieved from *http://www.sunday-guardian.com/news/nris-open-libraries-in-punjab*
9. Kumbar, B.D (2005). *Growth and development of Public library system in India.* Retrieved Nov. 19, 2005 from *http://www.nigd.org/libraries/mumbai/reports/article-4.pdf*
10. Lovely Professional University Library, Jalandhar. Retrieved from *http://www.lpu.in /the_lpu_advantage/world_class_infrastructure.php#library*
11. Misraa, Jogesh (1979). *History of libraries and librarianship in modern India since 1850.* Delhi: Atma Ram.
12. Punjab Agriculture University Library, Ludhiana. Retrieved from *http://web.pau.edu/ msrlibrary/*
13. Punjabi University Library, Patiala. Retrieved from *http://punjabuniversity.ac.in/ pbiuniweb/librarymain.html*
14. Rajiv Ghandhi National University of Law Library, Patiala. Retrieved from *http://rgnul.ac.in/lib_intro.htm*
15. Sharma, S.K (1996). *Public library in India: trends and status.* P.K.Mahapatra (Ed.), Public libraries in developing countries (pp.121-127). New Delhi: Vikash Publishing House.

20

Library Movement and Development of Rajasthan

Dheeraj Pratap Kanwar
Asst. Librarian
Baldev Nagar,Masuriya Jodhpur
Rajastan

1. RAJASTHAN: A PROFILE

Rajasthan, the largest state of India is located in the north-western part of the subcontinent. It is bounded to the north and north-east by the states of Punjab and Haryana, to the east and south-east by the states of Uttar Pradesh and Madhya Pradesh, to the south-west by the state of Gujarat, and to the west and north-west by Pakistan. The southern part of the state is about 225km from the Gulf of Kutch and about 400 km from the Arabian Sea. Jaipur is the capital city and lies in the east-central part of the state.

The history of Rajasthan is about 5000 years old and the mythological origin of this gigantic land is related to the famous myth of Ram, the seventh incarnation of Lord Vishnu. In the ancient period, Rajasthan was a part of different dynasties including the Mauryan Empire . The first batch of Aryans who came to India settled in the region of Dundhmer and the first inhabitants of this area were the Bhils and the Minas. The earliest Rajput dynasty that emerged around 700 AD was the Gurjara and Partiharas and since then Rajasthan was known as Rajputana (the land of the Rajputs). Soon, the Rajput clan gained supremacy and the Rajputs were divided into 36 royal clans and 21 dynasties. The armed conflicts and the struggle for supremacy among the Parmars, Chalukyas, and Chauhans resulted in a lot of bloodshed.

In the medieval era, the major regions of the state such as Nagaur, Ajmer and Ranthambhore became a part of the Mughal empire, which was headed by Akbar. The most famous Rajput warriors of this era were Rana Uday Singh, his son Rana Pratap, Bhappa Rawal, Rana Kumbha and Prithviraj Chauhan. With the end of the Mughal regime in 1707, the Marathas gained supremacy and captured Ajmer in 1775. The Maratha ascendancy ended in the late 17th century with the arrival of British. The present state of Rajasthan was formed in 1956.

2. LIBRARY MOVEMENT IN RAJASTHAN

Libraries were established in Rajasthan as early as 14th. Century and maintained in the form of Pothi-Khanas consisting rich collections of manuscripts on different disciplines. (Trikha;2001;57-59) Rana Kumbha's Saraswati Bhandar Library was established in 1448. Raja Man Singh established library, Pothi-Khana in 1592 by keeping rare and important manuscripts. Pioneer Public Libraries were established in Bharatpur in 1907, Sikar in 1908, Kota in 1910, Fatehpur in 1910, and Jodhpur in 1915. There are 5 Divisional libraries, 24 District Libraries, and 8 Tehsil Libraries with 600 Book Deposit Centers on 15 August 1956. Mobile van was also provided to Division Libraries to supervise library services in the state.

3. THE RAJASTHAN PUBLIC LIBRARIES ACT, 2006

Rajastan public library Act was passed in 2006. Before 2006 Some abortive attempts were happened in the state. Attempts for Library Legislation in the State have been made since 1965. The proposed Library Bill presented to the State Government was discussed threadbare by the then office bearers of the Rajasthan Library Association: Dr. Satish Chandra (President), Shri. N.N. Gidwani, Shri C.D. Sharma and Shri Mohan Rao with the concerned authorities in the State Education and Law Departments. Since then a little headway has been made in this regard. Financial constraints due to recurring droughts and other natural calamities are often posed as easy excuses by the State bureaucracy. The Ministers and Legislators mostly remain preoccupied with other priorities. Hardly any one of them can think for the development of Public Libraries.

In 1969 RLA initiated a fresh attempt for library legislation in the State. At the Executive Committee Meeting of RLA held on 10 March 1969 under the Chairmanship of the then President Dr. Satish Chandra, it was resolved to prepare a memorandum and submit the same to the Chief Minister. Accordingly, the Secretary of the Association Mr. Mohan Rao prepared a memorandum. A delegation of RLA met Mr. Mohanlal Sukhada, the then Chief Minister of Rajasthan at his residence in April 1969 and presented the memorandum and pleaded for his immediate attention. The delegation included Messers Satish Chandra (President), N.N. Gidwani, Mohan Rao (Executive Secretary), Giridharilal Sharma (Treasurer), and Himmatlal Sandhya.

The Act envisages promotion and development of

public libraries in the State. According to this Act, a Council to be called the Rajasthan State Library Council is constituted. The Council shall consist of the following members, namely:-Ex-Officio members (The Minister In-charge of libraries Chairperson, The Secretary to the Government responsible for the libraries -Vice-Chairperson, The Secretary to the Government Finance Department or his nominee not below the rank of Deputy Secretary, The Director, Collage Education, The Director, Elementary Education, The Director, Secondary Education, The Director, Panchayati Raj, The Director, Local Self Government, The Chairman, Board of Secondary Education, Rajasthan, The Secretary Rajasthan State Text Book Board, The Librarian, State Central Library, The Director and Public Libraries-Member Secretary. There are some Nominated members also in the council. They are Three members nominated by the Chairperson form amongst person having specialized knowledge and interest in matters relating to library service, among whom one should be a woman, One Librarian of District Library to nominate by the State Government, Two eminent scholars nominated by the Chairperson and Two members of the Rajasthan Legislative Assembly to be nominated by the Speaker of the Rajasthan Legislative.The Headquarters of the council shall be at Jaipur There will be a State Central Library for a division, District Library for a district Panchayat Samiti Library for a Panchayat Samiti and such other village libraries as it may think necessary. Every library establishment under sub-section shall be managed, organized and developed by the Director.

The Director shall prepare every year the annual budget proposal for Directorate of public Libraries of plan and non-plan expenditure and submit it to the State Government. There shall be a Fund to be called the State Library development Fund for modernization and development of public libraries in the State. The State Library Development Fund shall consist of- (a) Grant received form the State Government other than the grant specified in subsection (2) of 15;(b) Any contribution or special grants from the Central Government for modernization and development of public libraries;(c)All money received by way of contributions or gifts made by

4. ACADEMIC LIBRARIES IN RAJASTHAN.

The major academic libraries in the state are university libraries. The major university libraries have been given below.

4.1. Rajasthan University Library

The University of Rajputana was established by an act of legislature on 8 January 1947. The Library was created later on, after the availability of a small annex in the same compound in 1949. A budget provision of 20,000 Rs. was made for the Library and about 1,500 books were immediately acquired. The first book, Preface to Library Science by Dr. S. R. Ranganathan, was added on 11 May 1950.

The Library which was initiated in the corner of the office of the First Vice-Chancellor Dr. G. S. Mahajani in Kesargarh (a fort-like structure on Jawaharlal Nehru Marg, which now houses the offices of the popular Hindi newspaper Rajasthan Patrika). The Library moved to the completed portion of the new building in October 1958. Jawaharlal Nehru formally inaugurated the new building in October 1959.

4.2. Central University of Rajasthan - Library

University has a central library in its temporary campus Malviya National Institute of Technology, Jaipur on 16th February 2009. The University Library was relocated at the campus of the University at Sh. R. K. Patni Govt. P. G. College, Kishangah, Distt.-Ajmer and is presently functional at the permanent campus of the University at BandarSindri. Central Library plays a vital role for an institution for creation of new knowledge through acquisition, organization and dissemination of knowledge resources and providing for value added services. It's an essential component of the institute's outstanding research and education mission. It is a most lively place on the campus providing a safe, comfortable and friendly environment that enables learning and advancement of knowledge, and promotes discovery and scholarship.

4.3. Mohanlal Sukhadia University (erstwhile Udaipur University) Library

The University Library System has a Central position in the academic activities of the University. It is considered to be a heart of the University which should be injected with fresh blood continuously.The University Central Library was constituted in 1962 and the Extension Library of the University of Rajasthan working in the Udaipur was merged into it in 1966. The College Libraries were created gradually with the establishment of the Colleges. In 1987 the Rajasthan Agricultural University was spilt up from the University and all the College Libraries of Agricultural wing became the part of the Rajasthan Agricultural University. The Sukhadia University Library System consists of the following Libraries :

1. University Central Library
2. College of Science Library
3. College of Social Science & Humanities Library
4. College of Commerce & Management Library
5. College of Law Library, and
6. Faculty of Management Studies Library.

4.4. University of Kota – Library

The Central Library of the university is having the existing stock of nearly 6160 books worth Rs. 31.10 lacs (Rupees thirty one lac and ten thousand). These includes the reference books, text books, journals, competition books and books pertaining to the syllabus of the courses running by the university in Law, Commerce & Management, Social Sciences (Geography, History, Political Science, Sociology, M.S.W., etc.), Physics, Chemistry, Computer Science, Life Science, Wild Life Science, Heritage, Museology & Tourism Management, etc. disciplines and also for competitive examination aspirants. Very recently, the university has invited the tenders, vide No. UOK/Acad./Admin./2011-12/ 18883 dated 13.03.2012 (Annexure-03), for the purchase of the books of Rs. 23 lacs (Rupees twenty three lacs) for Law, Sciences, Social Sciences (Geography, History, Political Science, Sociology, M.S.W., etc.), Commerce & Management, Physical Education, Computer Science, Life Science, Wildlife Science, Heritage, Museology & Tourism Management, etc. subjects.

5. SPECIAL LIBRARIES IN RAJASTHAN

The majority of the special libraries in the state are academic special libraries. They are – Health sicnece university library – Jaipur, AIMS library Jodhpur, Rajasthan Univesity of veterinary and animal husbandry, Bikaner.

6. LIBRARY ASSOCIATION IN RAJASTHAN

6.1. Rajasthan Library Association

Rajasthan Library Association was set up in 1962. Its headquarters is at Jaipur. It was started under the guidance of Prof. Bashiruddin. It established braches in all divisions and district head quarters. The association drafted a bill in 1965 on libraries in the state.

7. LIS EDUCATION IN RAJASTHAN

Bachelor degree course and Master degree course in Library science are being offered in different universities in Rajasthan. They are Mohanlal Sukhadia University (MLSU) , Udaipur, Singhania University, University of Rajasthan, NIMS UNIVERSITY and Shobha Nagar. In addition to this university departments, B.N.P.G. College, Udaipur – offers

BLISc regular course and Jain Vishva Bharati University offers BLISc in distance mode.

REFERENCES

1. Dhyani, Pushpa, Public Libraries in Rajasthan. (in Vashisth, C Pand other ed. New horizons in library and information science, Madras: TR Pubs, 1999.
2. Mohammed Taher (2001). *Libraries in India's national developmental perspective: a saga of fifty years since independence*: New Delhi: Concept publishing.
3. Mohan Rao. Library service in Rajasthan. (in Ranganathan, SR and Neelameghan, A Public Library System, etc. Banglore: SR Endow for lib Sc, 1972. Chap Z R)
4. Sharma, CD. Public Libraries in Rajasthan. (All India Library Conference (30) (Jodhpur) (1990). Souvenir, p. 45-50).
5. Sharma, Sandhya, Rajasthan me granthalaya adhiniyam: Ek Sarvekshan. (Granthalaya Vijgyan v 13, n 1 & 2 Jan-Dec 1982).
6. . *www.uniraj.ac.in*
7. . *www.**rtu**.ac.in*
8. . *www.**jnvu**.edu.in*
9. . *www.**mgsu**bikaner.ac.in*
10. . www.ruhsraj.in

21

Library Movement and Development in Sikkim

Ashif KM
Librarian
W.M.O College, Muttil, Wayanad
Kerala

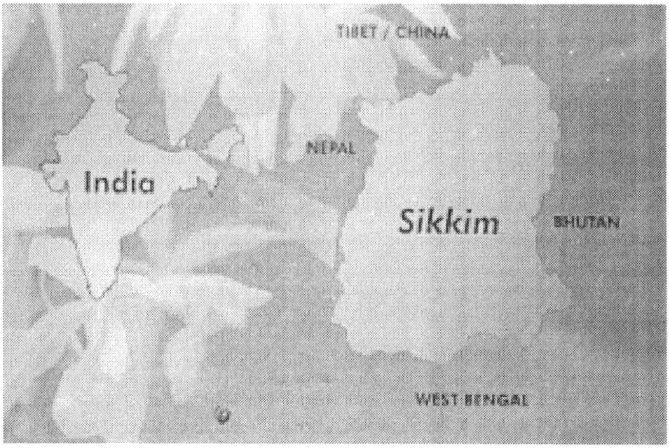

1. SIKKIM : A PROFILE

Sikkim is a landlocked Indian state located in the Himalayan mountains. The state is bordered by Nepal to the west, China's Tibet Autonomous Region to the north and east, and Bhutan to the east. The Indian state of West Bengal lies to the south. With 610,577 inhabitants as of the 2011 census, Sikkim is the least populous state in India and the second-smallest state after Goa in total area, covering approximately 7,096 km^2 (2,740 sq mi). Sikkim is nonetheless geographically diverse due to its location in the Himalayas; the climate ranges from subtropical to high alpine, and Kangchenjunga, the world's third-highest peak, is located on Sikkim's border with Nepal. Sikkim is a popular tourist destination, owing to its culture, scenery and biodiversity. It also has the only open land border between India and China. Sikkim's capital and largest city is Gangtok.

According to legend, the Buddhist guru Padmasambhava visited Sikkim in the 8th century AD, introduced Buddhism and foretold the era of the Sikkimese monarchy.Sikkim's Namgyal dynasty was established in 1642. Over the next 150 years, the kingdom witnessed frequent raids and territorial losses to Nepalese invaders. In the 19th century, it allied itself with British India, eventually becoming a British protectorate.In 1975, a referendum abolished the Sikkimese monarchy, and the territory was merged with India. Sikkim has 11 official languages: Nepali (which is its lingua franca), Sikkimese, Lepcha, Tamang, Limbu, Newari, Rai, Gurung, Magar, Sunwar and English. English is taught in schools and used in government documents. The predominant religions are Hinduism and Vajrayana Buddhism. Sikkim's economy is largely dependent on agriculture and tourism, and as of 2012 the state has the third-smallest GDP among Indian states.

2. LIBRARY MOVEMENT IN SIKKIM

Sikkim do not have a long history of libraries. The library facilities in the Sikkim State was initially set up during the reign of Maharaja of Sikkim probably in the 60s. However, it became functional quite actively in the society only after the merger of the State in the Indian Union. A community center library was set up with a full fledged custodianship of Mrs R.D Ralchung as Curator some times in 1964 and building of collections in the library began steadily. The library facilities in the State are much behind than others.

Persistent effort is, nevertheless being made to expand and popularize this important facility in the District and Sub-Divisions with the sole objective of promoting the public reading habit and creation of well informed civil societies. Some of the developments under this sector since 1977-78 onwards that deserve mention are as follows;

1977-78 : District libraries at Namchi in South, Galshing in West and mangan in North districts were established with one each librarian and a peon.

1994-95 : Sub-Divisional Libraries at Chungthang, North, Pakyong, East, Ravongla in South and Soreng in West District were set up in respective Sub-Divisional Administrative Complexes.

2001-02 : Then Community Centre Library at Gangtok was upgraded to State Central Library and Special schemes from ministry of Culture, Government of India through its Nodal Agency, Raja Rammohan Roy Library Foundation (RRRLF), Kolkata were initially introduced in the State. In order to strengthen the library movement as well as to monitor the schemes of the Foundation, a State Library Committee was formed in the same year.

2002-03 : A separate Childern Library was set up in the State Central Library.

2003-04 : Another sub-Divisional library at Rongli, East District was set up.

Total Public Libraries under Cultural Affairs & Heritage Department

1. State central Library : 1 Nos
2. District Library : 3 Nos.
3. Sub-Divisional Library : 5 Nos.
4. Separate Children Library : 1 Nos

3. ACADEMIC LIBRARIES IN SIKKIM

3.1. Sikkim Manipal Institute of Technology (SMIT) Library

The SMIT Central Library serves as a model of an

evolving and dynamic facility in technical learning since 1997. The Library's collection comprises hybrid resources (Print & Electronic) in the field of science and technology, engineering & management. The Library also has a separate Internet section consisting of a number of networked terminals for providing recent and most comprehensive access to e-journals and other e-reference resources to the faculty, students and staff under Intranet and Internet environment. The Central library has automated all its routine activities through library software called "ESYLIB" and also extended the scope of various services like CD-ROM database search, & EPAC.

Currently Central library has 50,000 volumes, including textbooks, reference books, 2,000 CD ROM, and non book materials 7947 project reports and other reports, 100 National & 80 International Journals & 3000 periodical back volumes. SMIT Central Library is an active member of DELNET & various e-Resources such as: IEEE, ASME, ASCE, Springer Link, Elsevier Science Direct, J-Gate (both Engineering & Management), EBSCO, ASTM Digital Library, and McGraw Hill. The Library is also having Internet, Reprographic and book Bank facilities.

3.2. Sikkim University Library

The Central Library was started in February 2008 with a floor area of about 1000 sq. ft. Presently it occupies more than 9000 sq. ft. Library is the heart of a university and it serves as an information and knowledge resource centre to support all academic activities of a university. Though the Library is still in its infancy stage it can be compared with any modern university library of the country so far as infrastructure facilities and adoption of new technology are concerned. The concept of modern library implies the adoption of new technologies to multiply and simplify the services to the utmost satisfaction of the users which the Library has successfully achieved. It provides web-enabled accessibility to its resources within the campus as well as outside. It has introduced self-check-out and check-in system of circulation of books, thereby making users independent regarding issue and return of books. For security purpose, it has installed CCTV covering every floor of the Library. It has more than 37000 books with more than 200 journals in addition to the e-resources available under UGC consortium. The Library also has a small collection of 1178 Braille books and subscribes to about 10 popular news magazines and 21 daily newspapers.

3.3. Harkamaya College of Education (Gangtok)

Harkamaya college library was setup along with the establishment of college in 2003. Library is functioning in college building from 9 am to 5 pm. The college library is closing in all state and national holiday. This library designed to support the information needs of college faculty, students and also researchers those who education field. Harkamaya college library is an eminent library in education field in Sikkim. Besides of education this college library has computer science books, History English, Geography, Sociology, Library and Information Science, Political Science and other discipline. The Library Collection consists of 9541 Books and more than 30 Periodicals covering all aspects. The library has a one reading room for students and one for faculty and research scholar. Harkamaya College of Education library has at present 10 computers and using SOUL 2.0 software for library automation and DDC 21st for classification.

3.4. Sikkim Manipal Instutute of Medical Sciences (SMIMS):

Sikkim Manipal Institute of Medical Sciences (SMIMS), located at Tadong, is a constituent college of the Sikkim Manipal University (SMU). SMIMS offers MBBS, B.Sc. Nursing and Physiotherapy courses, besides M.Sc Programs in Microbiology, Biochemistry, Physiology and Anatomy. The Central Referral Hospital and STNM Hospital in Gangtok offer clinical training opportunities to students. SMIMS library has 11500 books and approx 105 journals and 200 e-journals. Library provides 36 computers with 512mbps speed broadband connection for library users and 6 newspapers. The library opens from 9 am to 8pm in all working. During holydays and Sundays it works from 9am to 2pm and close only national holyday.

3.5. Layola College Library

Layola college is one of the reputed college in sikkim. It has a sound library with collection of 1,09,000. it is kept open 8.00 am to 8.00 pm.It is a fully automated library with autolib software. The library subscribes 160 journals. Approximate 500-600 ysers visit the library regularly.

3.6. Damber Singh College Library

The College has well equipped digital library wherein more than 4000 reference and recommended books are available. This is the one and only college which offers LIS course in the state.

4. SPECIAL LIBRARIES IN SIKKIM

4.1. The Namgyal Institute of Tibetology's libraries

The Tibetan library is situated on the first floor of the institute's main building. The NIT's library holds one of the largest collections of Tibetan works in the world outside Tibet. There are over 60,000 titles consisting of Tibetan translations of canonical and non-canonical works from their original Sanskrit or Pali, as well as tantric texts belonging to the four sects of Tibetan Buddhism. Among others, the library also has the collected works of Padma Lingpa, Mipham Rinpoche and the Great Vth Dalai Lama, and the hagiography of Guru Padmasambhava. To the right of the main building is the general library.

This library holds a good collection of books in different languages covering Tibet, Sikkim, Nepal, Bhutan and Ladakh, including a number of collections on religion

[Buddhism], History and Philosophy. In addition, journals and periodicals from leading institutions and organizations enrich the collection. Since it is a reference library, the institute does not lend or issue books for home use. However, readers and visitors can consult them in the library's reading room. The library allows photocopying although some restrictions apply to the rare books collection.

5. LIS EDUCATION IN SIKKIM

5.1. Damber Singh College

The College offering B.A Pass/Hons. and Bachelor Degree in Library and Information Science (BLISc.) is situated in the picturesque place of mountains at Samdur, Tadong, Gangtok, the capital of Sikkim. The college is connected by National Highway 31A. The nearest railway Station New Jalpaiguri and nearer Airport, Bagdogra are 117 km and 120 km respectively away from the college.

Since inception, the college has been serving as an alternative institution of higher learning in the capital city Gangtok. In 2004, the college was shifted to a more scenic place and in a spacious building at Samdur, Tadong in response to the need for both vertical and horizontal expansion. It provides three year honours degree course in Humanities and One year Bachelors Degree course in Library & Information Sciences besides B.Sc (IT), and M.A in many subjects.

6. CONCLUSION

The library movement and development in Sikkim state has to achieve many more things. There is no any active library and information association in the state. That is why the library legislation in the state is not yet fulfilled. The isolated endeavors are to be united for the development of LIS in the state.

REFERENCE

1. Seth, Ved (2001). Sikkim. *In.* Library and Information Services in Indian States and Union Territories edited by P.B.Mangla, *et.al.* New Delhi: Shipra.
2. Neeraj Kumar (2013) A study of ICR application in the libraries at the retrial levels in VOLUME NO. 3 (2013), ISSUE NO. 10 (OCTOBER)International Journal of Research in Computer Application and Management.
3. Kumar, PSG (2009). Library Movement and Library Development in Gujarat, Dadra and Nagar Haveli and Daman and Diu. New Delhi, B.R Oublishing Coroporation.
4. Venkatapaiah (2000) Indian Library Legislation : State Library bills and acts. Delhi, Daya Publishing House.
5. Mohammed Taher (2001). Libraries in India's national developmental perspective: a saga of fifty years since independence: New Delhi: Concept publishing.
6. http://www.sikkim-culture.gov.in/Libraries
7. *shodhganga.inflibnet.ac.in/bitstream/10603/1204/.../09_chapter*
8. http://www.nmlindia.nic.in

22

Library Movement and Development in Tamil Nadu

Kalyani KS
Librarian and Information Asst., Anna Centenary Library, Chennai (India)
Ashok Kumar A
Librarian and Information Asst. Anna Centenary Library, Chennai (India)

1. TAMIL NADU : A PROFILE

Tamil Nadu is one of the 29 states of India. Its capital is Chennai (formerly known as Madras), the largest city. Tamil Nadu lies in the southernmost part of the Indian Peninsula and is bordered by the union territory of Puducherry and the states of Kerala, Karnataka, and Andhra Pradesh. It is bounded by the Eastern Ghats on the north, by the Nilgiri, the Anamalai Hills, and Kerala on the west, by the Bay of Bengal in the east, by the Gulf of Mannar and the Palk Strait on the southeast, and by the Indian Ocean on the south. It also shares maritime border with the country of Sri Lanka.

Tamil Nadu is the eleventh largest state in India by area and the sixth most populous state in India. The state was ranked sixth among states in India according to the Human Development Index in 2011. It was the second largest state economy in India in 2012. The state has the highest number (10.56 per cent) of business enterprises and stands second in total employment (9.97 per cent) in India, compared to the population share of about 6 per cent. In the 2013 Raghuram Rajan panel report, Tamil Nadu was ranked as the third most developed state in India based on a "Multidimensional Development Index". The region has been the home of the Tamil people since at least 1500 BC. Its official language is Tamil, which holds a status of being a classical language. Tamil has been in use in inscriptions and literature for over 2500 years. Tamil Nadu is home to many natural resources, classical arts, classical music, classical literature, Hindu temples of Dravidian architecture, hill stations, beach resorts, multi-religious pilgrimage sites, and eight UNESCO World Heritage Sites.

2. LIBRARY MOVEMENT IN THE STATE: A HISTORY

According to Dr.S.R.Ranganathan, "Public Library system means an integrated nation-wide network of public libraries giving free library and information services to one and all of the citizens – literate or illiterate, rich or poor, rural or urban". Tamil Nadu can be proudly quoted as the pioneer of library movement in the country. Dr.S.R.Ranganathan, who contributed his life to the field of Library Science was the mastermind personality for the glorious history of public library movement in Tamil Nadu. In the words of Mr. Gardener, "Madras was one of the most advanced states in India in the field of library science". It was the first state to enact the legislation for public libraries and also formed the nation's first library association which paved the pathway and strong foundation for LIS education in India. The state has extended its splendid support for the widespread expansion of public libraries and has always been in a step forward to reach the public by the introduction of innovative new library services. The concept of "Library on Wheels" can be cited as the perfect example. The Saraswati Mahal Library at Thanjavur and the Connemara Public Library at Chennai stand as the hallmark of libraries in the state. It is the first state in India, which enacted the "Right to Information" for the common public.

A Good Beginning.

In the budget for 1920-21, the first foundation was laid by the Hon'ble Mr.K.Venkatattappayya's resolution in the local legislative council. The concern for public libraries was realized and to establish them a sum of Rs. 20,000 was allocated in the budget. It was on 12th July, 1926, Dr.S.R.R. who was acting as librarian of Madras University gave a detailed lecture about the history of libraries and shared his valuable experience about his foreign visit to libraries. The spark for public libraries act was first quoted only in this lecture, when he said, that a special library cess was charged by the Municipalities to meet the recurring expenditure at Britain. On 23rd December, 1927, he read a paper on 'Rural Library Service', in which he again stressed the levy of library cess and compulsory library legislation by each provincial government.

S R. Ranganathan – A Man of Mission and Vision

Dr. S. R. Ranganathan was a visionary who realized

the importance of library legislation for the promotion & development of library movement in India. He was the first person in India who ever thought about the need for library legislation in 1925. He drafted a 'Model Library Act' and presented at the First All Asia Educational Conference, which was held in Banaras in 1930. This 'Model Library Act' was published by the Madras Library Association in 1936. He also prepared a Model Union Library Bill in 1948 & redrafted it in 1957. India got the first Public Library Act through the ceaseless efforts of Dr. S. R. Ranganathan. Madras Public Library Act was passed by the Madras Legislature in 1948. SRR would be ever remembered by India for making people library-conscious.

3. MADRAS LIBRARIES ACT

The Madras Public Libraries Act, subsequently renamed as the Tamil Nadu Public Libraries Act, was enacted in Madras State, India, in 1948. The act was the first of its kind to be enacted in India after independence. The Connemara Public Library became the first library to come under the purview of this act, as a "State central library". Subsequently, nine district libraries were added during the Five year plan from 1951.The act was enacted based on research and activity by S. R. Ranganathan and the Madras Library Association. Other states have enacted public library acts modelled on the Madras Public Libraries Act.

Background

On 22nd February, 1948, the legislation for bringing about a co-ordinated system of libraries in the province with a central and local committee to assist in the work was introduced in the Madras Legislative Assembly by the Education Minister, Mr. T.S.Avinashilingam Chettiar. The next day the bill was under discussion in the Madras Legislative Assembly by the members such as Mr. A. Kameswara Rao who supported the motion for referring the bill, Mr. V. I. Muniswami Pillai, Mr.M.S.A. Majid, Mr. N.S. Varadachari, Mr. D. V. Ramaswami, Mr. M. Bapineedu, Mr. K. Koti Reddi, Mr.

Tenneti Viswanathan, Mr. Kanniappan, Mrs. Lakshmi Ammal and others. It was decided to levy of the library cess at quarter anna in every rupee of the property tax collected by the Corporation of Madras, Municipal Councils and Panchayat Boards. The motion referring the bill was finally accepted. On 27.11.1948, the Madras Public Libraries Bill, 1948 was passed by the Legislative Assembly. The Bill sought to provide for the establishment of public libraries in the Province and for the organization of a comprehensive rural and urban library service. Thus Tamilnadu became the first state to pass Library legislation in India.

Provisions

The Madras Public Libraries Act provides for overall governance by a State Library Committee, presided over by the incumbent Education Minister for the State. The committee comprises members from various walks of life, including representatives from universities and from the State Library Association, as well as a Secretary whose primary function is as assistant to the Director of Public Libraries (DPL). The latter role is assumed by the incumbent Director of Public Instruction.

Revenue is obtained via a cess, a tax which is collected by local administrative bodies such as the Nagar Palikas and Panchayats. Those bodies remit the tax to their Local Library Association (LLA), which operates as an umbrella organisation at the mid-tier District administrative level. The rate of taxation is fixed in law but the LLA can request a higher rate if the State government agrees to it. The State government matches the funds generated by the cess. The LLA determines the conditions of entry to the libraries under its control.

Cities with a population in excess of 50,000 must have a central library of their own and provisions exist for expansion to include branch libraries and other means of devolved access if demand should require such. In addition to libraries that are administered by the LLA, the Act provides for a register of other libraries. This is maintained by the DPL, who has the power to issue grants from State resources to those institutions listed. With the exception of the city of Madras, these grants cannot be less than the cess collected elsewhere. Further resources are obtained by a modification caused by the Act. The Press and Registration of Books Act of 1857 is amended such that a situation somewhat akin to copyright libraries exists. All publishers within the State are required to provide five copies of their output to the State government, which in turn passes on four of those copies to the State Central Library. Until various re organisations of States, the Act applied to parts of what are now Andhra Pradesh and Kerala.

After effects

Several perceived failings in the Madras Public Libraries Act have been addressed in subsequent Acts elsewhere. For example, the Hyderabad legislation, which later became the Andhra Pradesh Public Libraries Act, states that there should be a completely separate department of government to administer the libraries; that the head of the State Library Committee (in this case called the State Library Council) should be elected rather than defaulting to the portfolio of the current Education Minister; and that all local administrative areas should have their own library authority. Furthermore, the amount and extent of the cess collected was improved by extending the range of taxes upon which the surcharge was levied; and the government, through the State Library Council, has a duty to train the librarians. A key strategy which was embodied in the Act was the formulation of a hierarchical system whereby the local libraries were connected to the District libraries and they, in turn, were connected to the State Central Library and the National Library. Centralised acquisition and resource sharing was envisaged. This strategy had formed a part of the Second Five Year Plan but it appears not to have been enforced with any haste; Brahmanda Barua wrote in 1992 that throughout India "The network principle has nowhere been applied in organising the libraries."

4. PUBLIC LIBRARIES IN TAMIL NADU

Public Libraries are being opened in Tamil Nadu as per the "Tamil Nadu Public Libraries Act, 1948" with an aim to provide best reading for the greatest number at the least cost. A Directorate of Public Libraries under the direct control of Education Department was formed on 1st August 1972 in order to improve and administer the public library services, in Tamilnadu. In October 1974, a Library Re- organisation committee was formed under Shri.V.N.Subbarayan which gave valuable recommendations for the improvement. A qualified library professional for each district was appointed from December 1976 as "District Library Officer" shortly termed as DLO for each District. The DLO will be the responsible officer for the functions and administration of all the libraries which comes under the District. In November 1978, an official committee under the chairman of Shri. S.Srinivasan which reviewed the recommendations of the Subbarayan Committee and evolved certain norms for the number and category of technical and non-technical posts required for each library. From 1.4.1982, the Government of Tamil Nadu has provincialised all the staff members of the Department of Public Libraries, and the salary, allowances, pension etc., of the library staff are directly paid by the Government from the Treasury. The structure of the public library system corresponds to the structure suggested by the Advisory Committee for the Libraries set up by the Government of India.

The period beginning September 16, 2009, to September 16, 2010, was celebrated as the 'Library Rejuvenation Year' and the initiative was called as 'Our World, The Library'. There were 4042 libraries in the State, only 1,600 had their own buildings. More than 2,000 were functioning from rented buildings. State Government had allotted Rs.25 core for the construction of buildings for libraries and Rs.10

crore for repairs of existing buildings and Rs.25 crore for the procurement of books for rural libraries the year 2014 – 2015.

4.1. Connemara Library – A Legacy

The State Central Library is the Connemara Public Library and acts as the copyright library. Connemara public library is inaugurated on December 5, 1896. In 1890 then governor of madras, lord Connemara, felt the need for a public library in Chennai. On March 22 1890 the foundation stone was laid by lord Connemara for the public library. On December 5 1896 the library named after lord Connemara and formally opened.

The library came in to existence as organization by appointing full librarian in the year 1929. It was opened to all in the year 1930 by the same year the first lending and home delivery services were started. Under, Tamil Nadu public libraries act 1948, it was considered as state-central library in the year 1950. The United Nations recognized Connemara library as its depository center in the year 1955. The Tamil Nadu state's bibliography of children's literature and Tamil books publications were started in the 1963 and 1964 respectively. In the year 1965 it was recognized as information centre by UNESCO organization. Commencement of institute of library sciences had happened in the year 1966. It was in the year 1968 the merger of children and state bibliography had happened.

In 1974 the three storied new building added. In this building were all functions taking place now. Here we can find a vast collection of books in an arrayed manner. There are text book section, periodicals hall, a reference room, a video room, a large floor for Indian language books, a Braille library, I A S study centre, browsing centre, permanent book fair centre, Xerox facilities and the library had been fully computerized which access to book easy. The library has a rare books collections like "The bible published in 1608", "Accounts of the trade in India by Lockyer (Charles).

4.2. Anna Centenary Library

Tamil Nadu public libraries has recently established fully air-conditioned world class "Anna Centenary Library" located at Kotturpuram, Chennai to mark the Centenary celebrations of former Chief Minister Perarignar Annadurai. Hand carved bronze statue of Anna reading a book at the entrance of the library cordially welcomes the reader community. Spaciously built on 8 acres totaling a combined built up area of 3.75 lakh sq.ft has totally ground + eight floors and the storage capacity of 12 lakh books. The noteworthy sections are unique Braille section and kids special first floor spread over 15,000 sq.ft with colorful pictures and green tree, playing equipments for children. High-tech auditorium of seating capacity of 1250 persons spread over 50,000 sq.ft, parking facility for 417 cars and 1026 two wheelers, mini conference hall, amphi theatre and exhibition hall, residential facilities for research scholars, disabled friendly are the prominent features of the library. Exclusive interior decorations, carpet tiles imported from USA spreading 2 lakh sq.ft., interior structural glazing to the extent of 3.5 lakh sq.ft. exterior aluminum composite panels to the extent of 1.5 lakh sq.ft. Won the gold certified India's first green library. Wonderful collections of about 6 lakhs books invites not only the Chennai dwellers but also the user community all over India.

4.3. Madras Literary Society Library

The Madras Literary Society (MLS) located at DPI campus Nungambakkam stacks more than 83,000 books which is more than a century old. Established in 1812 as Asiatic Society of Madras, MLS is the oldest lending library in the south. It was started with Bengal Asiatic Society in Kolkata and Bombay Asiatic Society. The single-storey library building is a red-brick structure with intricate sandstone trimmings inspired by the Rajasthani style of architecture.

The oldest book is Aristotle's Opera Omnia in Greek and Latin published in 1619. Apart from first editions of several books, MLS has original documents and surveys of the Ganges Canal plain (1854) and Buckingham Canal project (1898). Old pictures of Pudukottai, Trichy, Thanjavur and Madurai, photographed by Captain Tripe, are preserved in a glass case mounted on a teakwood table at the entrance. The library, which has only 200 members now, once had a devoted readership that included Subhas Chandra Bose, Annie Besant, T T Krishnamachari and C P Ramaswami Iyer.

4.4. Thanjavur Maharaja Serfoji's Sarasvati Mahal Library

The pride of Tamil Nadu Libraries, Sarasvati Mahal Library deserves prominent place as it serves as the valuable treasure of Tamil ancient culture which was built by the successive dynasties of Nayaks and the Marathas of Thanjavur. It houses a rich and rare collection of both palm leaf and paper manuscripts of about 46.000 on art, culture and literature in Sanskrit, Tamil, Marathi and Telugu languages. Thanjavur is known for the art of painting. The library holds beautiful paintings on wood, glass, canvass drawn after 1750 and books exceeding 50,000. It follows various conservation and preservation techniques for the durability of the collections. In 1918 this Library was made as a public Library. The library is now administered by a body constituted by the Government and financed by the Central and State Governments

4.5. Government Oriental Manuscripts Library

This library is considered as a Treasure-house of Knowledge and is also designated as "Research Centre" under the affiliation of the University of Madras. It is located in the western side of the first floor of the Madras University Main Library. It was established in 1869 initially with huge personal collections of Colonel Colin Mackenzie, Dr.Leyden and C.P.Brown. It is headed by the Curator under the control of the Department of Archaeology, Government of Tamil Nadu. Many manuscripts have been acquired from time-to-time by purchasing them from the owners of the manuscripts or by transcription. It has grown to its present dimensions and it possesses 72314 manuscripts in the following languages (Refer Table). Apart from this, nearly 23,000 printed books are available for reference in the Library.

4.6. UV. Swaminatha Iyer Library

Within the Kalakshetra compound in Besant Nagar, close to the sea shore, is the Dr. U VS Library. A prominent and well known library amongst the learned and highly literary sections of the Tamil society in the State and beyond, this library was established on 5 August, 1943. A concern of literature enthusiasts of India's oldest continuously used classical language has been to preserve the gems of writing and thoughts from history spreading over several eras, centuries (millenniums even), rulers and tumultuous events. Taking this concern unto himself, Dr. UV Swaminatha Iyer, known as "Grandfather of Tamil", collected scripts and palm leaf inscriptions from the pre-sangam era in a single collection for history and knowledge sake. Literary contributions to ancient Tamil include Tholkappiyam from the pre-Sangam era, 10 idylls and eight anthologies from the Sangam era and five epics Silappathikaram, Manimekalai, Seevakasinthamani, Valaiyapati and Kundalakesi. According to sources in the library, all 10 idylls, four out of eight anthologies and three out five epics are stored in palm leaves due to the efforts of UVS. All the palm leaves are now published in a book format for use for scholars and other interested parties. The source further states that 69 of the 96 palm leaf manuscripts and 21 of the 47 paper manuscripts of sangam literature are in library collection. DR. UVS library is maintained by a society and supported by the Tamilnadu government.

5. ACADEMIC LIBRARIES IN TAMIL NADU

Some of the prominent academic libraries in the state have been given below.

5.1. Anna University Library

The University Library, which has been established in the year 1978 gained autonomy from December 2000. It is housed in a three storeyed new Building located at the eastern side in the main campus. The total area of the Library building is about 4122 sq.m. 30 video cameras are placed at strategic points in the library for surveillance. The MIT campus also has a library of area 1256 sq.m. Around 10,157 registered uses are in access of the library. Many knowledge-based services like that of Reference, Bibliography, MALIBNET service., DELNET, Reprography, CD-ROM Databases, Internet browsing and e-services are provided by the library for its users.

5.2. Annamalai University Library

The seed of the main library germinated in 1920 with a token deposit of 200 books, when Sri Meenakshi College was founded. it was shifted into its present abode in 1959, opening a new chapter in its history. The Annamalai University Library has the unique privilege of being selected as a full-fledged Depository for the World Bank Publications ever since 1986. The UGC Study Centre was established in 1975.

5.3. Madras University Library

The university has four libraries, they are – Madras University Library (Chepauk Campus), Cental library (Guindy Campus), Cental library (Marina Campus) and central library (Taramani Campus).

Central library (Marina Campus) : When the language departments were moved to the Marina Campus, the language collections were separated from the Madras University Library and moved to the Marina Campus in the late 1970s to form an Oriental Research Institute Library where books on Tamil, Telugu, Malayalam, Kannada, Samskrit, Hindi, Arabic, Persian, Urdu were housed.

Madras University Library (Chepauk Campus) : Madras University Libarary was established in 1907 in the Connemara Public Library. The existing library building, built in Indo-British style was opened on 3rd September 1936. This Building is built with the pointed arches in granite, domes with octagonal base. The kiosks resemble the Islamic Architecture in India.

Central library (Taramani Campus) : Situated in Taramani, in the vicinity of many Information hubs of our capital city of Chennai, this Library of the Madras University's Information System has a calm and serine atmosphere for peaceful study and research. The primary mission of this library is to support the educational and research programs of the University by providing physical and intellectual access to information, consistent to the present and anticipated educational and research functions of the University.

Central library (Guindy Campus) : The Guindy Campus Library is established in 1900. It is housed in the Science Campus of University of Madras comprising of the Schools of Physical, Chemical, Life, Earth, Energy and Environmental Sciences. The Guindy Campus Library has emerged as a Knowledge Resource Centre mainly catering to the information needs of the Faculty, Research Scholars and Students of Schools of Sciences, besides being an information hub to industries and research institutions.

5.4. Bharathiar University Library

The Library of Bharathiar University was established in the year 1981 at the Madras University Autonomous Postgraduate Centre of the University is an area of 11,750 sq.feet. The seating capacity currently is about 300, and has over 1,47,350 volumes covering all disciplines. The library subscribes to 153 National and International journals and seven leading news papers. 150 journals magazines and periodicals are received on gratis. Back issues of journals are available some dating back to 1880's. Photocopying facility is also available inside the library.

6. SPECIAL LIBRARIES IN TAMIL NADU

6.1. Roja Muthiah Research Library

The Roja Muthiah Research Library (RMRL) was founded in 1994 to preserve, catalogue, and expand the collection of Roja Muthiah Chettiyar, a private collector who put together one of the world's finest private libraries of Tamil publications during his lifetime. Located in Chennai, RMRL currently houses one of the most unique collections of Tamil imprints in South Asia. Some of the publications date from the latter part of the eighteenth century. With a collection of 3,00,000 items, RMRL provides research materials and facilities for research scholars of Tamil studies in a variety of fields spanning the humanities, social sciences, and sciences. Most of the publications date from the latter half of the nineteenth and the twentieth century. As per the annual report of RMRL (2013 -14), 1204 research scholars had visited this library 2322 times for their research work. An MoU was signed last year with the Franckee foundation, Halle Germany for exchange of literary material.

6.2. Central Leather Research Institute Library (CLRI)

The CLRI library provides the knowledge base on leather, footwear and allied disciplines, whether it be the science and technology, the economics and the commerce or the fashion and design aspects of leather and leather products. The library has in its leather collection rare books dating back as much as 100 years, the early editions of books authored by luminaries and doyens in the field and reports of various pre- and post- independence government committees. The library strives to be a "national library for leather" and houses about 20.000 books, 26,000 bound volumes, 150 periodicals and 200 dissertations besides unique monographs and government reports on leather and leather goods.

6.3. Knowledge Resource Centre -Combat Vehicles Research And Development Establishment (CVRDE - DRDO)

The Knowledge Resource Centre of CVDRE, previously known as Technical information Centre (TIC) was established in the year 1969. In 2010, it was shifted to new premises namely the Knowledge Resource Centre (KRC), which was formally inaugurated on 13th March 2010. Now, KRC is an ISO 9001:2008 certified with total area of is 1950Sq. and centrally air-conditioned which includes reading halls,VIP longue, data centre and Internet browsing centre. The environment at the KRC provides an ambient atmosphere for the existing stock (50000 Nos.) as well for the future expansion (100000 Nos.). The facilities at the KRC have paved a way for access of IEEE, Janes, Elsevier, JCCC, and Science Direct publications under DRDO Consortium for e-journals. KRC is providing A&I database, COMPENDEX and INSPEC (IP enabled) and Indian Standards, British Standards, SAE Ground Vehicles Standards, and National Technical Information Systems (NTIS) (IP enabled) on Intranet. Forty one rare and out of print books have been grouped as a separate collection namely 'Classic Books', preserved using a specialized technology (Photolam).

7. LIS EDUCATION IN TAMIL NADU

As far as Library and Information Science is concerned, Tamil Nadu is the birth place in India. All levels of courses (Diploma, Degree, Master Degree, Mphil and PhD) in this discipline are being offered by different universities in the state. The Universities which offer the course are – Annamalai University, University of Madrass, Bharatiar University, Bharati Dasan University, Periyar University, Gandhi gram Rural University, Alagappa University and Karpagam University. Some of the major teaching departments are given below.

7.1. Dept. of Library Science- Annamalai University.

The department have been offering BLIS (one year) ,

MLIS (Two year) and MLIS (Five Year integrated) programmes. In the last five years the faculty has earned 2 projects worth thirty three lakhs of rupees. Fifty eight researchers have successfully completed their Ph.D. programs and 44 their M.Phil Programmes. The department has carved a riche conducting five national seminars. The faculty have published 139 research papers in national and international journals. The faculty have won two awards and the endeavours of the teachers will make a positive continuum in the years to come.

7.2. Dept. of Library Science- Madras University

The origin of Library and Information Science education in the University of Madras starts with the Summer School by Dr.S.R.Ranganathan, the then librarian of the University in the year 1929 under the auspices of Madras Library Association. This led to the introduction of Certificate Course in Library Science by the University in 1931. In 1937, the Certificate Course was converted into Diploma Course. Dr.S.R.Ranganathan donated a Lac of rupees in the year 1957 (University's Centenary Year) for establishing a teaching Department in the University. The Sarada Ranganathan Chair in Library Science in 1959, which was the first Professorship in Library Science in the British Commonwealth. Department of Library Science was established in 196. This Department is the First Department in the country to have been awarded with SAP status since 1996 and in 2001 SAP Phase II was approved and completed in 2006.

7.3. Dept. of Library Science- Alagappa University

The Department of Library & Information Science (DLIS) was started in the 2006-2007 academic year. The department was having two permanent faculty members, and faculty support from the Central library of the University. Presently the department utilizes the services of five faculty members and four professionals in Library & Information Science. Four faculty members are having Ph.D Degree in Library &Information Science. Our University is the fifth university in the State to have this course. Even before the creation of the Department of Library & Information Science, Alagappa University has been offering B.L.I.Sc, and M.L.I.Sc programs (from 1998), M.Phil program (from 2002), and C.L.I.Sc and PGDLAN programs (from 2008) in the distance mode (DDE). The Department is offering 4 programs in Library & Information Science: B.L.I.Sc., M.L.I.Sc., M.Phil., and PhD.

8. LIBRARY ASSOCIATIONS IN TAMIL NADU

8.1. Madras Library Association (MALA)

During the early years the MALA launched many innovative programmes such as a mobile library service for the rural areas of Mannargudi and Cuddalore; hospital library service; publication of a collection of essays in English and South Indian languages on the "Library Movement" by several distinguished authors; compilation of bibliographical lists; promotion of school libraries and organising essay competitions among school children. A programme for training librarians was started in 1929 which was handed over to the University of Madras in 1931. This later developed into a post graduate diploma course and eventually the full-fledged Bachelor's degree course. Monographs on all aspects of library science such as *Five Laws of Library Science, Colon Classification, Classified Catalogue Code* and *Library Administration* were also published which gained international recognition. These publications form the basic works for the training programmes conducted by library schools in India and abroad. It took over two decades of perseverence on the part of MALA for the Madras Public Libraries Act to be passed in 1948. This act, the first in the country, proved to be the model for the later acts. To widen the Association's activities and concentrate on college, research and industrial libraries, the need for a permanent abode of its own was felt. Its former president, the late S.R. Ranganathan had earmarked for the building fund a part of the proceeds of the royalties earned by his books. These funds finally provided the MALA in 1976, with premises — a wing of the Gokhale Shastri Institue in Mylapore.

The main objectives of the Association were promotion of the library movement and creation of general awareness, especially among the rural public, of the benefits of using books and libraries. To achieve these, lectures, filmshows, exhibitions, and other activities were organised. The MALA's aims and activities were well received and appreciated both by the public and the government, and by the end of the first year its membership had reached 400, comprising mainly of the elites of Madras.

The MALA has been organising continuing education programmes, discussion groups, workshops, conferences and seminars. The Association maintains active liasion with academic and research institutions, book publishers, and many of its activities are planned in collaboration with local, national and international institutions.

9. CONCLUSION

Public Libraries serve as the strong pillars of nation's knowledge economy. Tamilnadu public libraries strives its maximum to satisfy its mission but still not an exception from criticisms. They claim the pride of implementing the policy of "centralized purchase of books" in India for all public libraries of the state. Interests of local readers are being ignored is the fact. Dr. SRR's dream was to offer free public library service to all which remains still a dream. Tamil Nadu is collecting membership fee for enrolment and renewal. It's really burden for the common people who pays library cess and also extra fee to use the public library. Lack of well qualified staff, and attractive collections, poor maintenance of village and rural libraries are the drawbacks which should be given due consideration by the concern authorities. The post of Director of Tamilnadu Public Libraries has been mostly held by the Directorate of School Education officials as an additional in-charge who possess nil experience in running libraries. A full time qualified Director with degree and experience in Library science is the long time demand of the department of TN public libraries. Amidst of all aspects, it leads in its own way in making the public of nation as intellectual citizens.

REFERENCES

1. Kumar, Satish, and Anil Kumar Mishra. "Collection Development Policy : an overview with referced to KRC, CVRDE, DRDO, CHENNAI." Indian Streams Research Journal 3.12 (2014).
2. Kumar, SK Asok. *Public Library System and Services in Tamil Nadu*. Bharathi Puthakalayam, 2008.
3. Ranganatha (SR). opening address to All India seminar on public library system. In S.R.Ranganathan and A.Neelamegham, Ed. Public library system. 1972. SREFL, Bangalore.
4. Ravi, N., ed. *The Hindu Speaks on Libraries*. (3, 10, 17, 71,74, 80) Madras: Kasturi & Sons, 1992..
5. www.rmrl.in
6. www.clri.org
7. http://biblio-thief.blogspot.in/2011/06/tamil-nadu-public-libraries-act-1948.html
8. http://www.hindu.com/2001/08/21/stories/1321017a.htm
9. http://www.thehindu.com/ebooks/html/hsl/hslcont.htm
10. http://timesofindia.indiatimes.com/city/chennai/Forgotten-library-200-year-old-Madras-Literary-Society/articleshow/31979699.cms
11. http://thanjavur.nic.in/sml/index.html

23

Library Movement and Development of Tripura

Saumen Datta
Senior Librarian, Tripura Public Service Commission
Agartala- Tripura

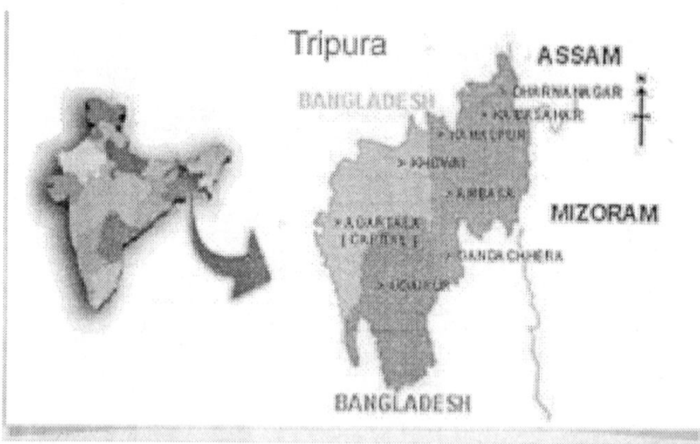

1. TRIPURA : A PROFILE

Tripura, a small state of North-Eastern part of India, is a land of forests, hills and rivers. Located in the rugged and hilly terrain of the tropical forests, the erstwhile princely state of Tripura in north-eastern part of the country was abode of about 1 million people in 1949 when it merged with Independent India as a Union Territory. It was granted statehood in 1972. It has an area of 10,492 sq.km and bounded by Bangladesh on three sides sharing about 80% of its boundary of its perimeter. The remaining 20% of its boundary is shared with the states of Assam and Mizoram through land routes, and have a narrow corridor with Assam to link the state with rest of the country.

As per the 2011 census, the state has a population in total 3,671,032 comprising tribal and non-tribal. Nearly two-third of the area of the state is hilly and about 59% of its total area is covered with green forests. Agriculture is the main source of livelihood. Severe constraints of cheap and convenient modes of transport, geographic isolation and poor economic growth have not deterred the people of the state from acquiring education, and have a literacy rate of 71% as per 2001 census.

2. PUBLIC LIBRARY MOVEMENT IN TRIPURA

Tripura has its great and glorious past of the King Dynasty. The kings of Tripura were great patron of arts, culture and literature. The subsequent kings like Dhanya Manikya(C.1490-1520A.D.), Rajdhar Manikya(C.1586-1680A.D.), Kalayan Manikya (C.1624-1660A.D.), Ramdev Manikya(C.1673-1660A.D.), Ramganga Manikya(C.1804-1809A.D.) and their successors established many institutions of public utility.

Birchandra Public Library of Comilla: A Historic Past : Maharaja Birchandra Manikya (1862-1896A.D.) was not only an able ruler but a great lover of arts, culture and university wits. He established a library at Comilla (now in Bangladesh) probably in the year 1896 A.D. which was then within his territorial jurisdiction and also a very culturally enlightened place. This library was popularly known as the Place Library. It was started with the collection of two hundred valuable books including manuscripts, palm leave puthy of Bangle, hand written Rajmala, Krishnamala, Champak Vijoy and the other chronicles of the Royal house of Tripura.

Library: From palace to public : The King Radhakrishna Manikya (1896-1909A.D.) constructed the

Ujjayanta Palace Library in 1900 A.D. The establishment of the Palace Library was the land mark of the library movement of Tripura, though the library was closed to the common people. Afterwards the strictness was relaxed and the men of letters were permitted to use the said library.

A great significant incident led to the bifurcation of the Place Library. In June, 1897 an earthquake shook the entire North-Eastern India and demolished almost all the important buildings of Agartala. At that time the library collection was temporary shifted in a separated shed. The public in general were for the first time got a chance to use the library. Subsequently important collections were housed in the Palace Library. After several shifting, the library was housed in a newly constructed building during the reign of Maharaja Bir Bikram Manikya Bahadur in the year 1924.Library was kept open for the four hours daily.

3. PUBLIC LIBRARIES IN TRIPURA AT PRESENT: AN OVER VIEW

At present, among 25 public libraries, 10 libraries have their own buildings. From the year 1896 to 1996, the total no of the reader was 25, 379 and the total no of books were 3, 95,122. From the year 1996 to 2012, the number of Library members has increased in 43,884 and the number of books has increased in 70, 2,649.

3.1. Birchandra State Central Library.

Very recently Birchandra state Central Library has shifted to the old Secretariat building of the state which is more specious then the old one. As a result, this Central Library of the state has excelled its opportunities of service towards its users.

Presently the Central Library of the state has been introduced the following services:

- Lending Service:
- Reference Service

- Childrens' corner
- Senior citizens' corner
- Free Internet service
- Womens' Corner
- Carrier guidance
- Reprographic Service
- News paper and journal service
- Archive of rare and old books
- Physically challenged corner

All other 24 public libraries of Tripura are trying to proceed towards modernization based on the Birchandra State Central Library and its services. But the necessary infrastructure of this modernization has not yet been made till today.

It is a matter of regret that after a long journey, the public library services in Tripura are not up-to-the-mark. There are only 25 public libraries in the whole land. Lacks of technical staffs and poor economic condition may be attributed to the present unsatisfactory functioning of the public libraries in Tripura. There are insufficient staffs, specialized in the field, no computer facility and poor collections of valuable books and journals. The Libraries have become merely a store house of knowledge out of limited collection of books and journals. In Tripura, public library has its more than one hundred year history but the improvement is far from the level of achievement to be reached.

The public libraries functioned under the Higher Education department of the Govt. of Tripura. It appears that the said department is not looking after the development of the public library as it deserves. It is also surprising that there is no public library Act for the public libraries of Tripura. The poor achievement of the state in respect of public libraries will be revealed from the information below:

According to Annual Report of 2005-06 of Union of Rural Development, Govt. of India, the number of rural libraries in some of the states of India is as follows:

4. LIBRARY LEGISLATION IN THE STATE

In Tripura, Library act is yet to be practiced. The Library act is not passed in Tripura still now. Though several attempts have been taken for passing the Act. It is hoping that in near future Library Act will be passed.

At last it can be said that several steps are needed for development of the Libraries in Tripura. Such as

1. Public Libraries of Tripura are lagging very much and requires immediate attention for computerization, networking and digitization.
2. The Library should immediately procure necessary hardware and integrated digital Library Software.
3. Soon after this, the Library should immediately take up the task of retro-conversion by creating the Library data base.
5. State Govt. should give top priority to create a Public Library Website which could allow the users to access digital collections. (e-books, e-journals,).
6. Once a Library website is developed a lot of rare collections could be digitized and be up loaded in the Website.
7. Digital Library collections can provide unlimited *access and huge* variety of contents with limited cost.
8. Immediate attention should be given to orient the existing Library staff (Professional, semi-professional) to the upgraded skills with regard to hardware, Library software, retro-conversion, database creation and search, networking, design and development and maintenance of library website.

5. ACADEMIC LIBRARIES OF TRIPURA

5.1. Tripura University Library

On 2nd July 2007, Tripura University has got the status of Central University under the Ministry of Human Resource Development, Government of India. Today Tripura University is spread over an extensive campus of about 83 acres and has the Faculties of Arts, Science, Indian Languages, Engineering and Technology, Information Technology, Education etc.

The University Library has a total collection of 75,400 text and reference books, and also subscribes about 120 periodicals and journals besides local and national dailies (as per 2006 records). The Library also has developed the e-journal facilities under the UGC INFONET. The Tripura University Library is the First and may claim to be one of the richest higher educational libraries in the State .The University Library also serves a crucial resource and learning centre of the Universality as well as in the State and eater the information needs of its various users for the growth and development of the university fraternity. The collection and dissemination of information and the creation and sharing of knowledge is the prime motto of the Tripura University Library.

5.2. College libraries of Tripura

At present there is 36 colleges in Tripura which are under the Tripura University. Financially Higher Education Department, Govt. of Tripura controls all of the 35 colleges except Holly Cross College. All of the colleges have their library though only few colleges have latest Library system. Most of the college library is far behind from the library automation and digitization. Lack of Library professionals in the library of all these colleges is the common problem.

6. SPECIAL LIBRARIES

In the field of special libraries, Tripura is going towards

in progress. There are several special libraries in Tripura and most of these are departmental. These libraries are continuously working for fulfilling the needs of their own organizations. The library of Law Department, Govt. of Tripura, library of Tripura Public Service Commission, Library of Tripura High Court, and library of Tripura Assembly are the important knowledge hub for their organizational goal and achievement. Most of these libraries are well organized and trying to keep them up to dated.

Library of Tripura Public Service Commission is one of the important library of Tripura. This library has serving its special kind of users since inception on 1972. The library is using egranthalaya as well as DSPACE for library automation as well as digitization of documents. The library is enrich with section like file achieve as well as permanent record.

Library of Tribal Research Centre, Govt of Tripura is also very important library for enlighting the knowledge power about the tribes of Tripura as well the tribes of North East.

7. LIS EDUCATION IN THE STATE

The education on LIS is in its mother womb in Tripura. In fact the degree course of Library and information science is yet to be introduced in the Tripura University. The Bachelor degree of Library and information science has been introduced in Ramthakur college of Agratala on 2010. But the infrastructure is not up to the mark still now. Most of the students acquire the BLISc and MLISc from IGNOU and from other university in a distance mood.

8. LIBRARY ORGANIZATIONS AND ASSOCIATIONS

At Tripura, there is only a library association namely Nikhil Tripura Granthagar Parisad. From its inception, the association is working for the development of the libraries as a whole in this state.

9. CONCLUSION

The academic libraries and the Public Libraries in Tripura in general are confronting with many problems due to lack of physical, human and financial resources as a result of which library is not in a position to provide effective and efficient services. This can only be achieved through modernization in the changing information scenario. Public Libraries as well as academic libraries in Tripura require a drastic change to keep- tune- with other developed state public Library system in India. A serious effort may be made by the state govt. to provide one time grant for the development of the academic libraries and the Public Libraries in Tripura which may be the new horizon of development in the libraries in Tripura.

REFERENCES

1. A. A. Alemna, 1995. "Community libraries: An alternative to public libraries in Africa," *Library Review*, volume 44, number 7, pp. 40–44. http://dx.doi.org/10.1108/00242539510147520, accessed 11 March 2013.
2. Zahid Ashraf Wani, 2008. "Library Philosophy and Practice"
3. R. Bhattacharjee, 2002. "Public library services in India: Systems and deficiencies," *Public Libraries Section — Country Report: India*, International Federation of Library Associations and Institutions, at http://www.ifla.org/VII/s8/annual/cr02-in.htm, accessed 30 March, 2013.
4. Patel and K. Kumar, 2001. *"Libraries and librarianship in India"*, Westport, Conn.: Greenwood.
5. S.R. Ranganathan, 1963. *"The five laws of library science"*, Bombay: Asia Publishing House.
6. Sinha, Manoj Kumar. 2007. Automation and Networking of Public Libraries of North Eastern Region of India with Reference to Rural Libraries of Assam: A Proposal. In: Rural Libraries in the North-East India: Problems and Prospects: Proceedings of the National Seminar held at Gauhati University, Guwahati ,jointly organized by Dept of Library and Information Science, Gauhati University, Guwahati and Central Reference Library, Kolkata during March28-29, 2007 (Eds: NarendraLahkar with a foreword by K. K. Kochukoshy), Central Reference Library, Ministry of Culture,

Govt. of India, Kolkata, Pp 350-367

7. KalpanaDasgupta, 2000. "Libraries and librarians in India on the threshold of the third millennium: Challenges and risks," *IFLA Conference Proceedings* (Jerusalem, Israel, August), at http://www.ifla.org/IV/ifla66/papers/039-120e.htm, accessed 17 April 2014.

8. National Knowledge Commission, 2007. *"Libraries, gateways to knowledge: A roadmap for revitalization"*, New Delhi: Government of India.

9. P. Varma, 2007. *"The great Indian middle class"*. New Delhi: Penguin.

10. *CIA World Factbook*, 2008. "India," at https://www.cia.gov/library/publications/the-world-factbook/geos/in.html, accessed 8 April 2013.

11. R. Seth, 2006. "Storehouses of knowledge to educate the masses: The Indian library system — a present day scenario," *Frankfurter Buchmesse*, volume 58, number 9, pp. 622–628.

12. Sinha, Manoj Kumar and Satpathy, Kishor C. (2006). Application of Multimedia and Mass Storage Technology for Library and Information Management and Services. In: Vistas of Information Management: Professor H.R. Chopra Felicitation Volume (Ed. P. VenkataRao.) Wisdom House Academic Publishers, AmbalaCantt, 255p.

13. K. Deshpande and B.B. Hungund "What Ails our Public Library System", ILA Bulletin, Vol. 24, No.1&2, 1998.

14. B. Ramesh Babu and P. Govinda Reddy, "Public Library System in Tamil Nadu with Reference to Circle Libraries" in Knowledge Management, B. Ramesh babu et.al (ed) New Delhi; Ess Publication, 2003.

15. Miao, Q. (1998). "To be or not to be: public libraries and the global knowledge revolution", (conference paper), Proceedings of the 64th IFLA International Congress and Council. Retrieved fromwww.ifla.org/IV/ifla64/082-78e.htmml, accessed 10 April 2014

16. Singha, Manoj Kumar. (2011). *"Design and Development of Regional Knowledge Network for North Eastern Region of India (RKNNER) : A Proposal" . In: Three Day National Seminar on Networking of Library and Information Centres of North east India in Digital Environment (NLICDE-2011) jointly organised by Central Library, NIT, Silchar and National Library, Kolkata*

(Ministry of Culture, Govt. of India) during March 21-23, 2011 (Eds: Kishor Chandra Stapathy and R.Ramchandran) NIT, Silchar ,Pp.56-57

17. Kaul, H.K. (2002). Knowledge centers: the key to self employment and poverty alleviation. *Delnet Newsletter*, 9(2), 17-18.

18. Arora, J. (2001).Indian National digital library in Engineering Science and Technology (INDEST): a proposal for strategic cooperation for consortia-based access to electronic resources. *International Information and Library Review*, 33, 149-65.

19. Bobby, M. S. V (2007). Developing Informational Professionals in the Information Technology: a study. In proceeding: 5th Convention PLANNER - 2007, Gauhati University, Guwahati, December 7 – 8 , 2007 . Retrieved from http://ir.inflibnet.ac.in:8080/jspui/bitstream/123456789/465/1/CALIBER%202008(15).pdf , accessed 10 April 2013.

20. E. F. Sandys,1999. "History of Tripura".

21. A.C. Bhattacharjee, 2009. "Progressive Tripura".

22. http://www.tripura.nic.in, accessed 21 March 2013.

23. http://www.tripurainfo.com, accessed 13November 2013.

24. http://cau.org.in , accessed 20 February 2013

24

Library Movement and Development in Uttar Pradesh

Nishat Fatima
Assistant Professor
Dept. of Library and Information Science
Aligarh Muslim University, Aligarh, UP

1. UTTAR PRADESH: A PROFILE

Uttar Pradesh (UP) is a state located in northern India. It was created on 1 April 1937 as the United Provinces, and was renamed Uttar Pradesh in 1950. Lucknow is the administrative capital of Uttar Pradesh. Ghaziabad, Kanpur, Moradabad, Aligarh, and Varanasi are known for their industrial importance in the state as well as in India. On 9 November 2000, a new state, Uttarakhand, was carved out from the Himalayan hill region of Uttar Pradesh.

The state is bordered by Rajasthan to the west, Haryana and Delhi to the northwest, Uttarakhand and the country of Nepal to the north, Bihar to the east, Jharkhand to the southeast, Chhattisgarh to the south and Madhya Pradesh to the southwest. It covers 93,933 square miles (243,290 km^2), equal to 6.88% of the total area of India, and is the fourth largest Indian state by area. With over 200 million inhabitants in 2011, it is the most populous state in the country as well as the most populous country subdivision in the world. Hindi is the official and most widely spoken language in its 75 districts. Uttar Pradesh is the fourth largest Indian state by economy, with a GDP of ₹7080 billion (US$110 billion). Agriculture and service industries are the largest parts of the state's economy. The service sector comprises travel and tourism, hotel industry, real estate, insurance and financial consultancies.

Uttar Pradesh was home to powerful empires of ancient and medieval India, including Magadha, Nanda, Mauryan, Sunga, Kushan, Gupta, Gurjara, Rashtrakuta, Pala and Mughal which many say was improved by the Nawabs of Awadh. The two major rivers of the state, the Ganga and Yamuna, join at Allahabad and then flow as the Ganga further east. The state has several historical, natural, and religious tourist destinations, such as the Taj Mahal, Varanasi, Piprahwa, Kaushambi, Kanpur, Ballia, Shravasti, Kushinagar, Lucknow, Chitrakoot, Jhansi, Allahabad, Budaun, Meerut and Mathura.

2. LIBRARY MOVEMENTS IN UTTAR PRADESH

The libraries were established in Uttar Pradesh during the Mugal period and Brititsh period, such as, Raza Library, Rampur in 1750, Allahabad Public Library (Azad Park Library), Allahabad in 1763, Maulana Azad Library, Aligarh in 1877, Bharati Bhawan Library, Allahabad in 1889 and Lyall Library, Aligarh in 1899. The state has a State Central Library at Allhabad, 69 District level libraries, 62 other prominent public libraries run by voluntary organizations.

3. UTTAR PRADESH PUBLIC LIBRARY LEGISLATION, 2006

The UP Public Library Legislation passed in the year 2006 by the Uttar Pradesh Legislature. The act provided for the establishment, organization, maintenance and development of public libraries in the state through various councils and committees:

State Library Council : The state has constituted a council which is known as the State Library Council which consists a member of Secondary Education Department acts as the chairperson, Vice-Chairperson who is the Principal Secretary or the secretary as the case may be to the Government of Uttar Pradesh and other members including one member who is nominated by the Raja Ram Mohan Roy Library Foundation, Kolkata. The work of the council is to advise the state government on all matters arising in the administration of this Act.

Standing Committee : The state is having a Standing Committee which functions to ensure the implementation of the decision and suggestions made by the State Library Council. The work of the Standing Committee is to plan, monitor and execute plans and projects in connection with the public library development in the state. It looks after the library work given by the Ministry of Education, Government of India, Department of Culture, the State Library Council or any other outside agency connected with the public library development. It has to also adopt measures for establishing co-operation and liaison among library services rendered by other departments. The committee has to organize the Continuing Education Programme for librarians in public library system such as refresher courses, etc.

District Library Committee : The State consists of a District Library Committee in each district of the state consisting of the District Magistrate as the Chairman and the Chief Development Officer as the Vice-Chairperson. The Member Secretary acts as the Librarian of the District Government Library and in the absence of the Librarian, the Principal of Government Inter College acts as the Member Secretary. The function of the District Library Committee is to prepare plans for the development of public library system in the district and monitor the progress of the district.

The Director of the Secondary Education, Uttar Pradesh is the Director of Public Libraries and he will be responsible for the proper administration and operation of the provision of this act. The director has to perform such functions which are subject to the control of the state government. He has to collect the reports and data on the working of all public libraries including government aided public libraries. He has to prepare and submit the reports, the annual budget and five year plans to the government for the development of public library system and services in the state. He has to set minimum standard for the library and information services rendered by various public libraries and he has to ensure that all the public libraries are maintaining such standards. He has to ensure, organize, support the in-service training of various types of library workers. Moreover, he has to exercise such powers and perform such other duties as may be conferred by the state government from time to time.

Structure of Public Library System : There are two state level libraries in Uttar Pradesh. These are:

1. State Central Library, Allahabad
2. State Central Reference Library, Lucknow

Functions of State Central Library : The State Central Library has to perform the duty of procuring and organizing all the reading material useful for the general public. It has to provide the facility of self-reading to the general public and also act as a supplement to other public libraries in the state. State Central Library has to organize book exhibitions, lectures, seminars and other activities for promoting reading habits among the public at large. The State Central Library also acts as an agency to disseminate information. The services for the handicapped is to be looked after by the State Central Library. Moreover, it will also look after the computerization of all the public libraries.

Functions of State Reference Library : The State Reference Library which is located at Lucknow performs the functions such as procurement of all useful materials, compilation of a computerized union catalogue of public libraries in the state, compilation and publishing of comprehensive bibliographies on various subjects for the benefits of scholars and researchers, providing of reference materials and acquisition of hand written manuscripts.

The State Reference Library is to compile a union catalogue of manuscripts available in different libraries of the state to promote co-operation in inter library loan among the public libraries and participate in various computerized library network such as DELNET for the benefit of the general public.

There is a Government District Library in each district. The District Library is to function as an apex library for the District Library system. In addition, it also functions as a lending and reference library for the district. The District Library collects materials of regional/local interest and also procures useful and standard materials and other reading materials such as audio-visual materials. It promotes mobile library services and establish book delivery systems. Moreover, it has to co-ordinate and supervise the activities of other government branch/tehsil/block/village libraries of the district and periodically performs inspections. In addition to it, it also performs such services which are entrusted by the District Library Committee.

Finance : For the development of libraries, the budget has its own importance. Development is not possible without a properly planned budget and this is the reason that the state budget should include the plan for the development of the libraries. The state government has to find the ways and means to increase the additional resources to support and develop the public library system. The financial assistance will be provided to any library run by voluntary organization registered under the Societies Registration Act 1860 and by local authority open for use to the general public.

The state recognizes any Public Library Association in the state registered under the Societies Registration Act 1860, for the purpose of payment of grant in aid or other financial assistance. Every person who is in-charge of the public library has to submit reports and give information as and when required by the state government.

4. MAJOR PUBLIC LIBRARIES IN UTTAR PRADESH

There are many public libraries in Uttar Pradesh. Some important libraries are listed below:

1. Allahabad Public Library established in the year 1864.
2. Carmicheal Library, Banaras founded in the year 1872.
3. The Lyell Library in Meerut founded in the year 1866
4. Rampur Raza Library,Rampur 1975

4.1. Allahabad Public Library

Allahabad public library established in the year 1872, is situated at Alfred Park. It is the symbol of friendship of Lord Thornhill, the commissioner of Allahabad and Mr. Mayne, the Collector. It is also known as Thornhill and Mayne Memorial. It was designed by Roskell Bayne. The public library is an outstanding Gothic style of structural design. In 1879, library was shifted to the present premises. It has about

75,000 books, besides a treasure trove of manuscripts and journals.

4.2. Rampur Raza Library

Rampur Raza Library was founded by Nawab Faizullah Khan of Rampur in 1774 AD. Later, it was taken over by the Government of India on 1st July 1975 which was declared as an institution of National importance. Rampur Raza Library has very important and rare manuscripts and valuable historical documents like paintings and very rare books in oriental languages like Arabic and Persian languages and besides all these materials it has around 80,000 printed books.Now the library work under the Department of culture, Government of India and funded by Central Government.

5. LIBRARIES OF MAJOR ACADEMIC INSTITUTIONS IN UTTAR PRADESH

Education sector in Uttar Pradesh is developing day by day. Following are some of the major universities located in Uttar Pradesh:

1. Sayaji Rao Gaekwad Library, B.H.U, Banaras
2. Central Library, Allahabad University, Allahabad,
3. Maulana Azad Library, Aligarh Muslim University, Aligarh.
4. Tagore Library, Lucknow University, Lucknow
5. Central Library, Babasaheb Bhem Rao Ambedkar University, Lucknow

These are the oldest internationally reputed universities located in Uttar Pradesh. These universities offer various courses such as undergraduate, postgraduate, doctoral, diploma and other courses.

5.1. Sayaji Rao Gaekwad Library, B.H.U, Banaras

The central library of Banaras Hindu University is named as Sayaji Rao Gaekwad library. The library was germinated from the small but precious collection devoted by Prof. R K Telang in the memory of his father Justice K T Telang in 1917 and housed in the Telang hall of Central Hindu College, Kamachha. The library was developed by the renowned historian Sir Jadunath Sarkar. It was shifted in 1921 to the central hall of the Arts College and then in 1941 to its present majestic building.

Now, the university has a central library as well as 3 institute libraries, 8 faculty libraries and 25 departmental libraries with the total collection of 13 lakh volumes to serve the students, faculty members, researchers and technical staff of the university.

5.2. Central Library, Allahabad University

The Central Library of Allahabad University, Allahabad started in the year 1916. It provides its services to all students, teachers, research scholars of the university. This library is developed out of main central college, Allahabad. The foundation stone was laid down by Sir John Hewett on 17th Jan 1910. The present building was constructed in 1974. The library has around 6, 85,110 books and 461 current journals. As far as e-resources are concerned it has around 2155 e-books and 11223 online journals. Library is providing different services to cater the needs of its users such as reference service, OPAC, internet facility etc. Moreover, different databases are available to facilitate the users.

5.3. Maulana Azad Library, A.M.U, Aligarh

Aligarh Muslim University, Aligarh has a very developed and beautiful library named "Maulana Azad Library" which is very famous for its collection of rare books and manuscripts. It was established in the year 1877. The library has around 11.5 lakh books. Apart from this it has very good number of digital resources also.

5.4. Tagore Library, Lucknow University

The name of the Lucknow University Library is Tagore Library. It is the central library of Lucknow University. It is located at the old Bennet Hall. It has total collection around 5,53,864 books, around 50,000 bound journals and 2,000 manuscripts and around 10,000+ online electronic resources.

5.5. Central Library, Babasaheb Bhem Rao Ambedkar University, Lucknow

The central library of Babasaheb Bhem Rao Ambedkar University, Lucknow was laid in January 1998. It has inherited approximately thousand reference books in Hindi donated by Uttar Pradesh Bhasha Sansthan Programme. Recognizing the role of library and information services in meeting the requirements of the university's academic and research programmes, the library purchases books and other information resources to satisfy the needs of the users. It has around 8500 books and 500 reference books, 40 periodicals and other e-resources. The university is the youngest one in the state.

6. SPECIAL LIBRARIES IN UTTAR PRADESH

Now Special libraries are acting as information center. They are for the special group of users that is why these libraries are always in the forefront to provide special services to the users such as current awareness services, selective dissemination of information services, Indexing and Abstracting services, document delivery services, online and CD-ROM serarch services, Referral services, translation services etc. In Uttar Pradesh state few special libraries are there such as:

- Knowledge Resource Centre of Central Drug Research Institute (CDRI), Lucknow
- CSIR-NBRI S&T Knowledge Resource Centre (Library) Lucknow
- Indian Institute of Toxicology Research Centre (TTRC), Lucknow
- Harish Chandra Research Institute, Allahabad
- Indian Institute of Pulse Research Library(IIPR), Kanpur

- UP Textitle Technology Institute library, Kanpur
- Dr. Shakuntala Misra University library ,Lucknow

7. LIBRARY ASSOCIATION IN UP

7.1. Uttar Pradesh Library Association

The Uttar Pradesh library association was founded in the year 1935 at Lucknow. The first President of the association was Dr. Wali Mohd. and General Secretary was Mr. Fazal Illahi. Due to the lack of interest the association could not survive for a long time but after that in 1948 librarians of Allahabad decided to revive the association and elected Col. N. Rehman, the then librarian of Allahabad University as President of the Association and Mr. M. M Goswami as its General Secretary. The constitution was drafted and adopted also but again could not survive longer and had to become defunct after sometime.

On 1st Sept. 1956, after a gap of almost seven years, in the presence of the then Chief Minister of Uttar Pradesh Dr. Sampuranand, the association again revived and a meeting of librarians was called by Dr. Radha Kamal Mukharjee. This meeting was procided over by S Bashiruddin, the then librarian of Aligarh Muslim University. In this meeting Mr. C. G. Vishwanathan, the then librarian of B. H. U. was elected as President and Mr. K Kumar, the then librarian of Amir-Ud-Daula Public Library, Lucknow as its General Secretary. Since then the association is discharging its function and fulfilling its objectives.

Presently, the association has more than 500 members from various places of the state as Life Members and 700 Ordinary Members.

Objectives of the Association

I. To develop library movement with in the state.

II. To improve the status and services conditions of library and information science professionals.

III. To generate an appropriate public opinion for public

library law in the satate.

IV. To create reading habit among general public in the state.

V. To co-ordinate with the Central Government and the social Organisations in the planning and execution of their policies towards mass education.

VI. To take all such actions as may be identical or conducive to the attainment of the objectives of the association or any of them.

7. LIBRARY AND INFORMATION SCIENCE EDUCATION IN UTTAR PRADESH

History of library education is quite old and advancing everyday. Quite a good number of universities are available in Uttar Pradesh like Banaras Hindu University, Allahabad University, Aligarh Muslim University etc. These universities are oldest universities in Indian history and got very good reputation in the world. The state has almost 60% literacy rate and is progressing almost all areas of education such as Agricultural Science and Technology, etc . Till today there are 354 universities and university level institutions in India. In Uttar Pradesh there are 34 universities and out of 34 universities 14 are offering Library and Information Education which present 41.17 % of the total universities of the state. The LIS education is started in UP since more than 72 years. The First department of library and information science was started at Banaras Hindu University in 1942. There are 4 central universities some state Universities and some deemed to be universities.

The name of the Central universities which offer Library and Information Science Education are listed below:

- Banaras Hindu University, Banaras
- Aligarh Muslim University,Aligarh
- Babasaheb Bhim Rao Ambedkar University, Lucknow

There are some state universities where Library and Information Science are being given these are:

Lucknow University, Lucknow, Bundelkhand University, Jhansi, Chaudhary Charan Singh University, Meerut, Chattrapati Shahuji Maharaj University, Mahatama Ghandi Kashi Vidhyayapeeth University, Varanasi, Sampuranand Sanskrit Vishvidhyala, Varanasi, Deen Dayal Upadhyay Gorakhpur, University, Gorakhpur and Veer Bahadur Singh Poorvanchal University,

In UP only one University which is providing Library and Information Science education through distance mode is also known as Open University i.e. Uttar Pradesh Rajshree Tandon University, Allahabad. The Uttar Pradesh State is also having one deemed to be university which is offering Library and Information Science education that is Allahabad Agriculture Institute at Allahabad. Different level of courses are being taught in these universities such as Bachelor, Master Diploma and M Phil/ Ph.D. Two years integrated course is also being taught in two universities that is Banaras Hindu University apart from regular BLISc, MLISc course and another one is Babashab Bhim Rao Ambedkar University, Lucknow.

Bachelor's degree course is offered by almost all the Universities of the State where as Master degree program is offered by AMU, BHU, and few state universities.

While M Phil /Ph.D is offered by AMU, BHU,BRAU, LU BU, UPRTOU. Almost all the Library and Information Science departments have included Information Technology in their syllabi. It has also been observed that the Central Universities have better resources and facilities in comparison to state Universities. The computer lab and Library both are fully equipped with information technology in these universities.

REFERENCES

1. Babasaheb Bhimrao Ambedkar University, Lucknow. Retrieved June 5, 2014 from bbau.ac.in Uttar Pradesh Library Association. Retrieved on June 5, 2014 from http://www.tagorelibrary.tripod.com/upla.html.

2. Banaras Hindu University, Retrieved June 5, 2014, from http://www.bhu.ac.in/

3. Maulana Azad Library. Retrieved June 8, 2014, from http://www.malibrary.com/index.html.

4. Rampur Raza Library. Retrieved June 5,2014 from http://razalibrary.gov.in/Razalibnew/index.html.

5. Rout, R.K.(Ed.) (1980). Library Legislation in India:problems and prospects. New Delhi: Reliance Publishing House.

6. Sharma, S.K. Pandey (1996). Public libraries in India: Trends and Status. In *Public libraries in developing countries: Status and Trends.* Ed. P. K. Mahapatra ,.125-127. New Delhi: Vikas Publishing House.

7. Status of Library Legislation in India. Retrieved June 4 , 2014, from rrrlf.nic.in.

8. University of Allahabad. Retrieved June 6, 2014, from http://www.allduniv.ac.in/

9. University of Lucknow. Retrieved June 4, 2014, from http://www.lkouniv.ac.in/

10. Uttar Pradesh Public Libraries Act, 2006, Act 21 of 2006. Retrieved June 5 ,2014 from rrrlf.nic.in.

11. Venkatappaiah , V.(1990). State Library Bills And Acts. In: *Indian Library legislation* Ed. P.S.G Kumar. V.2. Delhi : Daya Publishing House.

25

Library Movement and Development of Uttarakhand

Anil Kumar Dhiman
Information Scientist
Gurukul Kangri University
Haridwar – 249 404 (Uttarakhand)

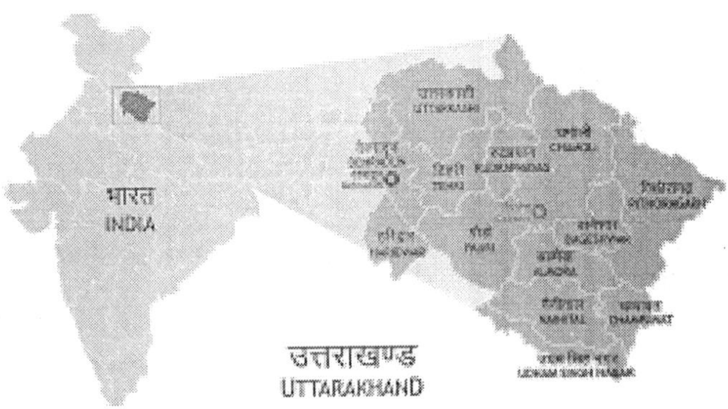

1. UTTARAKHAND : A PROFILE

Uttarakhand is a state in the northern part of India that came into existence on 9th November 2000. It borders the Tibet autonomous region on the north; the Mahakali zone of the far-western region, Nepal on the east; and the Indian states of Uttar Pradesh to the south and Himachal Pradesh to the northwest. Uttarakhand is mainly known for its natural beauty of the Himalayas, the Bhabhar and the Terai. The state is divided into two divisions – Garhwal and Kumaon. Its western part forms the erstwhile kingdom of Garhwal, while the eastern part is known as Kumaon.

Uttarakhand has an interesting history as it finds mention in the Hindu scriptures as Kedarkhand, Manaskhand and Himavant. It is often called the Land of Gods- Dev Bhoomi, because of its various holy places and shrines. Uttarakhand is 27th state that consists of 13 districts and its 90 percent part is hilly and rest is plain. It has most beautiful landscapes and natural beauty that is helping this nascent state in increasing its economy by bringing tourists throughout the year. Dehradun is the capital of the state. The places like Mussoorie, Nainital, Haridwar, Almora are some of attractive tourist places. The state also has many pilgrimage places. Kedar Nath, Badri Nath, Gangtori and Yamnotri are its most important pilgrimage places. Therefore, Uttarakhand government is also looking for developing pilgrimage tourism in the state.

2. LIBRARY MOVEMENT IN UTTARAKHAND

Library movement is a saga of organized growth and development of libraries giving the details of establishment, maintenance and functioning of libraries in a geographical proximity. These aspects viz., establishment, maintenance and functioning make a library a growing organization. No country in the world can progress without providing free public library services to the citizens. It is imperative on the part of the democratic country like India to establish the service institutions like public libraries in order to strengthen the democratization of information and to promote the social, cultural, historical and scientific and technical knowledge in the public at large.

Uttarakhand state itself does not have a rich past of its own, because the state has emerged as the bifurcation of old Uttar Pradesh. Some of the well established libraries by the state government of Uttar Pradesh were taken over while coming up into existence. But it is really appreciable that within five year duration of formation of the state there was seen a good movement towards development of library related activities in the state and Uttaranchal State Library Act was passed in the year 2005. However, it is yet to be implemented.

3. PUBLIC LIBRARIES IN UTTARAKHAND

Public libraries are largely regarded as the People's Universities. They are also considered as community information centers providing access at local level comprising of a wide range of knowledge and information for the benefit of the individual and society as a whole. Not very much is credited to the state as far as the public library system is concerned in the state. However, a few well established and old public libraries exist in the state, which are briefly elaborated below.

The very first public library in Haridwar was opened by Shri Kripalu Maharaj with 3500 books. But presently, there is a library in Sarwan Nath Nagar, Haridwar that is catering to the needs of local people. Another public library is at Municipal Building, Roorkee that is under municipal administration of Rookee (Haridwar). It houses general interest books on all subjects for local users.

3.1. Mahatama Khushi Ram Public Library, Dehrdun

This is one of the oldest public libraries of the state, which is situated at Dispensary Road, Dehradun. It contains a lot of books of vivid nature for public use. Newspapers are also subscribed in the library.

3.2. Doon Library & Research Centre

This is relatively a new public type library that was established at Dehradun in the year 2005. This aims to be developed as a reference library in social sciences with special emphasis on Himalayas as well as a public library. Doon Library has about 14,500 books which are catering to the needs of more than 1000 members. The library undertakes the initiation of a documentation service and indexing of articles on specific topics and issues, publication of an Abstract or Digest on Mountain Studies on a regular basis. The library is contributing to fostering a culture of book-reading and visiting and using libraries, especially among the youth and school children.

3.3. Durga Lal Shah Municipal Public Library, Nainital

The other public library is at Nainital that is known by the name Durga Lal Shah Municipal Public Library, Nainital. It is on the Mall Road and was founded in the year 1934.

3.4. Sri Dev Suman Public Library, Tehri Garhwal

It is the other public library of the state that has started its working on 01 March 2000 at its new present campus at Boradi (Tehri Garhwal). It is also the District Library of Tehri Garhwal. The main branch of the library was built by Raja Suharshan Shah of Tehri Garhwal, but now is maintained by government. This is housed in a three-storyed building and having over 1,00,000 book collection covering all major subjects. In addition, the collection has a very rich amount of manuscripts of all important old kingdoms of the state. Approximately 250 readers have the privileges of using this library on daily basis.

A branch library of Sri Dev Suman Library is established at Chamba (Tehri Garhwal) but its collection is very small in comparsion to main branch. It is having around 5000 books which have been received mainly as the donation from Raja Ram Mohan Library Foundation, Kolkata.

4. ACADEMIC LIBRARIES

Academic libraries are the libraries which are attached to their respective institutions. They are considered to be the nerve centres of academic institutions. These libraries serve two complementary purposes – to support the school's curriculum, and to support the research of the university faculty and students. Academic libraries are of three types - university, college and school level libraries. Each of them in Uttarakhand perspective is discussed below.

4.1. University Libraries

University libraries cater to the needs of undergraduate, postgraduate, research and faculty levels. University wise information with their libraries is detailed below.

4.1.1. Dev Sanskriti Vishwavidyalaya- Library, Haridwar

Dev Sanskriti Vishwavidyalaya was established on 11th April 2002 by an Act of Uttaranchal Government, Dehradun. The university is located at Haripur Kalan, a village located near the border of the districts of Haridwar and Dehradun. This vast institution is self- financed and managed through people's contribution and not by any grant from the State or the Central Government or UGC. The library is housed in five storey building called 'Aryabhatt Bhawan'. The library has a collection of about 25,000 books comprising of a varied collection 1,000 bound volumes of journals. It subscribes about 79 international journals in various disciplines of science, spirituality and humanities

4.1.2. Doon University - Library, Dehradun

Doon University is established by Doon University Bill, 2005 (Uttaranchal Adhiniyam Sankhaya 18 of 2005. It is a residential university. The library holds books, national and international journals, newspapers and many other resources like CDs and maps / toposheets. Online access to all relevant journals is also being provided by the library.

4.1.3. G. B. Pant University of Agriculture and Technology -Library, Pant Nagar

G.B. Pant University was established in the year 1960 as the first agricultural university in Asia under the name U P Agricultural University. University library has a highly specialized collection of documents in the field of Agriculture,

Veterinary Sciences, Animal Husbandry, Home Science, Fisheries, Basic Sciences, Humanities, Technology and other allied subjects

4.1.4. Graphic Era University Library , Dehradun

Graphic Era University, formerly known as 'Graphic Era Institute of Technology', is a deemed university located in Dehradun. The university has a well stocked library with over 79000 volumes of international and national books, journals, periodicals, reference books and other learning resources and it caters to reading and referral requirements of students and staff.

4.1.5. Graphic Era Hill University – Library, Bhimtal

Graphic Era Hill University (GEHU) is a sister concern of Graphic Era Educational Society. Its campus is situated at Bhimtal (Nainital). GEHU library is imparting its services to the students, faculty members and other staff members. Library, besides having a huge collection of books on engineering, science, technology, management and humanities offers library services through its various divisions.

4.1.6. Gurukul Kangri University Library, Haridwar

Gurukul Kangri University, Hardwar is a deemed university that was established in the year 1902 by Swami Shardhanand. It is under administrative control of Arya Pratinidhi Sabhas of Haryana, Punjab and Delhi. But University Grants Commission gives hundred percent grants to this university.

Gurukul Kangri University has a very good library. Besides, central library, there are also separate libraries for Kanya Gurukul Mahavidyalaya, Jwalapur (Haridwar) and Faculty of Engineering & Technology, Faculty of Management Studies, Faculty of Ayurveda & Pharmaceutical Sciences and Faculty of Computer Sciences.

4.1.7. Himalayan Institute Hospital Trust (HIHT) University - Library, Doiwala (Dehradun)

Himalayan Insitute Hospital Trust (HIHT) University was established by Swami Rama under the aegis of Himalayan Institute Hospital Trust, which is the sponsoring society of the University. In 1989, the founder, Shri Swami Rama after returning from the United States, started purchasing land for his dream project in the foothills of the Himalayas in the district of Dehradun and starting with a small OPD in 1989, a 250 bed hospital began functioning in 1994. Soon therefore, the construction of a medical college began. The central library of the University is well recognized for its specialization holding and services pertinent the academic and professional courses related materials provided. It is well equipped with books on different subjects in addition to Indian and foreign journals of different specialties.

4.1.8. Hemwati Nandan Bahuguna University - Library, Sri Nagar (Garhwal)

Hemwati Nandan Bahuguna University (HNB) a residential cum affiliating university that came into existence as Garhwal University in the year 1972. It is situated in Sri Nagar city (Garhwal) of the state. The library of HNB Garhwal University is housed in a three -storey building which has a sufficient area that is situated in the midst of the main campus of the University. It has a rich collection of about 2.0 lakhs books, 35 serials and non-book materials etc.

4.1.9. Himgiri Zee University - Library, Dehradun

Himgiri Zee University (HZU) was established in 2003 . HZU also owns a huge library with digital facilities, computers and photocopy machines. Besides, the campus is wifi, through which students can access Internet facilities round the clock.

4.1.10. Indian Institute of Technology (IIT) – Library, Roorkee

Indian Institute of Technology, Roorkee was established as Roorkee College of Engineering in 1847 at Roorkee which was renamed as Thomson College of Civil Engineering in the memory of its founder James Thomson, then Lt. Governor or North East Province and again as Thomson College of Engineering in the year 1945. After independence, in the year 1949, it was declared as University of Roorkee, Roorkee by Pt. J.L. Nehru, then the Prime Minister of India. In the year 2001, Parliament of India gave it the status of institute of national importance and upgraded as Indian Institute of Technology, Roorkee. Central Library of the institute that is known as Mahatma Gandhi Central Library, The library has over 3.45 lakhs documents in all forms and media. Its collection is chiefly rich in Science, Engineering and Technology, however, Humanities and Social Science have got due attention

4.1.11. Kumaun University - Library, Nainital

Kumaun University, a residential-cum-affiliating university that was established on 1st December . Nainital being its main campus has a very good library.

4.1.12. National Institute of Technology (NIT) Library, Sringar (Garhwal)

National Institute of Technology (NIT) Sringar (Garhwal) is among one of the ten newly sanctioned NITs in 2009 by the government of India. As the institute is newly established, it does not have very well structure and developed library.

4.1.13. Patanjali University – Library, Haridwar

Patanjali University was established in the year 2006 . It is situated near Bahadarabad on Haridwar – Rookee Highway in Uttarakhand state. The university got his name after the Ancient Yoga Guru Patanjali and is one of the largest yoga universities in India. The motive behind the establishment of the university was treatment, research and development in Yoga and Ayurveda. This university presently has no independent library but the library of Patnajali Yogpeeth is being used for university purposes. This has a very good collection on medical sciences and medical botany and other related subjects.

4.2. College libraries

College libraries are those libraries which are attached to the college- whether they are of academic interest or serving in the field of technical education. Uttarakhand has 13 districts where majority of the colleges are Government College, except that of Haridwar, Dehradun and Udhamsingh Nagar districts, where some of the colleges are private but government aided. Though, in Dehradun there exist some famous college, like MKP, Dehradun, DAV (PG) College, Dehradun and DBS College, Dehradun, but conditions of their libraries is also not good. The condition is worst in case of government degree / postgraduate colleges, where in most of the cases, there is no librarian. Overall, the condition of these college libraries is not good.

4.3. School Libraries

Welham Boy's School, Dalanwala Dehradun; Hopetown Girls' School, Rajawala Road Dehradun; Guru Nanak Vth Centenary School, Vincent Hill, Mussoorie; Mussoorie International School, Polo Ground, Mussoorie; Oak Grove School, Jharipani, Mussourie Hills, Dehra Dun; The Doon School, Dehradun; Welham Girls' School, Dalanwala, Dehra Dun: Wynberg Allen School, Mussoorie; Woodstock School, Landour, Mussoorie; The Selaqui School, Chakrata Road, Dehradun; Cambrian Hall, Dehradun Cantt; Canfield School Clement Town, Dehradun,; Carman Residential & Day School, GMS Road, Dehradun; Charmwood International School, Dalanwala, Dehradun; Children Academy International, OAK Hill Estate, Dehradun; and Constancia

School, Majra, Dehradun are some of the famous public schools near Dehradun and surrounding areas.

Nainital has also been known for its well reputed public schools. Four schools from the British period continue to exist today: Sherwood College, established in 1869; All Saints' College, established in 1869; St. Mary's Convent High School established in 1878; and St. Joseph's College established in 1888. In addition, a number of new schools have been established since independence. Major ones include: Birla Vidya Mandir that was established in 1947; Sanwal School, established in the year 1940s in Mallital; St. Amtuls Public School established in 1983; Parvati Prema Jagati Saraswati Vihar established in 1983; and Oakwood School established in 1989. Sherwood College is a co-educational residential school in Nainital that was founded in the year 1869. Its pastoral aims are to recognize and accept individual differences in ability and talent and to hold every child/ individual in esteem in his/her own right. Several Indian luminaries have attended these schools including prime ministers such as Rajiv Gandhi and film stars Amitabh Bachchan. Almost all of these schools have their own well settled libraries.

5. SPECIAL LIBRARIES OF UTTARAKHAND

Some of the important special libraries of Uttarakhand state are briefly detailed out below.

5.1. Alternate Hydro Energy Centre (AHEC) Library, Roorkee

Alternate Hydro Energy Centre (AHEC), an academic centre of Indian Institute of Technology, Roorkee was established in the year 1982. AHEC has well documented library of its own with latest literature on the topics related to small hydro power and other renewable energy sources.

5.2. Anthropological Survey of India, Library (AnSI)

Anthropological Survey of India was established in December 1945 by the Government of India in Benares and started functioning as a centralized institution.

Anthropological Survey of India (AnSI) is the apex Indian organization involved in anthropological studies and field data research for human and cultural aspects. AnSI Dehradun also has a very good library for its users containing documents of importance in related subjects. Around 20-25 journals of rare nature are also subscribed in the library.

5.3. Archeological Survey of India, Library - Dehradun

Archaeological Survey of India (ASI) is a premier organization for the archaeological researches and protection of the cultural heritage of the nation under the Ministry of Culture. The prime concern of ASI is the maintenance of ancient monuments and archaeological sites. Besides it regulate all archaeological activities in the country as per the provisions of the Ancient Monuments and Archaeological Sites and Remains Act, 1958. Dehradun circle of Archaeological Survey of India was established on 16th June 2003, after bifurcation from Agra Circle on creation of new state with a mandate of better maintenance of protected monuments and further researches in archaeological disciplines in the region. The library of the ASI is having a good collection of around 11,500 books of special nature for its users. Besides, the library is also subscribing 17-18 journals of archeological importance which generally are not available in other libraries of similar nature.

5.4. Aryabhatta Research Institute of Observational Sciences, Library

Aryabhatta Research Institute of Observational Sciences (ARIES) was set up in the year 1954 at Manora Peak, Naintal for carrying out research etc. in observational Astronomy & Astrophysics and Atmospheric Sciences. The library of the ARIES is known as one of the best libraries among similar types of the organizations in the country.

5.5. Botanical Survey of India, Library - Dehradun

Botanical Survey of India (BSI) Dehradun circle was formed in the year 1956 to carry out floristic studies in

Himachal Pradesh, Jammu & Kashmir, Punjab, Haryana and Uttarakhand along with UT of Chandigarh and NCR, Delhi covering Trans Himalaya Cold Deserts, the Western Himalaya, Siwalik Hills and Upper Gangetic Plain with the part of semi arid north west India. It has a library which has a good collection on flora, economic botany and other related subjects to cater the needs of scientists working therein and also to the research scholars.

5.6. Central Building Research Institute, Library-Roorkee (Haridwar)

Central Building Research Institute, Roorkee (CBRI) was established in the year 1947, with the responsibility of generating, cultivating and promoting building science and technology in the service of the country. The library of the institute is now renamed as Knowledge Resource Centre (KRC). It caters to the information requirement of Science &Technology community of buildings science and technology. The basic collection of library covers on the areas of Building Science & Technology comprising of Civil Engineering, Structural Engineering, foundation and Geotehcincal Engineering, Architecture, Earthquake & Landslides, Building Materials & Equipments, Building Physics, Mycology and Pestology and Chemistry & Chemical Engineering.

5.7. Centre for Tibetan & Himalayan Studies, Library - Dehradun

The Centre for Tibetan and Himalayan Studies had been a long held vision of His Holiness the Drikung Kyabgon Chetsang Rinpoche. It is named after the 33rd Tibetan King, Songtsen Gampo (617-650 A.D.) and is situated at P.O. Kulhan, Sahastradhara. The library of the institute is named as Songtsen Library, which undertakes support and publish urgent, necessary and innovative research projects. Resident Scholars Program as well as Lecture Series are arranged there in the institute. The institution also plan to host multi-disciplinary International Conferences and seek the participation of reputable scholars.

5.8. Central Soil & Water Conservation Research & Training Institute, Library - Dehradun

Central Soil and Water Conservation Research and Training Institute (CSWCRTI) was established in 1974, Dehradun (Uttarakhand). CSWCRTI library has a very rich collection of all types of literature relevant to the disciplines of soil and water conservation under one roof. It is one of the premier libraries under ICAR catering to the needs of scientists and scholars.

5.9. Forest Research Institute, Library - Dehradun

Forest Research Institute (FRI) made a humble beginning as Forest School established in 1878. Initially named as Imperial Forest Research Institute, F.R.I. came into being in 1906. Later, it renamed as Forest Research Institute and Colleges, with a number of centres located at different places all over the country administering research as well as training of Forest Officers and Forest Rangers. After reorganization of Forestry Research in the country and creation of Indian Council of Forestry Research and Education (ICFRE) in 1988, the training and research centres were given an independent status of institutes. Forest Research Institute that is now one of the institutes under ICFRE, was conferred the status of Deemed University in 1991 .

The library of the FRI that is known as National Forest Library & Information Centre (NFLIC), is one of the oldest library dedicated to the forestry and allied subjects in South and Southeast Asia. It is having about 2 lakh books and other reading material. The library also maintains grey literature on forestry which are neither formally published nor available commercially. It maintains excellent collection of back volumes of journals since 1835 and its current journal collection include Indian and foreign journals on all related subjects. Besides, 180 e-journals are also being subscribed by the library along with SCOPUS and Forest Science Databases.

5.10. Forest Survey of India, Library - Dehradun

Forest Survey of India is the successor of "Preinvestment Survey of Forest Resources" (PISFR), a project initiated in 1965 by the government of India with the sponsorship of Food and Agriculture Organization (FAO) and United Nations Development Programme (UNDP). Forest Survey of India came into existence in June 1981. FSI headquarter library at Dehradun is at Kaulagarh Road, Dehradun. It is a very special library, which has around 50,000 thematic maps in its library, which accounts for around 75 percent of the forest area of the country.

5.11. Indian Institute of Management, Library - Kashipur

Indian Institute of Management, Kashipur is a new entrant in the elite league of IIMs. IIM, Kashipur has a well-stocked library that is named as Learning Resource Centre (LRC). It is supporting the institute's academic and research activities in its quest to become a pioneer, research driven management institute.

5.12. Indian Institute of Petroleum, Library - Dehradun

Indian Institute of Petroleum (IIP), Dehradun is premier laboratory that was established in under Council of Scientific & Industrial Research (CSIR). IIP is engaged in research and development activity mostly in the downstream sector of petroleum industry. Library has more than 17,000 books, and 16,500 bound volumes of periodicals, in addition to international standards. This library also has a good number of Technical Reports, Thesis, Patents, Standards, Specifications, Reprints, Microforms, Microfiche, CD-ROM etc.

5.13. Indian Institute of Remote Sensing, Library - Dehradun

Indian Institute of Remote Sensing (IIRS), Dehradun is a premier training and educational institute that is situated at 4, Kalidas Road, Dehradun. It was set up for developing trained professionals in the field of Remote Sensing, Geoinformatics and GPS Technology for Natural Resources, Environment and Disaster Management), in 1966. IIRS central library has a wide range of collection of documents and information resources in print and electronic form to meet the requirement of its user community, especially on literature pertaining to Remote Sensing, Geographical Information Systems (GIS), Geospatial Technologies and their applications in various fields.

5.14. Indian Military Academy, Library - Dehradun

Indian Military Academy (IMA), Dehradun has a glorious past in the history of India. It was founded in the year 1932 to fulfil the growing needs for indenisation of the army. IMA library has its beginning with only 800 books which has reached up to 1 lakh by now. Its collection includes 91000 books, 11000 bound journals, 1600 CDs, along with numerous albums, and audio visual cassettes

5.15. Indira Gandhi National Forest Academy, Library - Dehradun

Indira Gandhi National Forest Academy was established as Indian Forest College in the year 1938 to train the forest officers in the country at Dehradun. It was renamed as Indira Gandhi National Forest Academy (IGNFA) in the year 1987 in the memory of Smt. Indira Gandhi, the late Prime Minister of India. IGNFA library has a very good collection of books, journals, magazines, CDs and Video cassettes in the field of forestry and allied subjects .

5.16. Lal Bahadur Shastri National Academy of Administration, Library - Mussoorie

Lal Bahadur Shastri National Academy of Administration (LBSNAA) was established in the year 1959 in Mussoorie as the National Academy of Administration by merging the IAS Training School, Delhi and IAAS Staff College, Shimla. The main purpose of academy is to train the civil service officers for the Indian Foreign Service, Indian Administration Service, Indian Police Service, Indian Forest Service, Indian Revenue Service, Indian Audits and Accounts Service, Indian Railway Traffic Service and other Government Agencies. LBSNAA has a very good library which is catering to the needs of probationary IAS officers as well as the senior administrative officers during mid-career training programme in the country.

5.17. National Institute of Hydrology, Library - Roorkee (Haridwar)

National Institute of Hydrology (NIH), Roorkee is the premier institute in the area of hydrology and water resources in India. Institute was established in 1978 with the main objective of undertaking, aiding, promoting and coordinating systematic and scientific work in all aspects of hydrology. Institute since its inception has been in the continuous process of building a good technical library with latest publications in the area of hydrology and water resources.

5.18. National Institute of Visually Handicapped, Library - Dehradun

National Institute of Visually Handicapped (NIVH) Dehradun is a premier institute in the field of visual disability that was established in the year 1943. and developmental activities ensuring emergence of disability inclusive policies, programmes and practices. Its R&D activities have contributed a number of useful tools and enabling technologies for equal participation by the visually impaired persons in different walks of life. NIVH is largest producer and distributor of Braille literature and devices in the country including talking books. NIVH library is designated as National Braille Library which has approximately 91000 volumes on its shelves comprising over 13,000 titles. National Braille Library collaborates with Library of Congress USA; Royal National Institute for the Blind, U.K.; and American Federation for the Blind, USA for providing a rich collection of Braille literature. There is a National Talking Book Library that is rendering invaluable service to the visually impaired persons including children. Being the largest library in the country, it has a rich collection of literature on possibly every subject. The library produces audio books in Hindi, English, Sanskrit, Urdu & some regional languages. With an elegant stock of over 4500 titles it is benefiting more than 18000 people across the country.

5.19. Oil & Natural Gas Corporation Limited, Library - Dehradun

Oil & Natural Gas Corporation (ONGC) has a long and cherished tradition of commendable initiatives, institutionalized programmes and practices of Corporate Social Responsibility which have played a laudable role in the development of several underdeveloped regions of the country. ONGC has its inception as the Natural Gas Directorate that was set up in 1955 under the then Ministry of Natural Resources and scientific. ONGC library housed very good resources comprising of books, journals and the CDs. It is also a member of CSIR-DST e-journals consortium.

5.20. Survey of India, Library - Dehradun

Survey of India, the National Survey and Mapping Organization of the country under the Department of Science & Technology, is the oldest scientific department of the Government of India. It was set up in 1767 and has evolved rich traditions over the years.

Library of Survey of India holds very good documents. More particularly it includes topographical maps, geographical maps, special purpose maps, project maps, tourist / guide maps and IAF maps & Charts etc.

5.21. Uttarakhand Academy of Administration, Library - Nainital

Uttarakhand Academy of Administration, Nainital, originally established as Officers' Training School (OTS) at Allahabad in 1951, and was shifted to Nainital in 1971. The institution was renamed as Administrative Training Institute (ATI) in the year 1974 and thereafter it was raised to its present status of the Academy in 1988. After the creation of the new state of Uttarakhand on 9th November 2000, the Academy has been designated as the 'Apex' training institution of the Uttarakhand State and is now known as "Uttarakhand Academy of Administration". Uttarakhand Academy of Administration also has a library that is known as Uttarakhand Academy of Administration Library & Documentation Centre. It holds a very collection of related documents on concerned subjects.

5.22. Uttarakhand Judicial and Legal Academy, Library - Nainital

Judicial Academy for the State was conceptualized by Hon'ble Mr. Justice V.S. Sirpurkar, the then Chief Justice of Uttaranchal High Court in the year 2004 for training to the judges of the state and was christened as Uttarakhand Judicial and Legal Academy (UJALA). Cradled in a valley of rolling pine filled hills of Bhowali, the academy became functional on June 14, 2008. The library of Uttarakhand Judicial and Legal Academy is the treasure house of eminent books and periodicals. The library is equipped with an audio-visual section and e-resource access facility. The library of UJALA has also acquired all major Indian electronic legal-data resources like AIR-Webworld, SCC online, Manupatra etc, which are available on both stand alone and online mode. Besides, the library services are being automated with the help of LibSys software.

5.23. Wadia Institute of Himalayan Geology, Library - Dehradun

Wadia Institute of Himalayan Geology (WIHG) is an autonomous research organization of the Department of Science & Technology that was established in June 1968 as a small nucleus in the Botany Department, Delhi University. Later, it was shifted to Dehradun in April 1976. Initially named as the Institute of Himalayan Geology, it was renamed as the Wadia Institute of Himalayan Geology in memory of its founder, the late Prof. D. N. Wadia, FRS & a National Professor, in appreciation to his contributions to the geology of the Himalayas. WIHG library is a medium sized special library that caters to the need of staff of the institute. Library of the institute is having a unique collection of about 28000 titles of the books, monographs, journals and seminar/ conference proceedings on Geology, mountain building processes with special reference to Himalayan Geology.

5.24. Wildlife Institute of India, Library - Dehradun

Wildlife Institute of India (WII), Dehradun is an internationally acclaimed institution that was established in the year 1982. It offers training program, academic courses and advisory in wildlife research and management. WII Library and Documentation Centre was established in line with WII's mission as multi-disciplinary information and learning resource centre on biodiversity conservation and management. It holds over 25,958 books, 20,600 newspaper clippings, 7,350 maps/toposheets and more than 6,225 bound volumes of old and rare journals. The centre also provides online access to all relevant journals and archives.

5.25. Zoological Survey of India, Library - Dehradun

Zoological Survey of India (ZSI) has its genesis as the Zoological Section of the Indian Museum at Calcutta in 1875.. Formally founded in the year 1916, ZSI is a premier national institute under the Ministry of Environment and Forests. ZSI regional centre also has a library.

6. LIS EDUCATION IN THE STATE

Uttarakhand being a new state does not have a good history of library education itself; however, it can be correlated with the Uttar Pradesh. Earlier, Certificate of Library Science (C.Lib.Sc.) under the aegis of Uttar Pradesh Library Association was running in three places – Roorkee, Dehradun and Nainital, which now are the part of Uttarakhand state. After formation of Uttarakhand, only 2-3 session of C.Lib.Sc. could be conducted. However, the course is closed now. But there are five universities in the state which are imparting B.Lib.Sc and M.Lib.I.Sc. Course). They are -

- HNB Garhwal University, Srinagar (Garhwal) – Central University (HNB)
- Himgiri Zee University- Private University (HZU)
- Uttarakhand Sanskrit University, Haridwar- State University (USU)
- Uttarakhand Technical University, Dehradun – State University (UTU)
- Kumaun University, Nainital – State University (KU)

However, Uttarakhand Technical University, Dehradun is an affiliating university in the state and it is not running these courses in its campus. It has many affiliated institutes which are conducting B.Lib.I.Sc. and M.Lib.I.Sc. in regular mode. Important of them are listed in following table. It is seen that Amrapali Institute is affiliated with KU, while others are affiliated either with HNB, Srinagar, or UTU, Dehradun. Thus, the conditions of Garhwal region seem to be better as compared to Kumaun region as first four universities fall in Garhwal region while rest one is in Kumaun region of the state. Besides, there are many institutes which are engaged in conducting B.L.I.Sc and M.L.I.Sc course to cater the needs of the students. Here, Garhwal region is ahead, there are many institutes conducting graduate and post graduate course in library science while in Kumaun region, only one institute is there conducting B.L.I.Sc and M.L.I.Sc course.

But there is no university in the state where research work is going on leading to M.Phil or Ph.D degree in Library Science. A few Ph.Ds were produced in HNB Garhwal University, Srinagar some times back but now there is no Ph.D. work is going on.

7. LIBRARY ASSOCIATIONS IN UTTARAKHAND

7.1. Uttara Library Association

Uttara Library Association was established in the year 2001 under the name "Uttaranchal Library Association" as a continuum of Uttar Pradesh Library Association (UPLA) Roorkee branch after the formation of Uttarakhand state. This association conducted Certificate Course of Library Science which earlier was running under the aegis of UPLA for one session only.

But this association is not very active at the moment and has restricted itself in organizing local level seminars on various occasions, especially on the birthday of Dr. S.R. Ranganathan. No other major activities are seen being carried out by it.

7.2. Uttarakhand Pustakalaya Association

Uttarakhand Pustakalaya Association is another library association which was formed in the year 2002 with great zeal and objectives. Certificate Course of Library Science was taken over by this association from Uttara Library Association later, but it could complete only two sessions of this course. After that, the course could not be continued. This association is not active now.

7.3. Uttarakhand Library Association

This is another state level library association which was formed prior to the formation of Uttarakhand state. Not very much contribution is its name except the some urges to the state to work towards promotion of library-oriented culture in the state.

7.4. Central Government Library Association

Central Government Library Association with its headquarter at Dehradun, is a national level association that was formed in the year 2004. All the library professionals working in different central government departments throughout the country are under its purview. This association organizes national level conference at regular intervals, where the problems of central government employees including their pay-related matter are discussed very well. This association seems to be very active in the state at the moment.

8. CONCLUSION

Concluding, it can be said that though Uttarakhand is comparatively new state which itself does not have a good past its own as such, but it has inherited a lot of Government of India Departments here from Uttar Pradesh. All of them like Survey of India, Forest Survey of India, BSI and ZSI etc. have a good past and prospects as well. They possess very good library infrastructure and collection there in. IIT, Roorkee is one of the exemplary libraries of the state that can be placed among one of the top most libraries in world as far as the infrastructure is concerned and can be set as an example. Gurukul Kangru University, Haridwar and Hemwati Nandan Bahuguna Garhwal University, Sri Nagar (Garhwal) libraries are also among the few best libraries in the academic arena.

REFERENCES

1. Anonymous. (2010). Souvenir of Seminar on E-Resource Management & North Zone Users Convention. IIT, Roorkee.
2. Anonymous. (2012a). Primary schools in Uttarakhand as of 30 September 2010 in Hindi. Government of Uttarakhand. Available at: http://schooleducation.uk. gov.in/files/statistics/ primary_ schools.pdf.
3. Anonymous. (2012b). Enrollment of (General) Children in Primary School. Government of Uttarakhand. Available at: http:/ /schooleducation.uk.gov.in/files/statistics/Primary.pdf.

4. Anonymous. (2012c). Status of Teachers (District wise) as of 30 September 2010. Government of Uttarakhand. Available at: http://schooleducation.uk.gov.in/files/statistics/teachers/ Primary_teacher.pdf.

5. Anonymous. (2013a). Souvenir of CGLA on the Occasion of 5th CGLA Conference. CGLA, Dehradun.

6. Anonymous. (2013b). Chayan: the Placement Brochure – 2013. G.B. Pant University of Agriculture and Technology, Pantnagar.

7. Dhiman, A.K. (2006). Information Literacy and the Role of Librarian. In T.A.V. Murthy et al., edited 'Dynamic Interoperable Web Based Information System (CALIBER-2006 Papers)'. INFLIBNET Center, Ahemdabad. Pp. 390-98.

8. Dhiman, A.K. (2007). L'enseignement de la bibliotheconomie et des sciences de l'information (French Language Article)-(Trends in Library & Information Science Education and Profession in India). *Bibliotheque(s).* 31 (March) : 34-36.

9. Dhiman, A. K. (2007). Information & Communication Technology Development and Changing Faces of Library & Information Science Education in India. *PEARL : A Journal of Library Science.* 1 (3) : 3-10.

10. Dhiman, A.K. (2011). Library Science Education in Uttarakhand: An Appraisal. In Jagtar Singh and Trishan Kaur edited "LIS Education, Research and Training : Vision 2020." IATLIS, Patiala. Pp. 499-509.

11. Dhiman, A.K. (2012). Privatization of Higher Education in India: Some Observations. In Doris Philip Singh and Naveen Samuel Singh edited 'Issues and Challenges in Higher Education. WordsWorth India, Delhi. Pp. 243-58.

12. Dhiman, A.K. and Gupta, S. (2002). Library Legislation: Need and Importance in Uttaranchal State. *Indian Journal of Information, Library & Society.* 15 (1-2): 38-43.

13. Dhiman, A.K. and Rani, Yashoda. (2005). Learn – Library and Society. Ess Ess Publications, New Delhi.

14. Dhiman, A.K. and Rani, Yashoda. (2008). Library & Information Science Education and Profession in India : Trends and Prospects. *Indian Journal of Information, Library & Society.* 21 (1-2): 1-27.

15. Dhiman, A.K. and Shrivastava, D.K. (2012). Public Libraries 2.0: New Expectancies in Digital Era. *Library Progress.* 32 (1): 73-80.

16. Dhiman, A.K. and Sinha, S. C. (2000). Computer Education

Centre at Roorkee: A Survey. *Indian Journal of Information, Library & Society.* 13(3-4): 257- 64.

17. Godiyal, Sunita and Nautiyal, R.C. Status of Teachers Education in Uttarakhand. Available at: http://www.aiaer.net/ejournal/vol20108/9.htm.

18. Lance, Keith Curry (2002). The Importance of School Libraries. http://www.laurabushfoundation.com/Lance.pdf.

19. Midda, Abdul Momin, Khan, Md. Alamgir, Khan, Bairam and Mukherjee, Sirpati. (2009). Changes of Activities in Academic Library System in India. Available at: crl.du.ac.in/ical09/papers/index_ files/ ical-53_153_336_1_RV.pdf.

20. RMSA. (ca2012). Rashtriya Madhyamik Shiksha Abhiyan (RMSA) Uttarakhand: Vision, Aims & Objective of RMSA. Available at: schooleducation.uk.gov.in/files/pdf/RMSA.pdf.

21. Mishra, Bibhash Kumar, Ahuja, K.K. and Harish Kumar. (2010). Library Services in Central Library of Kumaun University: A Study. *International Research Journal.* 1(12): 32-34.

22. Rani, Yashoda and Dhiman, A.K. (2012). Libraries at School Level in Uttarakhand. In P. Venkata Rao et al., edited "Libraries and Reading Habit in Electronic Environment'. B.P. Publishers and Distributors, Panchkula (Haryana). Pp. 230-36.

23. Sayeed, M. Abu (2009). College Library Information Systems : Status and Recommendations for Development to Meet Vision 2021 for Digital Bangladesh. ICAL – 2009 Paper. DULS, Delhi. Pp. 68-76.

26

Library Movement and Development in West Bengal

Niti Mollah

Librarian, K N C S, Berhampoe, Murshidabad
West Bengal

1. WEST BENGAL: A PROFILE

West Bengal is a state in the eastern region of India and is the nation's fourth-most populous state, with over 91 million inhabitants. Spread over 34,267 sq mi (88,750 km^2), it is bordered by the countries of Bangladesh, Nepal and Bhutan, and the Indian states of Odisha, Jharkhand, Bihar, Sikkim, and Assam. The state capital is Kolkata. Together with the neighboring nation of Bangladesh and parts of the state of Tripura, it makes up the ethno-linguistic region of Bengal.

Ancient Bengal was the site of several major Vedic kingdoms. It was part of large Indian empires such as the Maurya empire (second century BC) and Gupta Empire (fourth century AD); and part of the regional Pala Empire (eighth to 11th century) and Sena dynasty (11th–12th century). From the 13th century onward, the region was ruled by several sultans, Hindu kings and Baro-Bhuyan landlords, until the beginning of British rule in the 18th century. The British East India Company cemented their hold on the region following the Battle of Plassey in 1757, and Calcutta served for many years as the capital of British India. The early and prolonged exposure to British administration resulted in expansion of Western education, culminating in development in science, institutional education, and social reforms of the region, including what became known as the Bengal Renaissance. A hotbed of the Indian independence movement through the early 20th century, Bengal was divided during India's independence in 1947 along religious lines into two separate entities: West Bengal—a state of India—and East Bengal—a part of the newly created Pakistani Dominion—later becoming the independent nation of Bangladesh in 1971.

2. HISTORY OF LIBRARY MOVEMENT OF WEST BENGAL

The history of existence of library in the modern sense goes back to late 18th century. In 1780, Mr. John Andrews run a commercial library in of Fort William and the first public library; Calcutta Public Library was established during the British period in 1836, which is now known as National Library. Though library movement started at a quite slow pace but by 1900, we find 50 public libraries in Bengal.

There are very few examples of existence of library in the modern sense of the term in the 18th Century. The academic libraries established in the 18th Century are Calcutta Madrasah College Library in 1781, The Asiatic Society Library in 1784. Only special library established in 18th Century is Botanical Garden Library in 1787. Among the other academic libraries that existed in the 19th century with a flavor of becoming modern library in its richness of content and quality of services offered to their readers-users are Fort William College Library (1800), Hindu College (1817), Serampore College (1818), Kolkata School Book Society (1821) Oriental Seminary (1823), Sanskrit College 1823), Scottish Church (1830), St. Xavier College (1835), Hoogly Mohosin College (1836) and the University of Calcutta Library (1857) are among the mention worthies. Among the special libraries Botanical Garden Library (1787), Calcutta Medical College Library (1835), Geological Survey of India Library (1851), Bengal Engineering College Library (1856) and Indian Association for the Cultivation of Science (1876) are important to be mentioned. Calcutta Public Library established in 1835 is also a never to be forgotten development. Out of Calcutta and its vicinity, Nizamat Library attached to Nizamat College in Murshidabad is the earliest one. The college was conceived in 1823 and was approved in 1825. Finally the college became functional in 1826 along with its rich library (MHDS Website: *murshidabadheritage.org/*). Thus the Nizamat library became one of the first modern libraries in West Bengal (erstwhile Bengal).

3. PUBLIC LIBRARY SYSTEM IN WEST BENGAL TODAY

The state of West Bengal has a quite elaborate public library system. There is a seven-tier library development scheme, which envisaged setting up of public libraries at different levels- State Central Library; District Library; Sub-Division/Area Library; Rural Library; Village Library; and Delivery Stations/Book Deposit Centers.

Strictly speaking there are 6 Government District Libraries, 19 Government Sponsored District/ Additional District Libraries, 116 Town/ Sub-divisional Libraries, 2209 Rural/ Area/ Primary Unit Libraries, and 113 Upgraded Town Libraries. There are also two Government Central Libraries, two Government Town Libraries. Uttarpara Joykrishna Public Library is a Government Public Library of special status. District Libraries and Additional District Libraries are of the same status, Town and Subdivisional Libraries are of the same status and Rural, Primary Unit and Area Libraries are of the same status. Each tier of public library has a prescribed staff-structure and recurring grant system. Different tier of library in the state is mentioned below with their services.

District Libraries : District Libraries are at the apex of library system at the district level arrangement. The Government District Libraries such as, Taki Government District Library at Taki, North 24 Parganas; Deshbandhu District Library, Darjeeling; Barasat Government Library at Barasat, North 24 Parganas; Uttar Dinajpur District Library, Raiganj and 19 Government Sponsored District libraries at Howrah, Hooghly, South 24 Parganas, Bardhaman, Asansole, Durgapur, Bankura, Birbhum, Purulia, Purba Medinipur, Paschim Medinipur, Nadia, North 24 Parganas, Jalpaiguri, Alipurduar, Dakshin Dinajpur, Malda, Murshidabad render the following services: reading room service, lending service, career guidance service, service to children, periodical and newspaper service and reference and bibliographical service.

Town/Subdivisional Libraries : They are at the second tier of the district library system. These Libraries renders the following services: reading room service, lending service, career guidance service, service to children, text book service, and reference service.

Rural/Area/ Primary unit Library : These Libraries are at the lowest tier of the library system of a district. These Libraries render the following services: Lending service, Service to children, Text book and career guidance service, Reference service, and Reading room services.

Community Library-cum-Information Centre : These centres have been established in the C. D. Blocks. Each Gram Panchayat has one such centre where there is no Government or Government Sponsored Library. These centres are at the forming stage. These centres are to render the following services: Lending service, Reading room services, and Rendering of service to rural people related to their life & livelihood.

3.1. National Library, Kolkata

National Library, Kolkata is a centrally funded public library under the Dept. of Human Resource Development, Govt. of India. It started its journey as the amalgamated form of Calcutta Public Library (CPL) was established in 1836 and the Imperial Library founded in 1891. Initially it was not a Government institution. It ran on a proprietary basis. Any subscriber paying Rs 300 at a time or in three installments was considered a proprietor. Poor students and others were allowed to use the library free of charge for a specified period of time. The then Governor General, Lord Metcalf transferred 4,675 volumes from the library of the College of Fort William College to the Calcutta Public Library. These volumes and donations of books from individuals formed the nucleus of the library. Dwarkanath Tagore was the first proprietor of the Calcutta Public Library.

Both Indian and foreign books, especially from Britain, were purchased for the library. In the report of 1850 we find that the library has started collecting books in Gujarati, Marathi, Pali, Simhalese and Punjabi. Donations were regularly received from individuals and from the Government of Bengal and North Western Provinces. Calcutta Public Library had a unique position as the first public library in this part of the country. Such a tidy and efficiently run library was rare even in Europe during the first half of the nineteenth century. Thanks to the efforts of the proprietors of Calcutta Public Library, the National Library has many rare books and journals in its collection.

From the Imperial Library to the National Library : After Independence the Government of India changed the name of the Imperial Library to the National Library, with the enactment of the Imperial Library (Change of Name) Act, 1948, and the collection was shifted from the Esplanade to the present Belvedere Estate. On 1 February 1953, the National Library was opened to the public, inaugurated by Maulana Abul Kalam Azad. B. S. Kesavan was appointed the first Librarian of this Library. Indian Languages Collection: The National Library receives books and periodicals in almost all Indian languages. These are received under the Delivery of Books and Newspapers (Public Libraries) Act 1954 (D.B. Act). Language divisions acquire, process and provide reading materials in all major Indian languages. Hindi, Kashmiri, Punjabi, Sindhi, Telugu and Urdu language divisions maintain their own stacks. Other language books are stacked in the Stack division. Language divisions are also responsible for answering reference queries. The library has separate Indian language divisions for Assamese, Bengali, Gujarati, Hindi, Kannada, Kashmiri, Malayalam, Marathi, Oriya, Punjabi, Sanskrit, Sindhi, Tamil, Telugu and Urdu. Sanskrit language division also collects and processes Pali and Prakrit books. English books published in India are collected under D.B. Act.

Foreign Languages Collections : One of the aims of the National Library is to collect all the books published on India, anywhere in the world and in any language. At the same time it collects reading materials on other subjects in different languages for the use of the country. The Imperial Library had a good number of Arabic and Persian works and a few other foreign language books. In 1985 the European Languages Division was reorganized and five separate divisions were formed. These are East Asian Languages Division, Germanic Languages Division, Romance Languages Division, Slavonic Languages Division, and West Asian and African Languages Division.

Rare Books : The National Library has an impressive number of rare books and other reading materials. In 1973, a separate Rare Books division was established. At present the books published prior to 1860 are considered rare books, along with limited and first editions, books distinguished by their design, illustration or history, and a few other criteria. Along with rare books, manuscripts and microfilms of the library are also stacked in this division.The division also provides reading facilities to the users who wish to consult these items. At present the division has 4700 monographs, 3000 manuscripts and 1500 microfilms.

3.2. State Central Library, Kolkata

State Central Library is the apex body of the Library System in the State. It was established in 1956 at Emerald Bower at 56, B.T.Road. It has subsequently been shifted to its present location near Ultadanga, Kolkata in 1996. It was now a six stored building having all sorts of modern amenities situated in a well – populated area connected with well organized transport facilities to satisfy its clientele. Apart from these, it is the nerve centre of various other library activities of the State.

State Central Library along with 7 other Government Libraries and 19 Government Sponsored District Libraries are now connected in intranet. The bibliographical database of these libraries in the form of Union Catalogue will be available online through this portal along with various other services. All the public libraries of West Bengal [sponsored and non-sponsored] may share this bibliographical database at free of cost. A digital archive of rare books has been also build to cater the scholars and interested people of our society. Dissemination of information of various Government departments. In connection with life and livelihood of people is also a part of this portal along with various other library related information.

3.3. Uttarpara Joykrishna Public Library, Hoogly

Uttarpara Jaykrishna Public Library is the first free Public library in India. It was established by Jayakrishan Mukeherjee, famous son of Uttarpara. Influenced by Dwarkanath Tagore and guided by London Public Library act 1850 - Joykrishna initiated this novel venture in 1859 when modern public education was a far cry not only in Bengal but also India. Apart from its invaluable collection - it is also famous for its association with people like Michael Madhusudan Dutta, who spent last few days of his life in this library building, Rishi Autobindo - who delivered his famous 'Uttarpara Speech' and many others. The construction of library building started in 1856 on over one acre land at the cost of Rs. 85,000. The two storied library without house and flower garden formally opened on April 15, 1859 though it started working for scholars and researchers as early as 1851.The collection in this library contains very rare and old (publication discontinued) periodicals both in Bengali and English such as Dig Darshan (1818) the first Bengali periodical Bengal Chronicle (1821), Calcutta Monthly Journal (1798) etc.

3.4. North Bengal State Library, Coochbehar

North Bengal State Library is a pride of Cooch Behar. This Library has so many valuable manuscripts and Classic "*Punthis*" written on hand made papers and palm leaf. There are so many rare books, old journals Indian and Foreign rare documents, reports. The treasure is a cultural heritage of Cooch Behar Kingdom. The library has a long history of 125 years. During the minority of Maharaja Nripendra Narayan, Colonel Houghten came to Cooch Behar to act as Commissioner (1864-73). Colonel Houghten established State Library of Cooch Behar in the year 1870 by purchasing a stock of books at an auction sale of M/S.Rozario and Co., in

London. In a room of *Nilkuthi* the library was started. Later it was handed over to the Maharaja Nripendra Narayan who removed the library to Lansdown Hall in the year 1895. Worthwhile to note is that in the year 1882 the library was opened for public use.

4. WEST BENGAL PUBLIC LIBRARIES ACT, 1979 AND ITS SALIENT FEATURES

The West Bengal Public Libraries Act, 1979" is the fifth state legislation exclusively for public library. The West Bengal Legislature passed this Act and assent of the President was first published in the Calcutta Gazette, Extraordinary on the 7th January 1980. West Bengal enacted the Public Libraries Act in 1979 to become the fifth state of India with library legislation. Its preamble stated that, "An Act to provide for the establishment of Public libraries in the State of West Bengal and to regulate, guide, central, supervise and to grant recognition to the existing libraries in the State as also to provide for a comprehensive rural and urban library service in the State of west Bengal". The present form of the legislation have been in function after amendments in the years 1982, 1985, 1993, 1994, 1998, and 2003. By amending it has become more effective, operational and capable of handling new developments in the field of public library.

The salient features of West Bengal Public Libraries Act, 1979 are:

- The Act spreading over 5 chapters extends to the whole of state of West Bengal;
- The Act has not provided for any form of Taxation / Cess;
- The Minister - in - charge of Mass Education Extension & Library Services, Government of West Bengal looks after the affairs of library and information services;
- The act set mechanism for constitution of State Library Council for the purpose of advising the Government on the matters of public library services. Minister-in-

Charge of Library Services shall be the Chairman of the Council;

- State Library Council (SLC) is the chief advisory body to advise the Government on the policies and programmes concerning library services in the State. The Minister - in - Charge is the Chairperson of the Advisory Body;
- The act set forth mechanism for constitution of Local Library Authority for each district. The District Magistrate shall be the Chairman of the Local Library Authority. Provision for constitution of Executive Committee for Local Library Authority is there in the act;
- The Government is empowered to appoint District Library Officers and District Librarians in districts. The Government, in consultation with the Local Library Authority may place a person in charge of a District Library to be called as District Librarian;
- Directorate of Library Services is entrusted to implement the Act. The Director of Library Services under the supervision of the Mass Education Extension & Library Services Department administers the West Bengal Public Libraries Act, 1979 and as amended thereafter. The Department through the Directorate of Library Services, West Bengal also manages the State Central Library and other public libraries established or maintained by the Government and direct all matters relating to such libraries. It also directs and superintendents all matters relating to the work of all Local Library Authorities under this Act;
- Each Local Library Authority maintains a fund in which government grant as well as contributions received from other sources are deposited and payments are made from the fund for management, maintenance, improvement and development of library services or any other purpose as the Government may think fit;

- The Local Library Authority (LLA) for each district, except the district of Darjeeling, carries out the purposes of the Act. Financial management of local libraries rests upon the Local Library Authority.
- Means of augmenting funds as per provision of the act are:
  - (a) Contributions, gifts and income from endowments,
  - (b) Grants from the government, and
  - (c) Collection of Local Library Authority under the Act.
- Two separate Local Library Authorities have been created for Darjeeling district - One for Darjeeling Gorkha Hill Council (DGHC) and the other for Siliguri Mahakuma Parishad Area (SMPA). Normally, the District Magistrate of each district is the chairman of the LLA of that district.

5. THE MAJOR ACADEMIC LIBRARIES IN THE STATE

5.1. Calcutta University Library

Although the University of Calcutta was formally launched in 1857, it had no permanent building of its own, at least in the early years. It might be recalled that the University was initially authorized only to hold examinations and award degrees. In those rudimentary stages of its growth, library, museum and other common facilities did not receive as much attention as they deserved. It was only after the University got a permanent home of its own in 1872 that attempts were initiated for the setting up of a library. Its nucleus was formed out of a small gift of Rs. 5000 by Joykrishna Mukherjee, the public spirited Zamindar of Uttarpara. While donating the money in 1869 he expressed the hope that a small library could be set up by the University. At about the same time Esan Chandra Ghose donated a small collection of books to the University. These efforts marked a small but auspicious beginning.

5.2. Indian Institute of Technology (IIT) Kharagpur Library

The Central Library of IIT Kharagpur started in a small room of the Institute old Building (Shahid Bhavan) in the year 1951, and moved to its present premises in 1956. Since then, it has grown in size and content to take the present shape. With the developments in computers, microelectronics and communication technologies, the behavioral characteristics of the information seekers have been changing rapidly and the library is trying its best to adapt with the technological advancement. For the last six decades, the library has been the lifeline of the academic activities of the Institute. It is no exaggeration to state that the Central Library of IIT Kharagpur is one of the largest and finest technical libraries in Asia. The Library is well equipped with modem facilities and resources (print and electronic) in the forms of CDROMs, DVD-ROM, online databases, micro-documents, video cassettes, books, journals, patents, standards, theses, reports, etc.

5.3. Indian Institute of Management IIM Calcutta Library

Library of Indian Institute of Management Calcutta was set up in March 1962 and named as B. C. Roy Memorial Library in the memory of Dr. B. C. Roy, the first Chairman of the Institute. The Library has been primarily designed to meet the requirements of the Institutes academic programmes. The Library has a collection of more than 1.6 lakhs volumes of books and bound journals. It subscribes to 500 journals and provides access to more than 40,000 online full text journals. It is considered as one of the best management libraries in Asia. The functions and services of the library are computerized.

5.4. Indian Institute of Engineering Science and Technology (IIEST) Library

The University library has the distinction of being one of the oldest and the largest resourceful technical library in the south east Asia. The total area of the library is around

3,000 square meter and it is open from 8.00 A.M. to 8.00 P.M. The library not only caters to the basic information needs of faculty members, research scholars and students of this University but also provides information services to research workers of neighbouring universities and research institutes in the state.

5.5. Vidyasagar University Library

The Central Library of Vidyasagar University began its existence in the year 1986 with the commencement of six Post Graduate departments. Since then it has grown in size and content along with the university to take the present shape. All these years the Central Library has been the life line for the academic activity of the institute. It is one of the central facilities used by all the types of members and ex members of this University. It is housed in a separate building having four floors on a plinth area near about 11000 sq. ft. The library has a collection of more than 1 lakh volumes which includes Text Books, Reference Books & Bound volumes of Journals, Standards etc. Collection development, its organization and information retrieval are the basic functions of the library. The book collection has been supporting the teaching, research, development and other professional activities of these departments.

5.6. Jadavpur University Library

Jadavpur University Library was started along with the establishment of the University in 1955 in order to cater the academic and research needs of the faculty, research scholars, students, officers and non-teaching staff. Since then, the University Library has gone from strength to strength to live up to the expectations of its immediate clientele. It is one of the best-equipped libraries in the country.

The University is proud of its library system, which comprises the Central Library, Salt Lake Campus Library, 36 Departmental Libraries under the Faculty of Arts, Science,

Engineering and Technology, and also the Libraries attached with the Schools and Centres for studies. The Central Library of Jadavpur University is one of the central facilities used by all types of members of this University. This is the third largest library in West Bengal.

6. THE MAJOR SPECIAL LIBRARIES IN THE STATE

6.1. Asiatic Society Library (Kolakata)

Being one of the oldest libraries of the Asiatic Society is the grand stay, glory and honour of the Society. Its importance lies not in numerical strength but in its rich and unique contents. Certainly it is one of the richest libraries of collection of our collective past i.e. art, culture, history and heritage and one of the most important libraries to the researchers. The first accession of importance was a gift from the Seringapatam Committee (3 February 1808) being a selection from the Palace Library of Tipoo Sultan. The Collection contains many old and rare works. Special mention may be made of an illuminated manuscript of the Quran and old text of Gulistan, and manuscripts of Padshanamah bearing an autograph of Emperor Shahjahan. Similarly, Surveyor-General Colonel Mackenzie's collection of manuscripts and drawings were received in December 1822. The collection has been grouped into three departments; e.g.

(1) Printed Books and Periodicals (2) Manuscripts and Archives and (3) Museum Objects.

The Printed Books Department has four sections, viz;

(a) European Languages

(b) Sanskritic & other Modern Indian Languages

(c) Perso-Arabic and Urdu and

(d) Sino-Tibetan and South-Asian Languages

Printed books are there in almost all the major languages of the world. There are about 1,49,000 volumes, particularly rich in works on Indology and Asiatic Lore, and in standard philological and scientific serials. The printed books in this department range in date from the latter half of the fifteenth century A.D. and one of its special features consists in the many items of rare works, otherwise unavailable, or scarcely available, including books printed in India in the late 18th and early 19th centuries. Total number of Manuscripts in 26 languages is 47,000 (approx). The total numbers of Journals are about 80,000.

6.2. Saha Institute of Nuclear physics Library (Kolakata)

The Library was set up in 1950 with a meagre budget of a few thousand rupees and a generous donation of books and periodicals from Profs M N Saha, P C Mohanty, P N Ghosh, N N Das Gupta, A K Saha, S K Ghosh and others. Indian Science News Association, Indian Association for the Cultivation of Science and the National Institutes of Science in India made gifts of periodicals. Since then the Library has grown steadily in size (now 6500 square metres) and resources. Its budget, only Rs 50,000 in 1960, went up to Rs 2 lakhs in 1970 and 14 lakhs in the early eighties. It stands at 5 Crore now. The Library has the Libsys 6.1 (with the Web OPAC) software installed on a Linux platform to help access the Library Databases using any standard browser. On-line access to journals is available to the institute members only. Journal sharing facility exists among a few Libraries in Kolkata. The Library offers its reading room service to the outsiders on appropriate registration.

6.3. S. N. Bose National Center for Basic Sciences Library (Kolakata)

The Library of S.N. Bose National Centre for Basic Sciences i.e. SNB Library strives to evolve as a model and leading basic sciences library in eastern India. The collection comprises of more than 10,000 documents mainly in the fields of Physics (Astrophysics, Quantum Mechanics, Solid States, Optics, Particle Physics, Mechanics, etc.), Computer Science, Mathematics, Electronics, Laser, Chemistry, Biology,

Material Science, Nano Science and Technology, etc. It is primarily intended for the faculty, staff members, consultants, scholars, students of S.N. Bose National Centre for Basic Sciences. However, outside users *viz.,* professionals, *bona fide* research scholars, *bona fide* students, etc. also make use of the library. It has resource sharing arrangements with other similar organizations in Kolkata. The library also makes provision for general reading and thus subscribes Books in social sciences and humanities. Library subscribes 25 popular magazines and receives a good number of periodicals in exchange and also subscribes 13 newspapers are purchased towards this end. The institutional membership at the Library and Information Services, British Council also enhances this service. The library is fully computerized with the installation of LIBSYS 4 (on Linux platform). A server and 20 PCs, multimedia, scanners, colour printer, lamination machine, CD - writers, are also part of the set-up. The electronic databases at the Library cover monographs, journals, annual reports, CD/DVD-ROMs. The library subscribes to 234 journals. Most of the journals have online access.

6.4. Indian Association for the cultivation of science Library (Kolkata)

The IACS library has grown out of the research needs of the Association from its very beginning (1876). So it is the oldest library of its kind and occupies a unique position among the academia of the Eastern India. A measure of its social impact may be gained by noting that it caters to the needs of more than 3000 external users, while the staff and scholars of the Association would total to nearly 350. Yearly budget for the Library is more than five crore. An air-conditioned new building houses the library with all amenities to the users.

7. LIS EDUCATION IN WEST BENGAL

7.1. DLIS, University of Calcutta

The University of Calcutta is the first one to start a training programme in librarianship at the university level in eastern part of our country. The first Diploma Library Training Programme started in January 1945. In 1959, the Training Department was separated from the Library Department and was renamed as "Department of Library Science". A separate and independent Faculty for PG Studies in Library Science was created under which the department was placed. From the 1969-1970 session, the Diploma was replaced by degree of Bachelor of Library Science (BLibSc). In 1998 the department was renamed as the Department of Library and Information Science offering the course named Bachelor of Library and Information Science (BLIS). From the very beginning the course was conducted in the evening and the same is being continued. The department is presently under the Faculty of PG Studies in Education, Journalism, and Library and Information Science. A master degree course was introduced in 1973. The name of the course was Master of Library Science (MLiSc). Presently the department offers BLIS, MLIS, 5-year Integrated MLIS, M. Phil and 55, 24, 40 and 15 students respectively with varying number of Ph. D. Scholars.

7.2. DLIS, Jadavpur University

Jadavpur University was established in 1952. The Department of Library Science was constituted in 1964 under the PG Faculty Council of Arts to offer the BLibSc of one-year duration. In 2003,MLIS and BLIS courses were converted to the semester system comprising 2 semesters for each course. Considering the growth in digital library aspects, the department started a part-time (evening) PG Diploma in Digital Library Management in 2005 of two-year (four semesters) The department has also introduced PhD programme where intake vary year to year.

7.3. DLIS, Burdwan University

The University of Burdwan was established in 1960. In 1965, it started offering one year Diploma in Librarianship by establishing Institute of Library Science. In 1970, the name was changed to Department of Library Science, which started offering BLibSc. The nomenclature of the department was changed to Department of Library and Information Science in 1980. Subsequently, nomenclature of BLibSc was changed to BLIS. One-year MLIS and PhD were also introduced. The MPhil programme was introduced during 2007-08.

7.4. DLIS, Vidyasagar University

In 1985, Vidyasagar University was opened with six PG departments including the Department of Library and Information Science, which started offering BLIS. MLIS and PhD were introduced in 1987 and 1992, respectively. At present, intake for BLIS and MLIS is 35 and 15, respectively. Department of Library and Information Science is one of the six earliest departments of the University. BLISc. Course has been introduced from the session 1985 – 86. In the academic session 1987–88 MLISc programme is added. Research is part and parcel from the beginning of the journey. Presently the department admits 35 students for BLIS and 15 students for MLIS course with varying number of students admitted fo M. Phil and Ph. D. programme.

7.5. DLIS, Kalyani University

The Department of Library and Information Science of Kalyani University was established in 1991. A one year PG Course leading to the BLIS was formally inaugurated on 29 April 1992. Subsequently, a MLIS course was introduced during 1999-2000. The department has introduced the semester system for BLIS and MLIS courses from the academic session 2008-2009. At present, intake for BLIS and MLIS is 30 and 15, respectively. The Directorate of Distance Education (DDE), Kalyani University introduced MPhil in distance mode in 2008 with an intake of 55 which has been discontinued since 2011. In the academic session 2012-13 M Phil has been reopened with an intake capacity of 20. A Ph. D programme forms an integral part of departmental research activities with variable intake as per existing vacancy.

7.6. DLIS, North Bengal University

North Bengal University took initiative to establish Department of Library and Information Science and started offering BLIS since 1990-91 with intake of 56 students. The department has introduced one-year MLIS degree since 2005-06 with 40 seats. From 2009, the department adopted semester system for one-year BLIS course. The department has not yet started M. Phil or Ph. D. programme.

7.7. DLIS, Rabindra Bharati University

Department of Library & Information Science in order to cope with the professional manpower requirements for various types of libraries and information centres, Rabindra Bharati University, established the Department of Library and Information Science under PG Faculty of Arts in 1985 at Jorasanko Campus. Initially it started offering BLIS. BLIS was also started as evening course in 1986. The University has introduced M.L.I.Sc course on self-financing basis from 2007-2008 sessions. Intake for BLIS and MLIS are 40 and 10, respectively. Ph. D. programme has been introduced in 2013 with an intake of 14 scholars.

7.8. Netaji Subhash Open University (NSOU)

Seeing the ever increasing demand for LIS course, the NSOU came forward to offer LIS courses through open university system. NSOU is offering BLIS and MLIS in Open University (distance) mode. This university imparts LIS through several study centres spread over 19 districts in the state. It does not have, therefore, a fixed intake, and hence scope of producing a large number of LIS students is there. University record shows in 2007 a total of 1061 students were admitted in BLIS and 180 students in MLIS; in 2008 number of students enrolment rose to 5160 in BLIS and 225 in MLIS and subsequently dwindled down to 2750 for BLIS and 278 for MLIS in 2009. No. of study centres for BLIS in 2012 is 84. Total 96 (http://www.wbnsou.ac.in/wbnsou/ accessed on 07/11/12). Presently the University functions from 5 campuses in Kolkata and a regional centre at Kalyani (Nadia). As high as 1281 candidates are appearing in the BLIS practical examination in July, 2012 that is less than the previous years.

7.9. Indira Gandhi National Open University (IGNOU)

IGNOU is proved to be the pioneer in LIS education beyond doubt. LIS course offered by IGNOU considered to be one of the best in this part of the county and therefore fares quite well in all walks of LIS profession. The IGNOU has three regional centres in West Bengal namely, Kolkata, Raghunathganj (Jangipur) and Siliguri. A number of study centres are there under the direct control of those regional centres offering BLIS and also MLIS course.

8. LIBRARY ASSOCIATION (BLA): GENESIS AND ROLE IN LIS EDUCATION

Bengal Library Association formerly known as All Bengal Library Association was established in 1925 under the president ship of Poet Rabindranath Tagore and the first secretary of the Association was Mr. Sushilkumar Ghosh.

The major activities of the Association are -

- Propagating the importance of library and information services for individuals and for the society and developing awareness for the library and information services.
- Suggesting measures for improvement and expansion of library services for all categories of libraries in the state.
- Organizing movement for improvement of the service conditions and proper pay and status of the library workers.

- Organizing conference and seminars for apprising people of various aspects of the library movement and library services.
- Organizing training courses, refresher courses, workshops etc. and publishing books, periodicals, reports etc pertaining to library science and library services.

The Association has a library of its own with a collection of more than 5 thousand books on library and information science and reference tools. The Library is open to all members and students. The Association publishes a monthly journal in Bengali with English Abstract named 'Granthagar'. Besides this Association also regularly publishes books on Library and Information Science and library services in English and Bengali. The association also conducts Certificate Course in Library Science since 1937, Special course on computer application in Library Services and refresher course for working librarians.

9. CONCLUSION

In the development of library system in the state two organizations have contributed a lot. Raja Rammohun Roy Library Foundation is a central autonomous organization established and fully financed by the Ministry of Culture, Government of India has been playing very vital role in the development of public libraries in the state. This organization functions as a promotional agency, an advisory and consultancy organization, a funding body for public library development in the state as well as in the country. The Foundation works in close association and active cooperation with different State Governments and Union Territory Administrations through a machinery called State Library Planning Committee (SLPC/SLC) set up in each State at the instance of the Foundation. 'West Bengal State Committee for Implementation of RRRLF Programme under the chairmanship of Hon'ble Minister of State in charge, Department of Mass Education Extension and Library

Services discharges its function from State Central Library, Kolkata.

REFERENCES

1. Asundi, A. Y. and Karisiddappa, C. R. (2007). Library and Information Science Education in India: International Perspective with Special Reference Developing Countries, DESIDOCCC Bulletin of Information Technology. Vol. 27(2), pp. 5-11. Accessed from http://publications.drdo.gov.in/ojs/index.php/djlit/article/view/127 on 07/0/12.
2. Bandyopadhaya, Ratna & Panigrahi, Pijushkanti (2009). Towards standardisation of LIS education. In Library science education in West Bengal, edited by Goutam Goswami. Paper presented at the Fifty-first Bengal Library Conference, 18-20 December, (2009). Bantra Public Library, Howrah. Bengal Library Association, Kolkata, 2009. pp 120-2.
3. Chatterjee, Anjana (2001). Bihar and Jarkhand. *In.* Library and Information Services in Indian States and Union Territories edited by P.B.Mangla, *et.al.* Shipra, New Delhi.
4. Dutta, Bidyarthi and Das, Anup Kumar (2001). Higher Education in Library & Information Science in India, ILA Bulletin, 37(1), pp. 25-30.
5. INFLIBNET (?). Survey Report, INFLIBNET. Accessed from http://shodhganga.inflibnet.ac.in/bitstream/10603/1205/9/09_chapter%201.pdf on 10/09/12.
6. Krishan Kumar & Sharma, Jaideep (2009). Library and information science education in India. Har Anand, New Delhi, p. 312.
7. Mahajan, Preeti (2005). Academic Libraries in India: A Present-day Scenario. Library Philosophy and Practice, Vol. 8(1), pp. Journal Article (On-line/Unpaginated). Accessed from http://creativecommons.org/publicdomain/mark/1.0/ on 25/02/12.
8. Majumder, Krishnapada (2008). Development of public library system in West Bengal and Bengal Library Association. Bengal Library Association, Kolkata, p. 190.
9. Nagaraj, M. N. (1988). Indian association of special libraries and information centres. In Library movement in India, edited by Ramkrishna Saha (Bengal Library Association, Kolkata, pp. 12-17.
10. Panigrahi, Pijushkanti (2010). "Library and Information Science

Education in East and North-East India: Retrospect and Prospects", DESIDOCCC Journal of Library & Information Technology, Vol. 30, No. 5, September 2010, pp. 32-47.

11. Patel, Jashu and Krishan Kumar (2004). Libraries and Librarianship in India, Greenwood Westport.

12. Roy, Arun (1988). Bengal Library Association. In library movement in India, edited by Ramkrishna Saha. Bengal Library Association, Kolkata, pp. 149-52.

13. Roychaudhury, Prabir (1988). Public library development in West Bengal: A review. In Library movement in India, edited by Ramkrishna Saha. Bengal Library Association, Kolkata, pp. 135-48.

14. Saha, Ramkrishna (1988). Library movement in West Bengal. In Library movement in India, edited by Ramkrishna Saha. Bengal Library Association, Kolkata, pp. 153-59.

15. Saha, Ramkrishna (2009). Today's LIS education. In Library science education in West Bengal, edited by Goutam Goswami. Paper presented at the Fifty-first Bengal Library Conference, 18-20 December, 2009, Bantra Public Library, Howrah. Bengal Library Association, Kolkata, 2009. pp. 134-40.

16. Sarkhel, Juran Krishna & Das (2009). Standardization of LIS education in Indian universities. In Library science education in West Bengal, edited by Goutam Goswami. Paper presented at the Fifty-first Bengal Library Conference, 18-20 December, 2009, Bantra Public Library, Howrah. Bengal Library Association, Kolkata, 2009. pp. 27-30.

17. shodhganga.inflibnet.ac.in/bitstream/10603/.../10_chapter%202.pdf on 18/10/12.

18. UGC (2003). Higher Education in India: Issues, Concerns and New Directions, UGC, New Delhi. Accessed from http://oldwebsite.ugc.ac.in/pub/heindia.pdf on 08/09/12.

19. UGC-Review Committee (1965). Library science in Indian universities: Report of the UGC Review Committee. University Grants Commission, New Delhi. P. 86.

20. http://www.blacal.org/about.htm.